# KAUNDA'S GAOLER

# KAUNDA'S GAOLER

*Memories of a District Officer in Northern Rhodesia and Zambia*

D. G. Coe and E. C. Greenall

The Radcliffe Press

LONDON • NEW YORK

Published in 2003 by The Radcliffe Press
6 Salem Road, London W2 4BU

In the United States and in Canada
distributed by Palgrave Macmillan, a division of St Martin's Press
175 Fifth Avenue, New York NY 10010

Copyright © D. G. Coe and E. C. Greenall, 2003

The right of D. G. Coe and E. C. Greenall to be identified as the authors of this work has been asserted by the authors in accordance with the Copyright, Design and Patents Act 1988.

All rights reserved. Except for brief quotations in a review, this book, or any part thereof, may not be reproduced, stored in or introduced into a retrieval system, or transmitted, in any form or by any means, electronic, mechanical, photocopying, recording or otherwise, without the prior written permission of the publisher.

ISBN 1-86064-862-2

A full CIP record for this book is available from the British Library
A full CIP record for this book is available from the Library of Congress

Library of Congress Catalog card: available

Typeset in Sabon by Oxford Publishing Services, Oxford
Printed and bound in Great Britain by MPG Books Ltd, Bodmin

To My Dearest Daughters
Vivian and Lydia

E.C.G.

'*Prime Minister*: How does it feel to be sitting down to lunch with your former gaoler?'
  (Question from a journalist – *The Northern News*)

# Contents

List of Illustrations ix
Acronyms and Abbreviations xi
Glossary of Bemba Words xiii
Brief Chronology of Northern Rhodesia and Zambia xv
Acknowledgements xvii
Preface xix

1. The Letter 1
2. Indoctrination in Lusaka 11
3. Kasama 15
4. Ulendo and Witchcraft 33
5. Kawambwa 45
6. Mporokoso: An Idyllic Interlude 57
7. The Secretariat 68
8. Leave 72
9. Luwingu 75
10. Broken Hill (1952–55) 95
11. Ndola and Kitwe (1956–58) 107
12. Kabompo: The Garden of Eden 113
13. Distant Thunder 128
14. Confined in the Garden of Eden 132
15. Tribal Troubles 146
16. Ndola Rural (1962–64) 167
17. Kwacha: Zambian Dawn 180
18. Ndola: Yet Again 183

## Contents

| | | |
|---|---|---|
| 19. | The Missing Minister:<br>Acting Resident Secretary (1968–69) | 188 |
| 20. | Finale | 194 |

| | |
|---|---|
| Appendix 1 | 199 |
| Appendix 2 | 201 |
| Appendix 3 | 207 |
| Appendix 4 | 209 |
| Further Reading and Background Material | 212 |
| Index | 213 |

# List of Illustrations

1. Wartime wedding, 1943.
2. The DC's house, Luwingu.
3. Fisherman, Mpulungu, Lake Tanganyika.
4. The family, Kabompo.
5. *Boma* staff, Kabompo.
6. The bluff, overlooking the Kabompo river.
7. The Kabompo river in flood.
8. Some of Mwata Yamvwa's entourage outside Kabompo courthouse.
9. Mwata Yamvwa.
10. Lunda gathering to welcome Mwata Yamvwa at Kabompo.
11. Members of the Lunda royal family.
12. Kabompo football team.
13. Local Lunda craftwork.
14. Carved guardian spirit by DC's office.
15. Installation of the *ngambela* at Manyinga.
16. *Makishi* dancers.
17. *Makishi* dancer.
18. *Ndaba* of Kabompa district chiefs to meet the PC.
19. Preparing an alfresco meeting with Chief Nkana and his council.
20. *Kapasu*s parade for opening of Mushili courthouse, Masaiti.
21. PC Ewen Thompson with wife and VIPs.
22. Light-hearted moment with Kaunda at Luanshya airport.
23. Buttering up the press.
24. 'It's just a simple lunch' — Luanshya.
25. Messenger in the newly-designed uniform, 1954.

## List of Illustrations

26. The splendour of Victoria Falls and its rainbow.
27. The governor, Sir Evelyn Hone, with DCs of the Western Province.

# Acronyms and Abbreviations

| | |
|---|---|
| ADC | aide-de-camp |
| ANC | African National Congress |
| BSAC | British South Africa Company |
| CO | commanding officer |
| DA | district assistant |
| DC | district commissioner |
| DO | district officer |
| GH | Government House |
| HE | His Excellency |
| HU | higher up |
| IRA | Irish Republican Army |
| LegCo | Legislative Council |
| LSE | London School of Economics (and Political Science) |
| SOAS | School of Oriental and African Studies |
| MO | medical officer |
| NA | native authority |
| NAC | Nyasaland African Congress |
| NCO | non-commissioned officer |
| NR | Northern Rhodesia |
| NRAC | Northern Rhodesia African Congress |
| NRG | Northern Rhodesia Government |
| NRR | Northern Rhodesia Regiment |
| PA | provincial administration |
| PC | provincial commissioner |
| PPC | *pour prière congé* (away on leave) |
| RAF | Royal Air Force |

## Acronyms and Abbreviations

| | |
|---|---|
| RE | Royal Engineers |
| RFC | Royal Flying Corps |
| SAAF | South African Air Force |
| SNA | Secretary for Native Affairs |
| UFP | United Federal Party |
| UDI | unilateral declaration of independence |
| UNIP | United National Independence Party |
| V-E | victory in Europe |
| V-J | victory over Japan |
| ZANC | Zambia African National Congress |

# Glossary of Bemba Words

| | |
|---|---|
| *askari* | soldier |
| *ba Bemba* | the Bemba people |
| *ba Lovale* | the Lovale people |
| *boma* | local government administrative office |
| *bwali* | type of porridge made from finger millet, staple diet of the Bemba |
| *bwalwa* | native beer brewed from millet seed |
| *capitao* | foreman (Bemba corruption of 'captain') |
| *bwana* | Mr, master |
| *chi Bemba* | the Bemba (or Lovale) language, sometimes written '*ci bemba*' |
| *chipembele* | rhinoceros |
| *chitemene* | slash and burn cultivation |
| *Chitimikulu* | name of the Bemba paramount chief |
| *dambo* | water meadow |
| *filembwee* | beans |
| *fundi* | any local specialist, for example in making drums, repairing shoes, or skinning and curing pelts |
| *kapasu* | literally 'grasshopper', the equivalent of the district messengers employed by the native authority |
| *kashimi kapela* | the story is ended |
| *machila* | type of native hammock suitable for transporting invalids |
| *makishi* | masked dancers |
| *masaiti* | place name derived from many sides |

## Glossary of Bemba Words

| | |
|---|---|
| *mavirondongo* | chief's official Bemba executioners, otherwise known as 'the neck twisters' |
| *Mutende Momma* | Greetings, respected lady |
| *mofu* | very dense wood used for making dugout canoes |
| *mpende* | bream; very good eating fish (tilapia) |
| *mulombwa* | Rhodesian rosewood |
| *munani* | relish (used for flavouring, especially *bwali*) |
| *mutende* | peace |
| *mwana* | baby or young child |
| *mwata* | king or master |
| *ndaba* | tribal conclave |
| *ngambela* | head councillor |
| *nshiliyako* | I can't eat them (a phrase) |
| *ntipa* | marsh |
| *sampa* | giant catfish (heterebranchus) |
| *ubwamba* | fish basket (literally nakedness, especially female) |
| *ulendo* | tour |
| *unga* | the principal tribe then resident in Bangweulu (hence Lunga bank) |
| *via u tuzhi* | payment or reverse dowry to free oneself from the spirit of a departed spouse |
| *ya ba* | wonderful |

# Brief Chronology of Northern Rhodesia and Zambia

| | |
|---|---|
| 1889 | Charter granted to the British South Africa Company |
| 1891 | Commencement of annexation |
| 1898 | Sporadic resistance by the Ngoni |
| 1923 | Copper discovered in large quantities |
| 1924 | Transfer of authority to the Colonial Office; formation of LegCo, creation of Native Authorities |
| 1935 | First local welfare societies and associations |
| 1946 | Federation of African Welfare Societies |
| 1946 | A. Creech Jones becomes Secretary of State for the Colonies |
| 1947 | Comprehensive Development Plan |
| 1948 | Formation of African National Congress by Harry Nkumbula |
| 1950 | James Griffiths replaces A. Creech Jones |
| 1951 | Victoria Falls Conference |
| 1951 | Change of government in the UK, Oliver Lyttelton appointed Secretary of State for the Colonies |
| 1951 | Lyttelton decides to proceed with federation |
| 1953 | Lancaster House Conference |
| 1953 | Central African Federation with Southern Rhodesia and Nyasaland |
| 1954 | A. Lennox-Boyd replaces Lyttelton |
| 1955 | Imprisonment of Kaunda for two months |
| 1958 | Kaunda leaves ANC and forms Zambia African National Congress (ZANC) |
| 1959 | New constitution |

## Brief Chronology of Northern Rhodesia and Zambia

| | |
|---|---|
| 1959 | Kaunda becomes a restricted person, later arrested and transferred to Southern Rhodesia |
| 1959 | I. Macleod replaces Lennox Boyd |
| 1959 | Elections |
| 1959 | Formation of United National Independence Party (UNIP) |
| 1960 | Kaunda released from gaol, meets with Macmillan |
| 1960 | 'Winds of Change' speech by Macmillan in South Africa |
| 1960 | Monckton Commission |
| 1960 | The White Paper on 15:15:15 Constitution put forward by Mcleod |
| 1960 | Changed at Welensky's request |
| 1960 | Mulungushi conference (UNIP) |
| 1961 | Maudling replaces Mcleod |
| 1962 | Interim constitution |
| 1963 | Election leads to ANC/UNIP coalition |
| 1963 | Federation dissolved, another constitution |
| 1964 | Elections in which Kaunda wins a landslide victory and becomes Prime Minister |
| 1964 | October — Independence for Zambia; Kaunda becomes President |
| 1972 | One-party state declared in Zambia (UNIP) |
| 1990 | Opposition parties permitted |
| 1991 | Kaunda loses first multiparty election |

# Acknowledgements

First and foremost I must acknowledge the debt that I owe to Frances, my wife, who supported and encouraged me in good times and bad during the 25 years that I spent, first in Northern Rhodesia (NR) and then Zambia. I also recall those colleagues in the Colonial Service in NR, far too numerous to name individually, who trained me and taught me their own skills. Especially, I must acknowledge my dear friend Jo, who during the time while this book was written showed infinite patience in listening to me reading aloud the numerous drafts of the script, adding suggestions based on her own experiences in NR. For me it has been a personal tragedy that she has not survived to see this work completed. I cannot forget Father Etienne of the White Fathers, now long departed, who taught me Bemba and was a special friend for many years. Lastly, a special mention of my friends and former colleagues, John Blunden, Dennis Frost and Roland Hill who have taken the time to read parts of the book and offer their constructive comments.

It is impossible to avoid reference to the debt that I owe my co-author, Dr David Gordon Coe, without whose urging and occasional bullying this book would never have been completed. It arose from a casual conversation over dinner when I expressed the thought that I would like to write my memoirs, which possibly were of interest in view of my association with President Kaunda. To my delight he said, 'You write the memoirs and I will put them into a word-processor.' Little did he realize at the time that in the end he would wind up by completely rewriting most of what I put down. During the preparation of our script both he and I also

## Acknowledgements

bemoaned the fact that Frances was no longer with us as she had a magical touch with words as is apparent from the extensive quotations from her letters that appear in the book. Lastly, our special thanks to Jenny Hill for permission to use her delightful drawings.

# Preface

This was intended to be an account of my own and my family's lives and experiences in Northern Rhodesia and later Zambia. Nevertheless, it is totally impossible to divorce our personal lives from the historical changes that were unfolding around us, particularly as I was first the gaoler, as the local press put it, of the former president, Kenneth Kaunda, and later, I think, his friend.

Despite whatever civil unrest there might have been, the routine of life as a working colonial officer carried on and one tended to get on with it, particularly if there was no trouble in the immediate vicinity. Consequently, I have endeavoured to integrate the ongoing political changes into my story more or less at the appropriate times.

The detailed history of the last years of the federation is surprisingly complicated, when new constitutions arrived as regularly as one's pay cheque and nearly as frequently. Nevertheless, by no stretch of the imagination is this book intended to be a history and for that reason no attempt has been made to cite references. Needless to say, at a distance of time one's memory can become fallible but I have been fortunate insofar as I still have almost all the letters written by my wife Frances spanning that period of our life. My co-author and I have also sought to refresh my recollection of the precise timing of historical events by checking and through rereading the books of other authors mentioned under 'additional reading'. Their views and their interpretation of events have not always been the same as mine. It is also my good fortune to have in my possession part of an unpublished manuscript on

## Preface

Bemba tribal customs that was given to me many years ago by Father Etienne of the White Fathers (who also taught me Bemba). This has been invaluable as a source to draw on in order to confirm my own memories and to elaborate on some of the details of the ceremonies that accompanied the death of a paramount chief.

That the history is hard to follow is easily seen. If one first reads Kaunda's *Zambia Shall be Free* and then *4000 Days* by Sir Roy Welensky, I would defy anyone to realize that both books are talking about the same period of time in the same region. Only the reader can decide which version should be given more credence. To me both are superficially correct and one must look carefully at the nuances, the opinions expressed and especially the omissions to find the truth which, as is usually the case, lies somewhere in between. Welensky was adamant in blaming the British government for the failure of the federation and pointed to broken promises, which clearly were not kept. On the other hand, the proponents of federation made much play of partnership when advancing their case and it is interesting to note that at no time does Welensky's book refer to any benefits that federation brought to the natives. Nor did he once refer to partnership after the federation had come into being. For the convenience of those who may be interested I have included as separate appendices brief summaries of the history of Northern Rhodesia and the administrative setup there.

*Kwacha*! This was the slogan leading up to freedom in Zambia. It means 'the dawn'. Whether freedom has panned out as the native population had expected is another matter. There has been a price to pay. The first few years following the dawn were ecstatic but very expensive for the emerging nation. The mood of Kaunda's followers left no room to consider the words of caution from the ex-colonial officers such as myself who stayed on to help the transition. To spend, and when they got short, to borrow, was all they could think of and in this they were encouraged by some of the do-gooders who came in from outside to proffer their advice.

The growing financial problems were compounded by the strains put on the economy following UDI in Southern Rhodesia. Kaunda's decision to adhere rigidly to the blockade, brave though

## Preface

it was, took the country to the edge of bankruptcy and incurred colossal foreign debts. Only now are the developed countries contemplating ways to reduce this burden and so far contemplation has not yet produced a great deal of action.

It may well be that these were the problems that led President Kaunda to believe that they could only be dealt with by going down the slippery path to a one party state with himself as its leader.

Political correctness has become a popular expression since I retired and it is difficult to know quite where one is when writing a book that is devoted to Africa and the Africans. It is all too easy to make errors to which someone will take exception. For example we have found it convenient to use the word 'natives' quite freely. It is not used in any way in a pejorative sense, but rather in its truly literal sense the word that describes the indigenous people of a region. Looking back to some of those far off days, I seem to recall that the governor actually banned the use of the word long before it was deemed to have any special significance.

I am also fairly certain that at that time, if asked, I would have put myself firmly on the side of the natives, and this view makes itself felt in my script. It is generally accepted that the stated policy of the colonial administration was ultimately intended to lead to majority rule (even though the concept was sometimes ignored). The rules also called on us to be apolitical and there was surprisingly little private conversation that one recollects during the 1950s as to what the future had in store. My wife Frances and I agreed to differ about the best way forward. It was when I first arrived and spent a couple of days in Cape Town that someone said to me in a harsh South African accent — 'You don't have to worry about the bloody kaffir, man!' — it shocked me then as much as it would most civilized people today.

I also cannot forego the opportunity to rebut the denigration of the colonial service that has become so popular in recent years, sometimes in parts of the media that should have known a great deal better. Many DCs administered an area of hundreds of square miles by themselves, often with no one to help and just the moral comfort and support of their wives. They were not particularly well paid and the greatest encouragement that they had was their belief that what they were doing was genuinely for the long-term

## Preface

benefit of the local inhabitants. They tried with what limited means they had at their disposal to maintain law and order and to promote the well being of the residents of their area. In a private speech, referring to the DCs President Kaunda once said to UNIP officials, 'They acted like little gods but by heavens they were hard working little gods.' There was no question of adhering to a 'nine to five' routine and malaria and other problems of the jungle also took their toll, so that some paid the ultimate price. We ourselves lost a daughter. I personally did not escape from vilification. At the time when Kaunda was a restricted person and in my custody, he had hundreds of square miles where he could wander freely and this was well known, but it did not prevent ignorant, small minded people in the UK from sending letters addressed to me as the Commandant of the Kabompo Concentration Camp. Later a correspondent of the *Northern News* (subsequently to be named *The Times of Zambia*), who should have known better, could not resist the temptation to ask Kaunda when he was prime minister how it felt to have lunch with his former gaoler. Though I felt aggrieved at the time, now, many years afterwards I can feel some gratitude for the latter incident as it did at least provide me with the title of this story.

It is also not possible to omit a reference here to the district messengers — the unsung heroes of Northern Rhodesia. Without their loyalty and unwavering support it would have been impossible for any district commissioner to have administered the large area for which he was responsible. During the times of the troubles that led up to independence they were the backing on which the colonial officers relied. In my opinion they were badly neglected in the run up to independence by their ultimate masters at the Commonwealth Office in London — it was perfectly obvious to all that the district messengers were suddenly going to find themselves on the wrong side of the administrative fence but at no time that I am aware of was any advice or encouragement given them as to the kind of transition that they faced.

E. C. G. April 2002

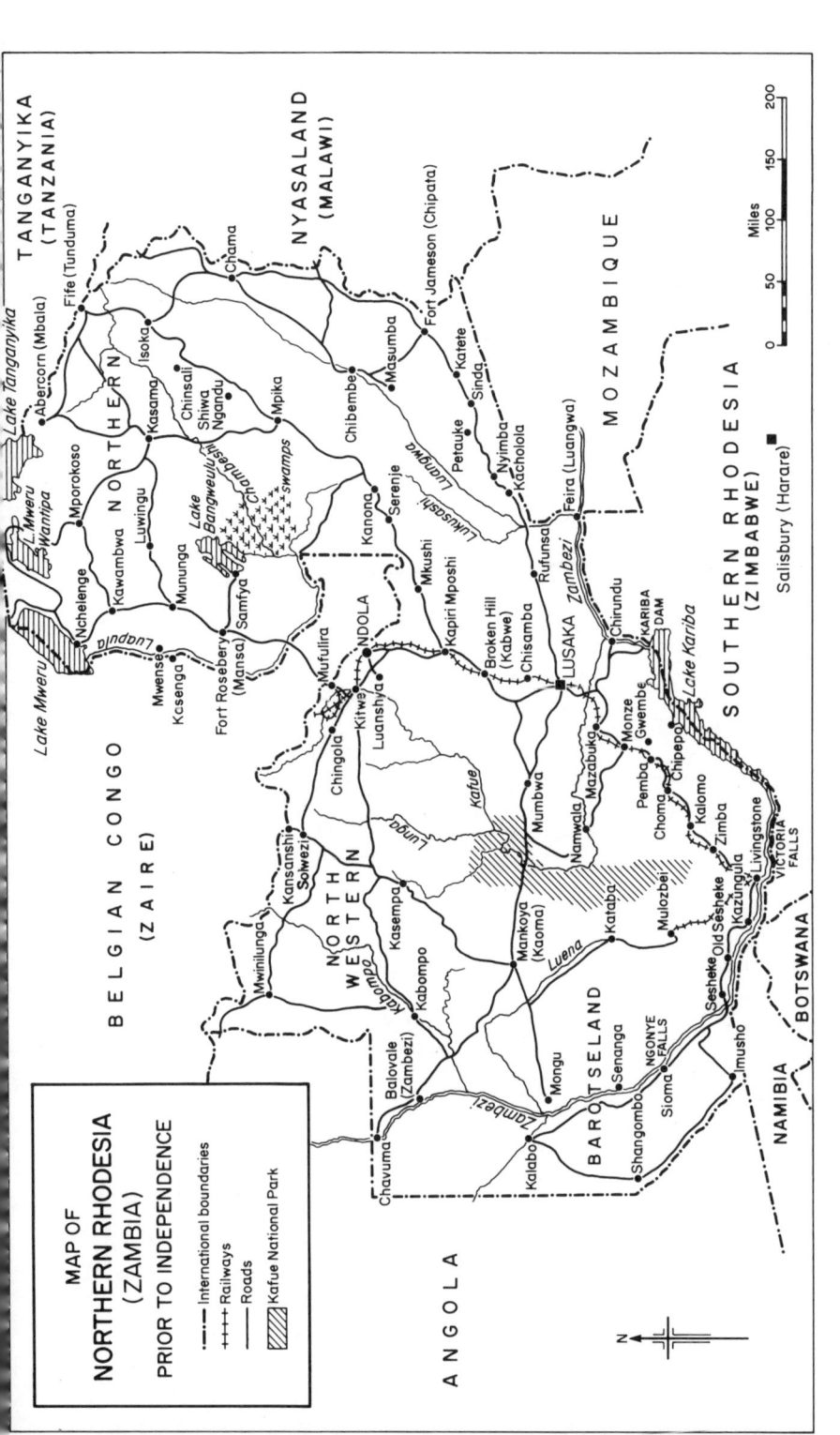

# 1
# The Letter

The arrival of THE LETTER created a sensation; to say that it came as a complete surprise is such an understatement as to be ludicrous, and it definitely requires capital letters.

It was the middle of the war and I was an officer in a bomb disposal squad. I had got married to Frances one month before and had only just returned from the brief leave grudgingly granted by the army so that we could go on a short honeymoon. We were living in a flat in Chiswick, which was close to the barracks where I was stationed.

The letter was from the Colonial Office and it stated that my name had come up in the course of a search of college records for people who had expressed an interest in working for them. It went on to enquire briefly if I was still interested in a position because if I were, then there would be no problems in getting me demobilized despite the war. To back up this surprising assertion there was an accompaniment in the shape of a copy of a letter from the Army Council; inevitably it was printed on the peculiar type of wartime stationery beloved of government offices and I have it to this day. It stated that the army recognized the needs of the colonial service and that if there were suitable recruits in the armed services they could be released with no stigma of any kind on their character. Indeed, it went further and said that anyone taking up this offer could assume that they would be doing a more valuable job as an individual looking after the needs of the Empire than as one of the herd in the armed forces (Appendix 1).

The letter is the real beginning to this story but what prompted it and the path that I had followed in arriving at a career in the colonial service are also an integral part.

In September 1939, when war broke out I was up at Cambridge with my closest friend Roy Knight, and we both enlisted, but whereas he was called up the same year, my papers did not arrive until February 1940. By that time I had completed my Part I Maths, and had got as far as two terms in geography, which resulted in the award of an MA under the wartime regulations without actually having to complete any further courses.

During our sojourn at Kings, Roy and I had frequently discussed the careers on which we proposed to embark. To him, the British Empire was like an article of faith and there was no doubt whatsoever in his mind that the only conceivable future for him was in the colonial service. His insistence that this was the best calling possible undoubtedly helped convince me that maybe my future too lay there. It was a great tragedy when he went down with his ship, HMS *Cornwall*, when it was sunk in action some years later in the Indian Ocean.

It was as a consequence of these discussions that one of the last things I did at Kings was to seek an interview with the university careers' officer. I was mindful of the problems that many ex-servicemen had in finding jobs after the First World War, and I wanted to get my name down right away for some kind of career at the conclusion of hostilities. I told him of my interest in the colonial service and specifically suggested the survey side since I was due to join a Field Survey Company when I reported for duty. He, however, proposed that my height would make me particularly suitable for the administration where 'presence' was a definite asset. I was initially intrigued by the suggestion and subsequently found the prospect immensely exciting, so I arranged for him to include my name with any others who had expressed an interest.

I had always felt a sense of admiration for those who served the country in the far-flung corners of the empire and was sure that I would not regret embarking on it as a career when the war was over.

It was then promptly and completely forgotten, as I went off to war.

As I was to discover, however, the war made no difference whatsoever to the wheels of imperial bureaucracy, which continued to grind away ceaselessly, added to which there was a staff shortage in the colonial service. This shortage was aggravated by the fact that quite a number of officers in the field, on hearing that

## The Letter

war had been declared, simply downed tools. They then headed for the nearest recruiting station although they were officially in a reserved occupation. The Colonial Office's approach to this problem had been to canvas the universities to see if there were any people who had expressed an interest in the service as a career. Of course my name had emerged.

This was the real start, which set the wheels in motion, but the background and thoughts that had culminated in my expressed interest went back much further.

I had been intermittently curious about the work that went on in the colonies since I was first gripped by the digressions of my Latin master. These were intended to help along a tedious subject when, as a young boy, I had followed in my father's footsteps to St Andrew's Preparatory School in Eastbourne.

My father Gerald Vyvyan Greenall was a self-employed marine insurance broker earning commission from the various shipping companies for obtaining cover for their ships with the Lloyds firms engaged in marine insurance. Since a young child he had always wanted to go into the navy but following an accident at his prep school when a broken arm was badly set he was considered unfit for the Royal Navy. He enjoyed telling the joke against himself that after his initial enthusiasm to join the navy he had accepted the opportunity to work with the underwriters solely because someone had said that Lloyds had something to do with ships.

He had married my mother Doris Truscott a few years before the outbreak of war in 1914. The Truscotts were a well-known family in the City, having provided two Lord Mayors, and the marriage was implacably opposed by her three brothers. Doris successfully overcame her brothers' objections by eloping.

During the First World War, Gerald was in the Royal Artillery and rose to the rank of captain commanding a battery and received the Military Cross. He was badly gassed towards the end of the conflict and had been demobilized by the time that I was born on 2 October 1919 at number 13 Hillgrove Road within spitting distance of Swiss Cottage. My grandfather and three of my uncles were also in the army. I was named after an uncle Cyril who had died during the carnage on the Western front at the Battle of Cavreille. Shortly after I was born, we moved to St John's Wood within earshot of the lion house of the London Zoo and for a few weeks the roars that could be heard at night were very frightening to a small boy.

Being sent away to school was considered an essential part of the process of being made into a man. The fact that it got the child out of the family home and made someone else responsible for their upbringing was conveniently ignored. My father had been at St Andrew's Preparatory School as a boy and I was duly packed off to the same establishment from the age of eight until I was nearly fourteen.

All that time the school was still in the hands of the same E. L. Brown who had also taught my father. He was over eighty with his white hair and supported himself on a stick, but he was a strict disciplinarian and would undoubtedly have got into serious trouble in these more permissive days. Over his years he had brought physical and mental cruelty to a fine art. I still recall him beating me and can truthfully say that at the time I hated him and wished him dead; dreadful thoughts indeed for anyone, let alone a boy just turned ten. He was of course getting too old for the job and finally died during my last year at St Andrew's.

I am now 6 foot 2 inches tall and weigh 15 stone, the army having trained me meanwhile in the gentle art of breaking a man's neck with my bare hands. In those far off days, however, I was a shrimp and at the outset when I entered St Andrew's I was bullied quite badly. Unluckily for my tormentor, his activities got noticed by those in a position to give him a taste of his own medicine and matters took a turn for the better.

These problems made me aware of the troubles that can be encountered in going through private school and a solution presented itself. I was an avid reader of boys' magazines such as *The Boys Own* and the like and one day saw an advertisement that greatly interested me. What had caught my eye was the caption: 'Don't be bullied'; it extolled the virtues of a book on jujitsu, or judo as it is more commonly called these days. Eagerly I sent off my postal order and awaited results; to my delight not only did the book arrive safely, but with it was a free gift of a spring grip that one could use to strengthen one's hands and wrists. Nowadays I can look back on this display of self-help with a degree of pride, but it is nothing compared with the boost the book gave to my self-confidence. Fortunately, the bullying had stopped so I had no

## The Letter

opportunity to put my new found skills into practice, which was probably just as well as one never knows where these things may lead.

Looking back from a distance of many years I suppose that life at St Andrew's was not too bad. In retrospect, it seems to me that every effort was made to look after us; we were well fed and there was as much variety in our lives as there was on the menu. We were taught to play fives as well as the usual school activities of athletics, cricket, soccer, hockey and rugby. At the weekend it was possible to take long walks to Beachy Head and Saturday evenings were enlivened by talks illustrated with slides on an epidiascope. Sunday nights we were able to visit Mr Brown in his house and to sprawl on the floor while he read to us books such as *The Woman in White* and the *The Moonstone*.

It was a Mr Hall who taught Latin, my least favoured subject. Nevertheless, he was my favourite master because he used to enliven his lessons by reading the letters he received from his son who was a district commissioner in Nigeria. I shall never forget a graphic demonstration of his when he strutted to and fro in front of the class demonstrating how to pace off a distance and the chipping of trees as a means of boundary demarcation. Maybe he thought Latin was as tedious as I did!

This was probably my first exposure to the concept of working in the colonial service and even then it sounded as if it was an exciting life. Further exposure came with the return to England of Peter Cunningham who was the son of settlers in Kenya and the ward of Roy Truscott, my uncle. Peter was one year my junior. It would be too facile to say that these experiences gave me the basic ideas for my future career although undoubtedly the seeds were planted then. The real inspiration was to come ten years or so later through my friendship with Roy Knight.

From the educational standpoint, I soon discovered a natural bent for mathematics and thoroughly enjoyed arithmetic, algebra and geometry. For its time the school took a surprisingly enlightened view of some aspects of education and actively encouraged me to take extra maths lessons from a Mr Bryant. When the time came to leave St Andrew's, I was already using logarithms and studying differential calculus and conic sections. The realization that I possessed a very useful short-term visual memory also enabled me to succeed academically. It was many years later that I discovered that the real way to learn a subject was through total immersion.

The extra lessons that I had received were of considerable assistance to me when the time came to take the entrance examination for Clifton College and, indeed, I was fortunate enough to win an exhibition of £40 — a not inconsiderable sum in those days.

During my fourth year at St Andrew's my parents were divorced. Gerald was very Edwardian in many of his attitudes and had a mistress. I forgave my parents for this rude shock many years ago but it was unfortunate for all of us (with the possible exception of the mistress) that they did not put it off for a while as he had only four years to live.

It had always been taken for granted by my mother's family that I was going to Clifton College and between them they successfully influenced my father. Clifton had been very popular with the Truscotts for a long time. My uncles had all been educated there including my namesake who had been killed during the war. It was a carefree time, which I did not realize had been made possible by grandmother Agnes, who was picking up the bills. It is a source of great regret that I did not know her better at the time, my recollections of her, being of a lady always dressed in 'widow's weeds' and who never took a holiday.

Nowhere could have suited me better than Clifton and those years were some of the happiest times of my life. I particularly enjoyed the sporting side of boarding school life and did quite well at boxing and rowing; I also took up fencing. It was through my sporting interest that I met and became a firm friend of Roy Knight who was the captain of boxing and whose short life was later to become inextricably intertwined with mine.

The public and grammar school systems of the day were one of the principal sources of recruits to the various government services such as the armed forces and the colonial and Indian civil services. One was subtly (and sometimes not so subtly) indoctrinated with the concept that one was privileged and that as a result one would be expected both to lead and serve. Clifton itself was highly oriented towards the army despite the fact that we were regularly taught that the First World War had been 'the war to end all wars'.

## The Letter

One year I took the role of Calpurnia in the school production of *Julius Caesar* and though I did not know it at the time, my future bride was sitting in the audience.

From Clifton, Roy and I went up to King's College, Cambridge and were freshmen together. It was in his rooms that I first met his sister Frances, who made a great impression on me from the moment that we met.

We had discovered that we were near neighbours and during one vacation, Roy called on us at Abercorn Place in St John's Wood and brought round with him one of the new gas masks intended for civilians so that we could try it on. We discussed the war that everyone felt sure was fast approaching. Shortly afterwards the masks were distributed to the population at large.

Living so close and lured by the prospect of seeing Frances, I became a frequent visitor at 56 Eaton Court in Hampstead where they lived. I was always made welcome, especially by Roy's mother, Christina, who seemed to take quite a shine to me.

All of this time as well as at college he preached the imperative virtues of working for the greater good of the empire.

These memories were still vivid in mind at the time I received the letter from the Colonial Office. I had no great difficulty in making up my mind and wrote back, replying that there was no question but that my interest was as great as ever. At a second interview shortly afterwards I was asked to indicate my first three preferences. Looking back in time, I have a wry sense of amusement as my choices; Cyprus and Palestine were almost the first territories to be granted their independence. As for my third choice, Uganda, its future was ill fated to say the least.

All of this time the war continued to rumble on around us, and it seemed totally unreal to believe that there was a possibility that I might be suddenly removed from it all.

After my call-up papers arrived in February 1940, I was sent initially for basic training at Fort Widley. This establishment had originally been constructed to resist a Napoleonic invasion, though how it was intended to have accomplished this I never knew as it faced inland. I was commissioned in June and then sent to 25 Field Survey Company of the Royal Engineers in Belfast. Subsequently I was given further training in surveying and map making.

Early 1942 saw me in the camp in Dalmeny Park outside

Edinburgh and later at Caergwrle near Chester but I was becoming bored with doing nothing and craved some action as well as the night life and excitement of wartime London. I volunteered for and was transferred to 24 Bomb Disposal Company, which was based in Chiswick.

All this time I had been courting Frances and we had become engaged. To call the banns at the parish church in Chelsea it was required that she had an official address in the parish so, in order to make everything lawful, she left a suitcase at the home of her sister.

We were finally married on 24 April 1943 before leaving for the Scottish Highlands for a brief honeymoon at Invershin. On returning to London we established residence that May in Chiswick. Although it was near the RE barracks we were not able to spend all our evenings together as I was sent off to a nearby training camp for a few weeks and it was there that the letter had come. Needless to say, I promptly informed my CO of its contents and my intended reply.

Despite all this excitement the possibility of a post still seemed enormously remote during hostilities and there was the business of winning the war to be completed. Time seemed to pass and nothing happened and it was yet another surprise when the next letter arrived that November when the CO was busy passing out mail. His reaction was quite amusing considering that he had been kept in the picture all along, 'Greenall!' he barked, 'What the hell is going on? These are your demob papers and we haven't even invaded Europe yet.' The letter in question was to advise me that my release from the army had been arranged and that I would be going to a posting in Northern Rhodesia.

From that time on matters moved along quite briskly, while Frances and I sat by the fire in the evenings and speculated on the future.

It is true that both of us were imperialists, though not I hope in the derogatory sense that the passage of time has seen attached to it. Both of us were members of the Royal Empire Society, subsequently renamed the Commonwealth Society. We both sincerely believed that Britain's mission in the colonies was to bring the benefits of civilization to the local populations and to prepare them for ultimate home rule. The concept of *Pax Britannica* was

## The Letter

well understood at home. We had no conception of the helter-skelter speed with which things were going to change following the cessation of hostilities.

The vast red blob of southern Africa might have been a uniform colour but at that time there were great differences between its various components. The Dominion of South Africa was still a part of the British Empire and under Field Marshall Smuts had its own armies in the field fighting alongside ours on the various African battlefields. Jan Smuts and Churchill had the highest regard for each other dating back to the conclusion of the Boer War and of course Britain had its high commissioner in Pretoria.

In contrast, Southern Rhodesia was a crown colony while Northern Rhodesia was a colonial dependency and protectorate. The unusual status of the latter was a legacy of the days when Cecil Rhodes had founded the British South Africa Company with a view to exploiting the lands that he planned to discover and colonize to the north of South Africa. It seems likely that he had in mind another chartered company like the East India Company, which had been the foundation of the fortunes of many British families.

Whatever our discussions may have dwelt on at the time, the fact is that they had little sense of the reality that was to unfold and all that lay in the future that was mercifully hidden from sight.

In a brief but pleasant interlude we went to the Senate House in Cambridge in January 1944 for my official graduation a few days before setting sail for a totally new life.

I departed from Hull the last day of January on the SS *Neleus*, a cargo ship of the Blue Funnel Line. We formed part of an impressive convoy that was making for the Mediterranean; at Gibraltar the *Neleus* left the convoy and headed on her own for Cape Town. It was not unusual for some ships to travel on their own if they were much faster than most other convoy ships as 'the powers that be' reckoned that speed was the best defence against submarines. The *Queen Mary* regularly made the transatlantic crossing as an unescorted troop carrier. In any case it was impractical to escort a single ship.

It was March before the ship docked in Cape Town. Having risen early, my first sight of the majesty of Table Mountain filled me with awe. I was warmly welcomed by an old friend of a relative of the family and had a few days in which to see something of Cape Town before I had to leave. Before the war I had travelled quite extensively on the continent, which had broadened my outlook considerably, and South Africa presented me with no great surprises, unlike Northern Rhodesia (NR), which had an altogether different culture.

From Cape Town the route to NR involved first travelling on the train to Bulawayo, a route that has subsequently become famous as a tourist run. After changing in Bulawayo one took the Rhodesian Railways to get to Lusaka. My arrival there in the early morning was nearly a disaster as in the half-light it was not apparent that the descent from the train was right down to the ground and I could easily have fallen flat on my face. At this distance in time I cannot recall whether there was in fact no platform anywhere or whether there was a platform but the train was too long for it all to be accommodated as has recently been suggested to me. Be that as it may I was fortunate that my long legs saved me and I was ready for my official reception by Johnny Walker and Robin Foster.

## 2
# Indoctrination in Lusaka

Lusaka came as something of a shock as I had neither been given a description of the capital of Northern Rhodesia nor seen any pictures of it. The capital had been relocated from Livingstone on the grounds that it was more central in 1935 when the date for the official changeover was intended to coincide with the silver jubilee of George V. Despite its status, it was what at first sight, in the parlance of the cowboy movies of the time, would have been described as a 'one horse town'.

The main street, Cairo Road, ran through its centre. It was never entirely clear to me how the street acquired its unusual name. There were two conflicting suggestions: the first being that it had been an optimistic reference to Rhodes's idea of a Cape to Cairo railroad, the other was that it was a convenient stopping place for the intrepid travellers earlier in the century who had tried to drive the same route. There were two hotels: The Grand Hotel and The Lusaka, which together with a few corrugated iron roofed shops were on one side of the road and looked across it to the railway that ran parallel on the other. A little way further along, Cairo Road curved to turn across the tracks to the start of a long sloping road that rose gradually until it reached Government House, which sat in solitary magnificence on top of a hill. Part of the way along the rise but still at a respectful distance from Government House were the various government office buildings collectively known as the Secretariat, together with the buildings housing the Executive and Legislative Councils.

The road joining them, which was one of only two sections of tarmac road in the protectorate in 1944, marked the separation of Government House from the Secretariat. The area of Lusaka between the station and the Secretariat was the European township, which was separated from the African township about two miles away. Household staff was usually accommodated in small houses located in the garden. Nearby were the airport, which was under the control of the South African Air Force, and the Gymkhana Club, which had squash and tennis courts, as well as a golf course as amenities alongside the Club House.

Nearly all the houses had corrugated iron roofs (in contrast to other towns that relied much more heavily on thatch). The few exceptions were referred to rather rudely as the 'HUs and Bloodies' signifying that the 'higher ups' got notably better housing.

I was accommodated at the Grand whose name hardly reflected the accommodation that was available. There was no water to be had in the bedrooms and the toilets were situated outside in a block at the back.

The initial training that I received in Lusaka was largely concerned with the treasury side of colonial administration. One of the more important duties of a district officer (DO) was to take care of local finances. They were responsible under the aegis of the district commissioner (DC) for keeping the district accounts. These recorded every item of expenditure made under the authority of the treasury warrant issued by the accountant general, who was, I suppose, the colonial equivalent of the paymaster general at home. The principal local source of revenue was, of course, the native poll tax, which the DC was responsible for collecting; details of all revenue were also recorded in the district accounts.

All of this sounds a great deal more complex than it really was, as in practice it was done very simply by the use of separate cashbooks for 'payments' and 'receipts'. There was also an expenditure ledger known as the 'votes' ledger and so called after the collective title of the heads of expenditure.

I have pleasant memories of those few weeks of training given in the Accountant General's Department in Lusaka by a very amiable gentleman by the name of Hatchwell. The instruction was both useful and informative, and provided an excellent introduction to the work that would need to be undertaken when one finally arrived on post. It was an open office and learning to understand the monthly operation of checking the cashbooks after they were sent in by the DCs was a straightforward matter.

The official policy of the Colonial Office towards Northern

## Indoctrination in Lusaka

Rhodesia was 'paramountcy', which meant exactly that, namely that the interests of the native African population were paramount. With the facile benefit of hindsight it is not too difficult to figure out how it was that the territory came to be so unprepared for independence when it eventually occurred. The woeful lack of higher educational establishments meant that there were few people with any background or experience, let alone training, to run a country. In contrast, India, which was inherently far more wealthy, had a well developed school and university system and, as a result, a comparatively large well educated class to draw on, so consequently was far better prepared for independence than any of Britain's African territories.

It can of course be said by way of excuse that independence arrived far sooner than even the most optimistic minds in the Colonial Office had ever envisaged. At the time when I arrived in 1944, Standard VI was the highest level of schooling that could be reached by the general population. There was some teacher training at Chalimbana, but even there the level attainable was restricted. Although there was a noticeable improvement over the following twenty odd years, it was still far from adequate. Subsequent to independence, President Kaunda wrote a review in the 1970s for the *Daily Telegraph* of a book called *Reap the Whirlwind* by Geoffrey Bing. In it he said: 'A damning indictment of British colonial policy and the neglect which led to the handing over of independence with only the minimal preparation ... which prevented the build up of the financial or economic civil service machine which was essential.'

Needless to say he did not point out that the minimal preparation was at least in part due to the fact that once he had the bit firmly between his teeth, he would not have been prepared to consider any delay to independence to provide for such niceties as training. However, this is anticipating a lot of history and I was still a novice.

The provincial administration, or PA as it was usually known, was where I worked initially as a cadet in the provincial and district offices. It was also responsible, among other things, for recruiting suitable school leavers from the local population. These were then deployed either into the clerical service or the offices run by the tribal councils and treasuries — a rather crude form of what is known nowadays as 'on the job training'. This was a standard procedure and was followed by each government department, as well as by the mines and other employers.

The PA also employed a sort of paramilitary police known as district messengers, which had powers of arrest. The district messengers were usually based on the local government administrative office or the *boma*, as it was universally called, using the native word for a protected enclosure. The same term was used all over most of the southern part of the continent and as far north as Kenya. A few rifles were held at every district station for their use in an emergency, though the only times that I ever saw these guns used were for protection against dangerous animals or occasionally to shoot game to provide meat for government labourers who were entitled to rations as a part of their contract of service. For example, under a typical contract of service they could have been employed to act as bearers for district officers when they went on tour and needed to sleep under canvas.

On these occasions suitable firearms were essential; lions would normally keep their distance in the daytime, but at night a large campfire was an essential precaution. Everyone who travelled had heard of and taken note of the experience of one party in the bush that had failed to travel with a gun. The fire had burnt low and a lion took one of the bearers from beside the dying embers; the rest of the camp had to take to the trees. All attempts to drive off the lion by shouting failed and they had the gruesome experience of having to remain in the trees all night while the lion was feeding below on their erstwhile companion.

Ultimately, the news came for which I had been waiting — my appointment to take up a post at Kasama. On hastily referring to a map this place turned out to be the capital of the Northern Province, which was the home of the Bemba, the largest of the native tribes in the territory.

# 3
# Kasama

A married cadet on his first posting was officially entitled to hire a car *once* for travel. This meant that had I done so then, there would not have been one with which to meet Frances when she arrived, so alternative travel arrangements had to be made. After I set off, it quickly became apparent that life was not going to be a bed of roses all the way — here I was, a specially released ex-officer of His Majesty's armed forces who had been used to first-class travel, sitting in the front seat of a mail lorry for a three-day journey that could have been completed in under ten hours in a car.

Although being driven in the lorry was uncomfortable, the slowness of the journey made it a wonderful way to see the country and get to meet some of the people *en route*. The route we followed was known as the Great North Road and during my entire time in NR, I never found out who had christened it thus or whether it was intended as a joke. Nothing could possibly have had less resemblance to the broad tarmac road that led north from London past Hatfield and Welwyn. During the course of the journey it was necessary to cross the Chambeshi River (meaning the great water) that was not bridged but had to be traversed on a Heath-Robinson type of ferry. This consisted of a pontoon raft constructed from a mixture of sawn and unsawn timber, which had been lashed and nailed together and was floated on some empty 44-gallon drums. This contraption was fastened to a strong sheet anchor cable fastened to both banks and could be hauled across by a gang of a dozen or so 'ferry men' complete with their *capitao*.

This was a free service that was paid for from the road vote of the DC Kasama. Innumerable stories used to circulate about the various purposes to which the road vote was put, although this

## Kaunda's Gaoler

one certainly was legitimate — I must say that during my sojourn in Kasama I never ran across any examples of misuse.

One of these stories came to light when it was repeated to the supposed perpetrator. Sir Arthur Benson arrived to take up a new appointment as governor and naturally received a large number of congratulatory letters, one of which had a twist to it. As near as I can paraphrase the contents it went something like this:

Dear Sir Arthur,

It goes without saying that, like all your friends, I was delighted to hear the news of your appointment and send my warmest congratulations.

I hope, however, that you will not take it amiss if I remind you of an occasion some years ago when I passed through Kawambwa on my way to Abercorn to take charge of an important trading store. The day was a public holiday and when I arrived at the Kalungwishi River I discovered that the road had been closed until further notice due to the fact that the pontoon was being used by the DC for a fishing trip.

I trust that now you are governor there will be no more need to interfere with the Kalungwishi pontoon when you wish to go fishing!

Anecdotes in Northern Rhodesia were more common than sunsets, the time of day when they were generally repeated as an accompaniment to the traditional sundowners.

Reverting to the Chambeshi pontoon, there was an occasion early during my stay that made a great impression on me as regards the realities of life for the native population.

I had arrived at the south bank and, having a few minutes to wait for the ferry, decided to consume the sandwiches that had been provided for my lunch. Finding them more than required and thinking the area to be deserted I threw them into the bush alongside the road. To my horror this nearly precipitated a riot as about a score of native children appeared from nowhere and descended on them fighting like vultures over the crusts.

It had not entered my head that bread was a great luxury, even if soiled, however unintentionally by contact with the ground.

## Kasama

I was given a very warm welcome to Kasama by the DC, Bill Williams who introduced me to Simon Simpson, with whom I was to share a bungalow. Bill and his wife also took me to the Gymkhana Club where I soon made the acquaintance of the rest of the European community and became accepted as an established resident. For a while I was treated as something of a curiosity, as indeed had also been the case in Lusaka. The war had cut off the colony from British visitors for several years and first-hand news of life and conditions in the homeland was at a premium.

Simple Simon, as he was known, was a good companion and gave me a lot of tips on local life; he was also very helpful in other ways such as introductions. He was formerly a member of the Malaysian police who had been fortunate enough to escape just ahead of the Japanese invaders. Unfortunately, he was moved to another post shortly after I arrived.

The capital of the Northern Province was a rather grandiose name for Kasama, a small township that, apart from about three dozen European settlers, was the home for somewhat rather fewer than 300 Bemba who lived in a separate compound. One of its claims to fame was that it had been captured by the Germans about a week before the end of the First World War and was where they had received the news of the armistice. Apart from my colonial service colleagues, Kasama and its environs were well stocked with old colonial hands, traders and missionaries. Most government departments had their own provincial offices there, including agriculture and public works such as roads and engineering, as well as the hospital. It was also the home to one of the half dozen airfields in Northern Rhodesia that had been set up for military purposes and that were run by the South African Air Force. Kasama had been the principal administrative centre for the Northern Province for around 35 years and the principle Bemba settlement for far longer, almost certainly more than two hundred years and predating Livingstone's visits to the area.

It was not too many years after independence that a railway was pushed through linking Zambia with Tanzania and it would be very interesting to see the changes that have taken place in Kasama with the arrival of the railway and the passage of time.

Generally speaking, an outstation or *boma* was a largish oval area cleared of bush. The length typically was between a third and three-quarters of a mile and the width around a quarter of a mile. The government office was located at one end, while either side of the road leading up to it were the houses (thatched bungalows) of the staff and the few European traders living there. Most households had a cook, a cleaner and a gardener though not full time. These would live with their families in very small houses at the bottom of their employer's garden. Wherever possible a *boma* would be located at a high point, though these were few and far between in most of the Northern Province. Kasama was no exception and was situated on the side of a hill.

Not too far away was the African township that housed all the families of the local people associated with the *boma*. These of course included the district messengers, office clerks and government labourers. The clinic with its dispensary and the prison were also located in the township.

Despite being positioned on a hill there was remarkably little to be seen from the *boma*, since all the buildings were of single-storey construction and were set in the midst of the bush. Despite the lack of moisture throughout the dry season, there were plenty of trees and, although they were very misshapen, they were considered sufficiently tall to provide a place of refuge from a lion if needs be, although I never had occasion to put it to the test.

The main office (also loosely referred to as the *boma*) itself comprised two or three good-sized rooms together with smaller quarters for the clerks; the size of the offices was dictated by the fact that they sometimes had to double as a courtroom. Work started at the *boma* at 8.00 a.m. on weekdays. The district messengers would parade outside the offices under the direction of the senior messenger present, and fall in, ready for inspection by the DC or whoever was in charge on that particular day.

The messengers were hugely proud of their status and this was reflected in the smartness of their uniforms and general appearance. At that time the uniform was a plain blue tunic with red facings and matching blue drill shorts topped off with a red fez, which had a long black silken cord tassel, and gleaming brass NRG (Northern Rhodesia Government) badge. They used to oil and polish their arms and legs until the skin shone and glistened in the sunlight, like their shining faces; fresh from my army days it added an entirely new dimension to the term 'spit and polish'.

## Kasama

There were no regular police in the northern territory at that time and the messengers also constituted a local police force under the control of the provincial administration that also had responsibility for the prison service. They carried handcuffs and had powers of arrest, but unless there were special circumstances did not carry arms. In the absence of any other mode of communication one relied on the messengers to live up to their title; locally they would go on foot, but they would travel by mail lorry or bicycle to outlying areas. They lived in the compound in their own housing, provided by the government.

I was kept extremely busy on what nowadays would be termed a steep learning curve. Bill Williams provided the principal training in my regular duties and it could not have been bettered. There was also a lot to pick up from the head clerk and the head messenger as well as my interpreter. Bill's and my paths were to cross again a few years later, when I was posted to the Secretariat where he was then chief secretary.

In my spare time it was essential for me to obtain a grounding in Bemba and very importantly to increase my proficiency at shooting with a .350 sporting rifle and a shotgun, both of which would be needed when I went on tour.

The kind assistance of the Simms family helped me to meet the language requirement. Mrs Simms had devoted her life to the mission field and to raising, Edna, her clever young daughter who worked in the health department and who undertook to teach me the rudiments of Bemba, which she did very efficiently. If the kindness I received from this small family were insufficient to engrave them permanently on my mind then there is no doubt that the ear trumpet wielded by the mother would have.

I already rather prided myself as a marksman before my arrival, having started shooting with a .22 in my days at St Andrew's and subsequently with a .303 at Clifton before joining the army. While in the services I had qualified as a musketry instructor. Under the circumstances there was an enormous incentive to do what so many of my predecessors had done and go hunting.

Every book that could be found on the subject and was available in the excellent local library was eagerly consumed, especially any relating to F. C. Selous (1851–1917) who had been the acknowledged master of the craft. There was much to learn; for example, one needed to know where to aim to achieve an immediate fatal shot, a matter of great importance with dangerous species. There were also other matters it was essential to know such as the fact that elephants compensated for their poor sight by having an exceptional sense of smell and that wounded lions had a nasty habit of doubling back to take an unwary hunter from the rear.

It did not take long to track down other like-minded individuals; probably the foremost of the local exponents was the provincial commissioner himself, Mr Gilbert Howe.

One evening a leopard broke into the *boma* cattle kraal and killed a calf. This provided an opportunity to test my shooting skills on the basis that leopards usually returned to their kill. In the unlikely eventuality of missing, I took the precaution of injecting the carcass with some of the strychnine held in the safe against such possibilities. According to the books, the next step was to look for a convenient tree in which to lie in wait for the shot when the leopard returned. It came as a rude shock when it dawned on me that, 'convenient trees' are not always where they are needed. The alternative was to spend a very uncomfortable night squatting on a makeshift platform precariously perched on the fence surrounding the kraal. By this time the rush of adrenalin that had galvanized me into a search for adventure had subsided and it seemed a lot easier to let the leopard get on with it in peace. The big cat duly returned and the poison did its work. My reward was a magnificent pelt unmarred by any bullet holes. It was possible to have the animal skinned by the local *fundi* and many years later it was sold in the UK by the Hudson Bay Company as part of a collection of skins.

In passing I learnt that all animals can easily be blinded or possibly hypnotized at night by a powerful light. This could be capitalized on by wearing a specially designed torch strapped to the head, known as a Bulala lamp. Several local residents had them though I never tried to get one myself.

Leopards were quite common around Kasama, although they were rarely seen due to their natural shyness. There was a celebrated occasion, the year before I arrived, when one that had been raiding the *boma* chicken run had been trapped but managed to get away. Pursued by some Africans, the animal, instead of

## Kasama

making good its escape bolted in the wrong direction and into the garden of Gilbert Howe, the PC. From there it went on and made the further mistake of jumping clear through the mosquito netting of the lounge into the room from which Mrs Howe and another lady had been watching the chase. The creature cowered in one corner while the ladies all scrambled to get out of the room led by the houseboy, who unceremoniously bundled Mrs Howe out of the way in order to lead the way. The poor leopard then proceeded to compound its errors by remaining in possession of the room, where shortly afterwards Mr Glieman, one of the local traders, found it and promptly shot it. A detailed account of the incident was given in the *Northern Rhodesia Journal* a few years subsequently.

My initiation into some of the rituals of social courtesy required of one had taken place in Lusaka. There it had involved finding the various books that one was expected to sign on first arriving in lieu of leaving one's card. The most important of these books was the one at Government House. The governor's household included an ADC whose duties included arrangements for entertaining. He was responsible for the custody of the visitors' book and the compilation of the lists from which were selected the names of the guests to be invited to various functions.

Whenever one was away from Lusaka it was most important to sign the book with the entry 'PPC' (*pour prière congé*) to signify one's absence and ensure that no invitations were issued by accident during that time.

In Kasama it was much less formal; one met colleagues at work and invitations generally followed. These social occasions usually took the form of getting together for sundowners, especially on public holidays and red-letter days such as the King's Birthday or a royal wedding, which were also public holidays unlike in the home country. Sundowners were invariably consumed as long drinks and, during the war, the principal tipple was brandy coming from the Cape. One of the local customs was that the bottle or decanter was passed with the invitation 'help yourself'. The ostensible reasoning behind this was that no one could blame the host if a guest got rather too merry.

It transpired that Gilbert Howe, the PC, was also an old Cliftonian and I was welcomed with what seemed like open arms.

## Kaunda's Gaoler

He was a real old-timer and greatly enjoyed describing how as a young man he had wanted to go big game hunting. Someone had told him that the best way to do this was to join the British South Africa Police and so he applied for an interview with the directors of the BSAC (British South Africa Company), as it was then known, in London. When asked why it was that he was applying, he immediately replied, 'Because I want to shoot an elephant'.

He was an invaluable ally and gave me a great deal of advice of the sort that could not be found formally, such as which people in the administration in Lusaka could be trusted and which could not be relied upon. He told me that of all the areas in the Northern Province it was Luwingu that was the jewel of its crown and some years later I was delighted to be posted there after my return from leave in the UK.

As a cadet I was sworn in as a class IV magistrate under the supervision of the DC, who was himself a class II magistrate, and found myself presiding over my own court. It was not normally required to administer tribal customs and when they arose from time to time such disputes were referred to the nearby court of Chief Mwamba. Fairly soon I found myself scrutinizing the somewhat sketchy case records of various disputes that the DC passed on, leaving me to seek further elaboration of the case through my interpreter, the tribal assessor or court clerk.

Before my studies were so rudely interrupted by the Second World War, one of my course subjects was anthropology. I had never anticipated that it would be relevant and it was a bizarre sensation to discover that it was now to be closely interwoven into my daily life. Indeed, I had hardly arrived and become accustomed to life in Kasama before an event occurred that left me on the receiving end of a crash course in the tribal customs of the Bemba.

The Bemba had reached a crisis in the development of the tribe. The paramount chief, Chitimukulu, had died and was due for burial in the sacred grove of Mwalole.

Ordinary members of the tribe would have a simple village funeral, where the body would be wrapped in a sleeping mat and buried. Alternatively, it might be folded in a blanket so that it took on the position it had originally occupied in the mother's womb and was then interred in a niche hollowed out from one of the walls of the grave. It was believed that in this fashion the deceased would leave this world in the same manner as he or she had entered it.

A much more elaborate procedure was required for the paramount chief of the Bemba, who was not only the chief but also the religious head of the tribe. It was the latter aspect that largely accounted for the absolute respect and obedience that he received from all the Bemba people. He was believed to have supernatural powers, which were important for maintaining the fertility of the land, and it was important that these powers had no chance to escape from his body. At one time in the old days of the nineteenth century it was customary for the expiring chief to be strangled or smothered on his deathbed by one of his faithful councillors to ensure that the last breath remained in him. Custom required that the chief's body should undergo a process comparable to mummification and, for this purpose, it had to remain in his own hut for a year. The mummification was achieved basically by smoking the corpse — the local people were well used to this process as it was extensively used for the preservation of the meat from game.

The partially mummified body of the chief was then escorted by a multitude of people on the way to his last resting place in the sacred grove, which was several days' travel away. Numerous traditional ceremonies were involved, including a make-believe pitched battle at the edge of the river that marked the boundary with the Chinsali district tribal area. At the entrance to the sacred grove the cortège would halt and only those authorized by tribal custom were allowed to enter Mwalole. This of course did not include a DC and his assistants.

This presented a considerable problem, for ancient custom also dictated that the chief should have company when he went to the after world. In earlier times the ritual was decidedly more sinister. Upon the death of the chief, the principal wife, together with his pipe bearer and other members of his immediate entourage would all have been arrested. The body would have been borne by slaves and each time the funeral party stopped to rest, the body would have been placed in a hut and one of the slaves would have been sacrificed and his body lain across the doorway. The significance of this was that stepping over a corpse was extremely unlucky because the spirit of the body would be able to look at the genitals of the person that had committed this sacrilege. The thought of what the spirit might do with this knowledge was too appalling to be contemplated. The villages through which the path led would be totally abandoned by their inhabitants during the passage. Finally, on arriving at the sacred grove, the remaining pallbearers and his chief wife would have been buried with him, she in a sitting position cradling his body on her lap.

In the middle of the twentieth century, of course, the colonial administration did not look favourably on human sacrifice, no matter how customary. This disapprobation, however, did not mean that the Bemba might not have other ideas.

Two of the most experienced DCs in the territory were deputed to attend the funeral and took with them a strong force of district messengers. Effectively, they conducted a census at all the villages along the route and then sealed off the sacred grove so that they could carefully check the entry and egress of those officiating, members of the family and so on. The officers had been clearly instructed that there was to be no interference with lawful tribal rites but, on the other hand, the tribal authorities were made well aware of the precautions that were being taken to ensure that they complied with the law.

As far as the authorities were concerned all went off without any problems and it appeared that the same number of persons came out of the sacred grove as had entered it; nevertheless, some time after the new paramount chief had been selected, there were rumours that perhaps the old traditions had been observed in some manner after all.

The first piece of gossip was that the old chief had not actually been buried at the time of the funeral but had merely been covered and concealed in some way until such time as the correct ritual could be carried out without interference. This did not seem to be very probable.

The second story was much more worrying; a hunting party had come across the remains of a teenage girl who had apparently been killed and then partly eaten by scavenging animals. What added a particularly sinister aspect was that the corpse had no hands and these appeared to have been severed deliberately. The missing hands could easily have been transported secretly into the funeral ceremony and buried when they could have been interpreted as symbolic of the service to be provided to the dead chief. It was also suggested that the girl was of the right age required by custom and that she could have been sacrificed by the dreaded *mavirondongo* (a Bemba word meaning 'neck-twisters'). These were the official tribal executioners and they were invariably blamed for being responsible whenever there were any suspicions of ritual sacrifice. They could have killed the young girl well away from the area of the sacred grove before the funeral and removed the hands to use in the rites at Mwalole and left the body to be eaten by wild animals.

Interestingly, a somewhat similar sequence of events had followed the funeral of a previous *Chitimikulu*, which had taken place back in the 1930s. It appeared that some while after the government approved obsequies, officers were chatting casually to one of the locals and he told them that he had just been to the funeral of the chief. Superficially, it is easy to suggest that the DCs could have insisted on being present at the final rites, but it was well known that by custom entry to the sacred grove was forbidden to unauthorized persons at all times. Broadly, Colonial Office policy was that we should not interfere in local customs unless it was absolutely necessary to prevent criminal activity or to ensure natural justice.

There was a story told of another DC who passed by Mwalole while on tour and instructed his porters to pitch his tent nearby. Later he went with one of the non-Bemba natives and entered the sacred grove in blatant defiance of the ban — thus seriously offending the guardian spirits of the burial ground. He compounded his offence by killing a snake there, a place where all snakes were protected by taboo. The rest of his porters were horrified and when a lion killed the native who had escorted him, no one was at all surprised. Shortly afterwards the DC was killed when a flagstaff he was helping to put up at his *boma* fell on him. Latterly, I became acquainted with the officer's brother, who reached a high position in the administration, but always found myself reluctant to ask for confirmation of the story. I can, however, vouch for the fact that *boma* flagstaffs were not always stable, for many years later during my period at Kabompo, the staff there was blown down by a gust of wind and it narrowly missed Frances.

One of the characters of Kasama was Sister Elaine Slater who ran the local hospital. She would cycle around the villages rather like a district nurse back at home apart from the fact that she carried an army issue .450 revolver with her. Many were the life saving operations she performed in the wilds. There was one celebrated occasion when she went out one night to visit a very expectant mother to be; when she arrived at the hut it was to find the entire family in a state of hysterics. A leopard had got onto the roof and decided to stay there, so no one dared to go out and the frightened patient had gone into labour; Sister Slater took matters into her own hands and resolved the problems by first shooting the leopard and then delivering the baby. She married Derek Peachey, the Kasama accountant, shortly after I arrived. They were madly in love and years later were to boast that they had never spent a night apart since their marriage. He too had led an unusual life. Of independent means he had been in the Household Cavalry between the wars. After being disappointed in his pursuit of an actress in a musical, he had hired a plane complete with pilot to enter in the Cape Town Air Race. The plane had crashed in the Abercorn district, killing the pilot. Feeling himself very much to blame, Derek had sworn to remain in the area where the plane had crashed. This he did, buying a farm on a piece of crown land nearby. There he was to remain until some time after independence when the two of them seized an opportunity to get out of the country in an inconspicuous fashion.

I had been in Kasama for some months before the good tidings that were eagerly awaited arrived. It was news to overshadow all other considerations. This piece of intelligence was, of course, the impending arrival of Frances to join me.

\* \* \*

Back in England, Frances had been maintaining a gentle but constant pressure (her own words were 'by being a shameless nuisance') on the Colonial Office and the Department of Manpower to obtain her release from a wartime job in the International Telephone Exchange. Scarcely a day went past without her picking up a pen to send me the latest word on progress. She lobbied unremittingly for support and many people were sympathetic.

## Kasama

Her time there had not been without its interesting moments and she had been instrumental in the apprehension of a spy who was subsequently arrested and shot. We, of course, knew none of this until the publication of *The Autobiography of Sir Patrick Hastings* in 1948. In the book, Hastings describes how the spy used to go to an isolated telephone box on a hill overlooking Londonderry harbour where he could observe convoys assembling. He then placed a telephone call to a 'friend' in Dublin with whom he carried on a conversation, disguising the information about the convoy under the guise of discussing supposed clues in a crossword puzzle. The book went on to say that he had come to the attention of the authorities through the alertness of the telephone operator who we realized must have been Frances. Working in the International Exchange Frances had listened to a number of these conversations and thought them odd; she checked where the phone box was and, realizing its strategic location, had promptly reported the matter to the relevant authorities. The book did not record that her report was initially ignored and it was only when she threatened to complain about their lack of interest to an MP of her acquaintance that they finally said they would look into it.

Frances was a gifted correspondent and I still have every letter she ever wrote me as well as many written to our parents. Our separation at this point in our lives had lasted for nearly nine months and, as a consequence, I have an enviable collection of love letters, a genre at which she was particularly adept. In total, the collection covers the whole of our time in Northern Rhodesia and most of it in Zambia, a period spanning over 25 years.

In preparation for her departure she had given up the lease of our flat that April and had returned to Eaton Court, but some time was still to elapse before she was able to make preparations to join me. In one of her letters she said that she was contemplating putting up a wanted sign with my picture on it. There were endless bureaucratic regulations to be complied with, some so far fetched as to be quite ludicrous. Part of her baggage was some very old family silver that was rarely used; indeed the individual pieces were wrapped in a *Times* of 1907 vintage. After inspecting her baggage, the censorship authorities insisted that each piece be rewrapped in plain paper. A query as to whether or not the enemy might not have already read that particular edition of *The Times* was answered with, 'We must comply with the regulations.' In the end, I had been working in Kasama for five months before receiving the magnificent news that she had already sailed from England on the *Empress of Scotland* and was *en route* to join me.

At last I was able to hire the car. Nothing like a Hertz existed in Northern Rhodesia in those days but there was a company always willing to oblige with a vehicle and driver. They duly picked me up and transported me to Broken Hill where she arrived on the train. There were no words to describe my joy at our reunion and we talked non-stop for the first few hours. Frances's impressions of the voyage were varied; first was the marvellous comfort of the trains in Africa, as her last journey on the train in England had been sitting on the seat in the toilet of the train as the only place available. Then there was the cleanliness and pleasantness of Bulawayo, which was in stark contrast to the derelicts whose presence always marred the joy of a brief visit to Cape Town.

Later, we were overpowered by the welcoming reception we had in Kasama as a couple. It was not until years after, when reading some of the letters she had written home, that I was to discover that Frances's initial views were mixed. The cottage, which I had been at some pains to make ready, was described as 'a rather dilapidated thatched house' in a letter. I was pleased, however, to see that she had thoroughly approved of the white uniforms of the servants and the greeting that they gave her '*Mutende Momma, Mutende Momma*!'

She also was very pleased by the extent to which everything inside had been polished in anticipation of her arrival. However, in my enthusiasm and having lived there already for some weeks, I omitted to tell her that the house had other residents besides ourselves. We were sitting having a quiet drink that first evening when she said, 'How is it that when everything is so clean there is that funny musty smell?', 'Oh, that's the bats my dear,' 'Bats?', 'Yes this is an old house and they all have bats. I find a squash racquet is the best thing for knocking them out.' Frances did her best to look nonchalant about the bats and finally after dinner that night confessed that on the strength of her first sirloin steak in four years, she would try to overlook them.

The following day she was very perplexed by how in a place where there was no electricity she could hear a vacuum cleaner running. Fuming, I exploded, 'It's those blasted bees again'; 'What, Bs as in bats?' 'No wild bees — buzz, buzz, buzz, up the bedroom chimney.' I explained that we could easily solve the problem by lighting a fire in the fireplace, whereupon all the bees would fly out of the chimney. Aided by some paraffin we soon had a good fire going in the grate and a sound of movement could be heard above. Next, there were a few drips of wild honey, eagerly consumed by the houseboy, and then with a rushing whirring noise, the whole swarm stuck in hot honey landed in an angry glutinous mass in our fireplace. At that point we decided that the problem was best left to the staff to sort out.

Over the ensuing few weeks Frances rapidly familiarized herself with her domain and the life of a cadet's wife.

The first time she went calling, she was very concerned not to commit any social gaffes and went complete with a large hat, handbag and gloves. Her new friend cautiously pointed out that people did not normally wear hats in Kasama, also stockings and gloves tended to be ignored; having made these observations she then said that she hoped Frances would not take it amiss that she had mentioned these matters but that local people tended to be rather critical.

The household staff had been hired well in advance of Frances's arrival as I was anxious to have everything spick and span. This produced some problems, for she was reluctant to interfere in what appeared to be an established routine. Our cook's name was Size and it was some while before she ventured to enquire directly into how two people managed to get through a five-pound tin of butter each week and how a 100-pound bag of sugar only lasted for six weeks.

Size was not particularly inventive in culinary matters. Anything to do with meat produced the suggestion, 'I tink I mince' and vegetables a similar thought, 'I tink I mash.' The latter could produce remarkable results, especially when applied to something like lettuce. On one occasion he stated that he was going to make marmalade and would require 20 pounds of sugar. After watching suspiciously for a while and seeing that he was cutting up copious numbers of oranges, spilling juice and shooting pips around the kitchen, we concluded that this was genuine and retired to let him get on with the mess he was obviously creating. It therefore came as quite a shock the following day to be presented with a single bottle of tobacco coloured fluid with a few slices of peel floating around like tadpoles. The explanation was 'Not set, Momma. The sugar's no good.' Several years were to elapse before we finally realized that marmalade never did set in Africa — unless one added the sugar oneself and watched personally while it dissolved.

The friendships we formed then in Kasama have lasted a lifetime. During our stay we made friends with members of every ethnic group. Of course it has been easier to maintain contacts with fellow Britishers, but we have never lost the feelings of goodwill towards numerous tribal folk that we got to know. Similar sentiments were reciprocated between many of the Africans and other district officers. Those who have doubts about the warmth of these feelings can refer to the fact that the local Bemba tribal council actually wrote to the Department of Native Affairs, as it was known then, requesting that they might in due course bury Gordon Tredwell (DC Mpika) in the sacred grove of Mwalole where only the *Chitimukulu* paramount chiefs had been interred until then.

\* \* \*

Despite its distance from the theatre of action the war impacted on Kasama in its own way. The local population had been invited to enlist to fight in the war and a considerable number did so. Half a dozen battalions of native troops from NR served outside the territory in various theatres of war. The Northern Rhodesia Regiment (NRR) had originally been established as a local defence force. It was officered by whites and had a leavening of British NCOs, but the *askari*s, as they were generally known, were all natives. The regiment had been involved previously, in the First World War campaigns with Germany's African colonial empire, and had served with such distinction that, after the armistice, von Lettow, the German commander, had praised the fighting qualities of the NR *askari*s. In the present conflict they had participated in the liberation of Abyssinia (as it was then known) and had seen action in Italian Somaliland. Some were also involved during the Free French occupation of Madagascar. Later, with the cessation of fighting in Africa some units of the NRR were sent to India where they became involved in the Burma campaigns. Apart from the usual campaign medals, several members of the NRR won decorations for gallantry.

There was no conscription, as such, and all of them were volunteers. Perhaps we would be deluding ourselves by thinking that many of these men joined up as a result of any particularly patriotic motives, although the king in England was still at that time regarded as mystical 'super-chief', living far off. It has been suggested that the thought of regular pay and good meals may have inspired them, but the prospect of adventure seems to have been more likely together with a liking for military life. Whatever their motivation, many made the ultimate sacrifice and first NR, then latterly Zambia can be proud of their record.

What was not anticipated at the time the call went out was the potential effect of this prolonged exposure to the outside world on the ideas and latent ambitions of the returning troops. They had been exposed to the realities of life in other colonies, and seen for themselves how it compared with the state of affairs back at home. They had also been living at close quarters with white British and especially Indian troops and would have had ample opportunities to observe something of their cultures and to hear their views on many subjects. The demobilized British armies of the First World War found that the reality of life back in the United Kingdom was a far cry from the 'land fit for heroes' that had been promised. In the same way many of the returning *askari*s must have found the homecoming to the routine and humdrum life of their villages a singularly dispiriting experience.

The African National Congress (ANC) had not yet been founded but it seems reasonable to believe that it must have found receptive ears among the old soldiers when it did come with its message of nationalism and promises of benefits for all. This, however, was looking considerably into the future and in any event it was generally malcontents rather than the ex-*askari*s who were responsible for the civil disturbances that later erupted.

The regiment made provision for *askari*s to write home while on active duty and the postbag usually had one or two letters addressed to the DC with requests of one kind or another, some of which were quite incongruous, for example the letter that read:

'Dear Mother and Father of all the Africans in the district,
I am writing to tell you that I am (name) from (village) in the area of (chief). I am single and I wish to get married. Please, please *Bwana* DC, I want you to look for a wife for me. I want you to choose a suitable young girl.'

At this point the letter entered into a detailed description of the characteristics he was hoping for; and was finally signed off

This is me Writing,
Pte Charlie Aaron, No. ...'

A similar letter complete with the original spelling is included as Appendix 4. In these more enlightened times the letter could have been passed on to a dating agency but that was hardly practical then.

Tragedy and loss also occurred, the occasion seeming somehow more poignant by its comparative rarity and when everyone knew the grieving parents. I still recall the shock when the news arrived that the only son of one of Kasama's local traders, fresh from university, had perished in Burma. It was a stark reminder in a tiny white community, insulated from the outside world in many ways.

# 4
# Ulendo and Witchcraft

Tours, or going on *ulendo*, were an integral part of a DO's job and it was not long before I was called upon to undertake one on my own. The preparation and organization of *ulendo* was quite a major performance. It started with plotting on a map the best route that would take in the villages that it was proposed to visit and deciding on suitable campsites and the number of days that would be required to complete a full tour of the selected area. The next stage was to send off one of the district messengers to advise the local chief that one was planning to make a tour through his domain and to extend an invitation that either he or his representative might like to accompany the tour.

Even a small tour required quite an entourage, at least 25 porters plus the head messenger and clerks. All would have to be fed while on the journey. The chief would have alerted the headmen of the various villages of our plans and it was their responsibility to warn the villagers of our impending arrival. They also had to ensure that there was food in the shape of a chicken or maybe eggs for the DC and mealie-meal, possibly with meat for the carriers if there was any game available. The money to pay for these provisions was carried along with the tax books and register in a tin box. A table and two chairs were carried along as essential office equipment. A visit to the *boma* stores would provide tents and a ground sheet together with a camp bed, bath, basin and a toilet seat.

The messengers had plenty of experience and were very skilled at setting up a camp in next to no time. At dawn on the day of departure the head messenger and his team plus the carriers would all assemble on the back veranda where Frances would have everything that I might personally want packed and ready. Finally, we would get under way with my bicycle plus a water sack and me.

One indispensable item, of course, was my rifle, as there was always a chance (however slight) of game that would provide a very welcome addition to the pot. Accompanying us was our cook, Size, wearing white tennis shoes, a pair of blue slacks and a khaki bush shirt, which looked very incongruous in the bush, even without the crowning glory of a chef's white hat that he insisted on wearing and that had been starched and ironed so that it stood perpendicular.

The main entourage would head directly for the place where we planned to pass the night and would set up camp there. In the meantime, I would proceed together with the head messenger, my clerk and the chief's representative to the first village on our itinerary. Normally there was no road as such, just a simple path that always followed the line of least resistance, meandering its way around the trees in the bush. The maintenance of these paths was the responsibility of the villages that they served.

During my absence one of the district messengers was assigned to keep guard on the house with Frances in it. He slept on the veranda where he snored so loudly that Frances declared that when I next went on tour she would prefer to sleep undisturbed by such precautions.

Right from the start, when I was making my first local tour of the villages in Chief Mwamba's district, I could see for myself the problems created in the villages by the departure of the menfolk who had gone off either to join the army or to work in the copper mines some 200 miles to the southeast on the 'Line of Rail', as everyone referred to the region around the railway. Of course the cash flowing in from the miners was a very welcome contribution to the vagaries of a subsistence economy, but the absence of virtually all the men apart from the elderly and youths was not conducive to a happy atmosphere.

The collection of the native poll tax was an important part of the business undertaken by the DO when he went on tour. He would have with him the necessary registers of all those liable for tax in each village and would expect to be greeted by the local headman. Apart from his own entourage, which would include a *boma* clerk as an interpreter and district messengers, there would also be the local chief or his representative. Their presence was necessary since the chief was the local delegated authority.

## Ulendo and Witchcraft

The whole village would be there, having been summoned by the headman, and they would sit around the DO. He would then go through the names of the people listed as living in the village and where necessary collect the tax. If any persons were missing it was necessary for the headman to explain their absence satisfactorily. If the explanation were considered to lack credibility then an investigation would be initiated. The presence of district messengers was very useful as they ensured that one did not get led up the garden path. The visit was also an opportunity for those who were old or infirm to seek exemption from tax. I was greatly taken aback the first time it happened, for the lucky exempted person promptly lay on his back and clapped his hands while ululating — a traditional greeting for a chief in certain tribes. In the case of youths who were deemed to be sufficiently adult to be added to the list, it was customary for them first to be taken to see the chief. If he approved, the youth would be provided with a note and would then be brought to the *boma* by his guardian, the headman or a *kapasu*, where he would be inspected and if it were thought that he was sufficiently mature he would be added to the tax register. Apart from the inspection aspect, tours were an extremely useful way of learning how the local people of the Northern Province lived and survived.

The soil around Kasama was very poor with only a few inches of topsoil and the local population practised a subsistence economy, growing only what they wanted for their own consumption. As a result, there was an ever-present risk of crop failure and famine, especially in some areas. In these districts it was the DC's responsibility to ensure implementation of the famine prevention regulations by insisting an additional 50 mounds of cassava were grown by each woman to provide food in the event of any emergency. The women did nearly all the routine work on the vegetable patches. The main exception was the annual burning of the *chitemene* gardens, which was men's work. All the local tribes practised this variant on the 'slash and burn' technique employed by most primitive peoples. The inherently poor quality of the existing topsoil meant that the soil was quickly played out. As a consequence, the gardens slowly moved further and further from the village. The *chitemene* system slowed down the depletion of the soil. Having selected a suitable area for a new garden early in the dry season, the man would proceed to cut down to ground level everything within that area and leave it lying in place to dry out completely. He would then go into the surrounding area and cut back all the bush and lop some of the branches off the trees, though leaving them standing. Any useful timber together with some firewood was removed and the remainder then left out until the end of the dry season. As the rainy season approached all the dry material from the surrounding area would be moved so that it covered the area to be cultivated, where it would be piled several feet high.

Finally, when the men decided that the rains were due and the time right, they would set light to the pile and up it would go with a gigantic whoosh of white flame visible for miles. After it had cooled the women would return with their hoes and scuff up the surface so that the ash was well mixed in with the soil. Because of the thinness of the topsoil, they would also build it up into mounds to increase its depth. At that stage the garden was also free of all insects and parasites that might eat the new crops that were to be planted when the rains returned.

A great deal of the ash from these enormous bonfires would get into the atmosphere and produce the most spectacular red sunsets that one can imagine. One evening when the display was unusually splendid, I was talking to an officer who had something of a reputation as an oil painter; I enquired, 'How would you like to put that on canvas' to which I got the succinct reply 'No one could convey it properly on canvas — and if you could, nobody would believe it anyway.'

Where practical, the villagers would grow vegetables such as beans, tomatoes, sweet potatoes and groundnuts, together with fruits like bananas, papaws and various citrus. The main crops, however, were cereals, especially finger millet, along with some maize. When ground, the finger millet was used to make the staple food, *bwali* — a kind of porridge that would be eaten by hand from a communal bowl. The porridge would be rolled into a ball and then dipped into one of the side dishes, which were known as *munani*.

Of course a lot of the millet was made into the popular and highly intoxicating native beer *bwalwa*. Parties at which large amounts of *bwalwa* were consumed were an essential feature of

## Ulendo and Witchcraft

the intricate and ritualized village culture. Since no attempt was made to clarify the *bwalwa* it contained all the protein and other nutrients from the millet and thus formed an important part of the diet. Copious drinking marked all occasions such as weddings and funerals, as well as births and the rites of pubescence. There was a great deal of competition over who could make the best beverage and women who could make good beer were very highly regarded. I am ashamed to admit to never having tasted *bwalwa*. It is particularly embarrassing as I am a direct descendant of the Thomas Greenall who founded the famous brewery of that name in 1762.

\* \* \*

There was little by way of livestock reared but apart from the staple diet of *bwali* the natives always enjoyed collecting wild fruit and hunting game or trapping small mammals and birds. Locusts and other insects were also consumed when available. Wild honey could be found by those with the courage to collect it, which was not too often as the African bee has a fearsome reputation. There was game (especially various species of antelope) to be hunted, though it was very rare around Kasama.

The absence of livestock could be attributed to tsetse fly (*glossina Rhodesiensis*). The fly, which looked rather like an over large horse fly, spread disease by consuming the blood of infected animals. The blood contained the trypanosome protozoa and was passed on when the fly bit later victims. The disease was invariably fatal to cattle and horses, as well as causing sleeping sickness (trypanosomiasis) in humans. Attempts were made to control the worst effects of the fly by cordoning off the areas where it was prevalent. The Department of Game set up barriers in places along the principal roads to stop cars and other vehicles and then sprayed them inside and out. The flies were only to be found in forested areas and were relatively unknown in the *boma*s where all the land had been cleared for some distance around. It was also well known that they were not active after dark or if the temperature fell below 60°F, which had practical consequences. It was impractical to move herds of cattle from one area to another so the only way to improve the stock was by bringing in superior bulls. These could be moved from one *boma* farm to another under cover of darkness with the aid of an experienced herder plus a couple of heifers to keep the bull calm. Photographs exist taken at the time when the railways were being built showing horses and cattle wearing pyjamas when they were being moved around. History does not recount whether this technique worked. They were very hard times for all and the workers had the grim satisfaction of being offered a made-to-measure fitted coffin for potential use as a part of their working contract. Even now some fifty years later there is no satisfactory control of the fly and attempts to discover a natural predator or antagonist have failed.

\* \* \*

These infrequent visits by DCs and DOs on *ulendo* were also, in their own way, of some reassurance to the villagers who were permanently worried about the possibilities of witchcraft.

Although the life of the natives living in the villages might have appeared to be uncomplicated, nothing could have been further from the truth. The missionaries studied the subject of witchcraft very carefully and I was fortunate enough to have the opportunity to talk about these matters often with Father Etienne, one of the White Fathers. He considered that much of what was believed in could be ascribed to two factors that he called 'transference' and 'causation'.

For transference it was thought that the essential attributes of anything existed in all parts of it and could be transferred to someone else by possession of some artefact. Thus a hyena was considered to be very strong and tireless; therefore, wearing a hair of a hyena would to some extent imbue the owner with these characteristics. 'Causation' meant that nothing happened in the lives of the Africans without some causative factor. It could have been good spirits or bad spirits, the evil influence of a witch or the breaking of a taboo but to their minds it was always there. Even those who had accepted Christianity were generally very reluctant to give up their inborn beliefs and superstitions and tended on the whole to think of Western religion as yet another layer of spirits (fortunately, usually benign) to be grafted onto the existing structure.

## Ulendo and Witchcraft

The most immediate spirits in their lives were those of deceased members of their own families, with the parents, not surprisingly, being helpful though still in need of prayer and being placated. Grandparents on the other hand were much more likely to be bad, although cantankerous is probably a fairer description.

Whether it was a good crop or a bad crop some entity had a hand in it, or if drinking dirty water made you sick then clearly something or someone was to blame and if someone was taken ill then it definitely needed investigating.

Witches were believed in and heartily disliked in NR in a similar manner to Europe in the Middle Ages. They had their own special gang of evil entities ready to work ill upon the luckless population and could easily make you become ill or even die. Where charms and incantations failed it was always possible that a few herbs in one's food or beer could produce the right outcome. As a result the local population usually found it necessary to have their own equivalent of a coroner's enquiry whenever someone died, as it was well known that nobody died as a result of natural causes not even an accident or of old age. This was rather clearly reflected in the fact that no word for 'accident' exists in Bemba. Clearly in the case of an injury it had to be established either which spirits were responsible or if someone had cast a spell to make it happen. While it was accepted that elderly people were ultimately going to die, they were still suspect since it was obvious that they must have had help of some kind from somewhere in order to survive that long. This was where the witch doctor entered the picture, though his true name might better have been 'witch finder'. It was his function to fill a similar role to that of a coroner to determine which spirits had been upset. One of the other important functions of the witch doctor was to sniff out witches in much the same way as the witch finders operated in Europe not so many centuries ago. The local people would have thought the witch doctors pretty useless if they could not find a witch. They, in turn, made sure that they did.

European and missionary protests that witchcraft was a load of nonsense were simply not believed. The fact that the white *bwana*s had made laws for the suppression of witchcraft clearly proved that it did exist and was to be feared. Besides, the converted Christians could find plenty of evidence for witches in the bible —

how could Moses bring about the plagues in Egypt if he was not a witch?

Strangely, people accused of witchcraft frequently ceased to deny it after undergoing whatever form of ritual investigation the witch doctor prescribed. Not many years before, witches were almost certainly killed and it would be a brave man who said it never happened in the 1950s or 1960s. It was all too easy to tell the visiting DC that someone had died following a snakebite.

The witch doctor was also the person to consult in the event of problems, for he would be able to tell if someone had offended the spirits and if so which ones and why. This was generally done by divination, which could be achieved by such simple means as throwing a handful of bones or less frequently by entering a trance. Some types of divination were altogether more sinister, such as divination with the aid of the coffin of a person alleged to have died as a result of witchcraft. If true, the following story implies the exercise of remarkable powers of suggestion or mass hypnosis. A missionary from the Swedish Baptist mission told me that one of his colleagues had learned of a funeral that was about to take place and where it was rumoured there would be a divination. He volunteered to be one of the coffin bearers – no one objected to his presence, he recounted, but when they started to carry the coffin it acted as if it were possessed, having a mind of its own, travelling a zigzag route off the path and past thorny bushes; yet, when it was finally put down, no one had any scratches. Robin Short, in *African Sunset*, recounted a somewhat similar incident of divination by coffin, only on that occasion the coffin was 'told' to find the evildoer and, having 'found' someone, proceeded to butt her to death. It was sometime later that the pallbearers were charged with homicide but got comparatively light sentences because the judge suggested that there was no evidence that they had deliberately manipulated the coffin to hit someone sufficiently hard as to cause their death. This evidence was all sworn to and attested in court.

Witch doctors also claimed to be able to cure people of various medical problems, which they would do both by transference and through herbal medicines of which they often had a fair amount of experience (there were also some people who practised solely as herbalists). This knowledge was usually handed down and the

## Ulendo and Witchcraft

herbs were apt to be compounded with remarkably unsavoury ingredients. Transference played a very significant part in the formulation of medicines. All of this combined with a considerable amount of mumbo jumbo sometimes worked, which shows the virtues of mixing gullibility with crude psychology. There is little doubt that the witch doctors were profound observers of human nature and knew how to play on weaknesses. Politically, they were very powerful in the tribal society, for their advice would be sought on all manner of matters. Of course, with the existence of laws against witchcraft, even consulting a witch doctor tended to be done in secrecy.

My own brushes with witchcraft were comparatively rare. This is perhaps a convenient place to recount them although they are well out of place in the time frame and the context.

\* \* \*

The first occasion was when I was a magistrate in Kabompo and a man was brought before me charged under the Witchcraft Ordinance. He had been found in possession of various evil charms, though there was no evidence advanced that he had in fact used them. After he had been sentenced to six months' imprisonment with hard labour, the witnesses and all the others present in the court departed, leaving a very smart and intelligent district messenger and myself with the charms still on the table. I proceeded to unlock the cupboard in which the court exhibits were stored and told him to put them away, at which point he took one look at them and bolted through the door as if the devil himself had appeared. I discovered afterwards that my experience was not unique, for Peter Snelson in his book *To Independence and Beyond* tells of how a PC talked to a number of teachers and other educated natives about the follies of believing in witchcraft and that they all along had agreed with him. At the end of his talk he produced a bag and tipped a heap of charms out and said, 'just look at all this rubbish,' only to discover that he was talking to an empty room.

There was an interesting aftermath to this when we had the privilege of entertaining Lord Dalhousie, when he was the governor general of the federation. After the exchange of the usual

## Kaunda's Gaoler

pleasantries in my office he delicately worked the conversation around to witchcraft and remarked that he had been approached by a very distinguished professor in England who had said that local DCs were likely to have in their possession collections of charms and various other *curiosa* that would be of inestimable value in the search for world knowledge. It was almost as if he knew what was in my evidence cupboard. Be that as it may, I was suddenly seized by the thought that it was impossible for me to unlock the cupboard; there they were and there they were going to stay, so I proceeded to look blankly back at him. It was neither the first nor the last time that I had reason to be grateful for a poker face.

The other occasion was when I was at Masaiti. The village headman and some of the local tribes people brought a man before me and accused him of witchcraft. As I remarked earlier, once accused these people often freely confessed and he did just that. He did not appear to be in any way mentally unsound but acknowledged that he practised it, saying that he had learned the art of sorcery from his father. He went on to say that through his spells he had in fact been responsible for several deaths that appeared to be from natural causes. Apart from his confession there was no real evidence to support a charge of homicide and in the end I concluded that all he could be sentenced for was practising witchcraft. I sentenced him to the maximum within my jurisdiction, which was 12 months' imprisonment with hard labour. This may sound excessive to some, but removing him from the village was of real benefit to him; if I had let him go free the residents might well have been tempted to take matters into their own hands.

There were also many taboos that could produce evil results if broken. In one tribe near Kabompo, a bridegroom was absolutely forbidden ever to see the face of his mother-in-law — possibly a new angle for the classic line of jokes. In some areas, if a child cut its upper teeth before the lower ones, taboo demanded that it should be disposed of promptly; otherwise, every time it lost a milk tooth someone would die.

In the case of the Bemba a widow or widower was not allowed to remarry because the spirit of the departed was still in possession of the partner. The only way that the spirit could be returned to its

## Ulendo and Witchcraft

own family was for the survivor to have sexual relations with the closest relative of the deceased. Usually it was accepted that the relations could be conducted symbolically by touching one another. Sometimes, however, there were problems if the real thing was insisted upon, as I discovered on one occasion when I was DC at Mporokoso.

A young and nubile widow had refused to cooperate with the rather elderly nearest male relative of her husband who promptly complained to the chief's court requiring 'specific performance' (if I recall the term correctly). The court accepted the plea and passed judgement that the widow must comply with the custom. The case was referred to me for review. In point of fact I was not there to act as a court of appeal but was only supposed to intervene where the native court had exceeded its jurisdiction or acted in a manner that was contrary to natural justice.

I used my discretion to refuse to grant specific performance but took care at the time to give no reasons. Somewhere I had run across a maxim that when exercising discretion it was much wiser never to give reasons and indeed, in this particular case, I was particularly relieved that I had not when it appeared in the law reports for that year. In point of fact the young woman was one who obviously took a pride in her appearance and dress, whereas the expectant beneficiary of the specific performance appeared to me to be nothing more than a randy old codger. If I had upheld the native court I felt that I would have been legalizing an indecent assault.

Another interesting superstitious custom deeply entrenched in some other tribes was that of *via u tuzhi*, which is almost untranslatable. In essence, it means that if someone's husband or wife dies it is necessary for the survivor to pay a sort of reverse dowry to free himself or herself from the spirit of the departed. This was of course vitally important if one wished to remarry and was sufficiently important to be regularly determined and enforced by the native court.

Sometimes the superstitions could be put to practical use. Because of the hot climate, it was very important that deceased persons were buried promptly. This could present a problem for Europeans, for suitable wood for a coffin was not always easy to find. To overcome these difficulties it was not unknown for settlers to have their coffins made in advance so that they would be available in an emergency. This was not good news for the house staff; they were accustomed to spirits outside and in the village but to find a ready built home for them (generally under the bed) where one worked was too much. They shunned them like the plague, leading one person to remark that a well-made coffin was far better than a safe any day.

In the midst of so many superstitions, it is not too surprising that the visit of a DC or DO on tour injected a temporary break of commonsense into the overheated minds of the villagers.

# 5
# Kawambwa

Nearly two years had passed in Kasama and it was time for a transfer and to leave the 'provincial capital'. This was for an infinitely more exciting destination in the shape of an outstation: Kawambwa.

It was our first experience of packing up our entire belongings and trying to load them on the back of a truck. Any thought that it was a job that could be done by our staff rapidly vanished as it became apparent that they had not got the slightest idea of how to do it. In the end we had about seventeen crates, some tin boxes and an assortment of golf clubs, gun cases and tin baths, mixed in with flour and paraffin. These were all loaded onto a lorry in a higgledy-piggledy fashion the morning we were due to depart. From the middle of this haphazard mountain came the mewing of a terrified kitten, 'What have you done with the cat?' 'It's in one of the little tin boxes with the crate of paraffin' was the reply.

In the process of unloading the lorry it soon became apparent that curious sounds were also coming from an old petrol can. Investigation disclosed that it was a live turkey (for Christmas) that had arrived the morning of our departure and been packed and stowed away without our knowing.

Once again I was allowed to hire a car to transport Frances and myself from Kasama to Kawambwa, a distance of about 200 miles more or less along the edge of the Chimpili Plateau. Not too great a distance on paper but through the bush on dirt tracks and with Frances pregnant it did not make for a fast drive. Consequently, we were glad to have an opportunity to stop at Mporokoso where we were entertained by the DC and his wife — the Macraes. They gave us a friendly welcome before seeing us off on the final leg of our journey, refreshed both in body after a hearty meal and in mind after having been regaled with much anecdotal information.

## Kaunda's Gaoler

Living on the tropic of Capricorn as we did, sunset barely varied by more than an hour between midsummer and midwinter and the skies were already darkening when we finally arrived at our destination and were met by Florence and Bryan Anderson who were to give us our first introduction to outstation life. We were to become the very best of friends and have remained correspondents right up to the present day when I still write to the now widowed Florence in Zimbabwe.

Much to my surprise, the entire district messenger force had turned out and was lined up on the lawn where I was introduced to each of them. It was a heart-warming experience and I mentally committed myself to their welfare. The following day I met my youthful clerk cum interpreter, Bellington, who readily agreed to continue my instruction in Bemba. He used to come to the house every morning between 6.00 and 7.00 a.m. to build on the foundation in the grammar that I already had. Thanks to his efforts following on Miss Simms's earlier teaching, I was able to pass my language exam in quite a short time. It transpired that the explanation for my interpreter's unusual name was that it was due to the inability of the native population to distinguish between the letters B and W and his name was meant to be Wellington. This lack of distinction also carried back over into European writing and it is not uncommon to find Bemba written as Wemba.

Bellington was enormously helpful and a considerable degree of mutual respect developed between us. Then, 24 years later, while sitting in my office in Ndola where I was then an acting resident secretary in the independent state of Zambia and coming to the end of my stay, he turned up one day out of the blue. I was totally amazed when he walked in and sat down and started recalling our times in Kawambwa. I never discovered how he knew where I was, but despite the fact that we had not seen or heard of each other for all those years he had wanted to come and wish me goodbye on my retirement. He was by no means the only one who turned up out of the blue. A former houseboy, as they were known in those days, came all the way from his home in Broken Hill to see me. While visiting, he related how his son (only just born when I first knew him) had become a pilot in the Zambian Air Force, which goes some way to show the extent to which the country had changed in the intervening years.

## Kawambwa

The district took in some splendid countryside, for the surrounding area abounded with rivers, lakes and numerous waterfalls, the one at Kalambo being especially famous as having a drop of nearly 1000 feet making it one of the longest drops in the world.

It was on my first tour in Kawambwa that I finally managed to achieve success in the hunting field. It was a thrilling experience to stalk and finally shoot the reedbuck that fell to my .350 Rigby. Over the years I must have worn out a considerable amount of shoe leather looking for game and it was a constant source of annoyance that what by all accounts had been so plentiful in the past was now hard to find.

Pregnant as she was, Frances had to remain at home when I went on tour; nevertheless, she took a keen interest in the domestic housekeeping arrangements that went with it. She did her best to ensure that I should travel in the maximum of comfort, even going so far as to send our cook along.

It was during our stay in Kawambwa that we acquired the first of what were ultimately to be a succession of pets. Smarti was a local mongrel puppy; though perhaps the description of 'mongrel' is rather flattering as it was a most unusual hybrid with a tail that grew at an alarming rate and seemed to be totally unrelated in size, length or colour to the rest of its body. Rather belatedly we pondered the possibility of docking but had no idea how the process was done. It did not seem appropriate to take it to the local butcher who had a sharp knife, although this was seriously discussed. Upon making enquiries we were told that the local procedure was to give the dog to the kitchen boy and to instruct him to bite off the required length. In her condition, Frances found this concept to be rather upsetting and nothing was done, although I believe that in Australia farmers sometimes castrate newborn sheep by biting off the testicles.

Smarti unfortunately did not survive for long enough for us to discover what he would look like when fully grown. We had just got him housetrained when he decided to go outside one evening. Shortly after we heard a low growl and a whimper, Frances jumped to her feet and headed for the garden while I rushed for my rifle. By the time it was in my hands and I had reached the doorway the leopard, for such it was, had headed down the path with Smarti in its jaws hotly pursued by Frances shouting 'drop it' and completely blocking any chance of a shot. Leopards were plentiful around Kawambwa and there were plenty of people who had the experience of finding one in the garden.

It seemed that each time I went on *ulendo* in the Luapula Valley there were unusual experiences. On one occasion I met a very old man who claimed that as a child he had met Dr Livingstone. There were also pointed out to me a number of women who had been mutilated by removing the nose and upper lip together. While the local population tended to attribute this to Arab slavers, my more sceptical colleagues pointed out that this was the Lunda penalty for adultery before the arrival of the British administration.

Apart from the business of tax collection and checking the registers to make sure that there was no one missing and unaccounted for, a tour also had the extremely important function of maintaining grass roots contacts with rural life. It was part of the DO's job to ensure that everything was running smoothly, whether it was matters devolved to the chief such as paths for bicycles, or matters directly the concern of the government such as road maintenance or the running of local schools by the missions under the aegis of the education department. The practice may seem complicated but there is no doubt that it made a significant contribution to law and order in the villages.

I was doing a considerable number of tours and along the way getting to know the mission areas, which was no mean feat as there were no less than nine different denominations in the field. As my wife dryly remarked on one occasion, they ranged from Plymouth Rock to the Rock of St Peter.

There was of course considerable rivalry between the various missions and I once had to arbitrate in a dispute over which should be allowed to establish a new primary school in a village that was midway between a Catholic mission and one run by the Plymouth Brethren. In order to make my decision I made a hasty survey of attitudes in the village and had to start by getting my question translated into Bemba — 'Whither do you pray? Is it to Mambalima or to Lomu?' thereby identifying the site of the Johnstone Falls mission on the one hand and Rome as the alternative choice.

On the whole I found the Roman Catholic missions the most impressive to visit because of the natural way in which one was

## Kawambwa

admitted into the routine of their daily life. The bare cell with its crucifix and the long refectory tables and benches were faintly reminiscent of dining in hall at Cambridge, which in my day was also quite a monastic experience. Meals were served in huge dishes that were placed at the head of the table and passed or maybe slid along from hand to hand and then to mouth so to speak.

Staying with the various local missions was not an entirely one-way affair; whenever they had occasion to visit Kawambwa to discuss schooling, sickness and so on, we would put them up as a matter of course, though preferably not different denominations at the same time.

During one tour I stayed at Johnstone Falls with the first of the Plymouth Brethren to arrive in the district. Willie Lammond had walked the entire distance from the west coast around the turn of the century despite supposedly having flat feet. He also suffered very badly from toothache from time to time and during his first furlough spent nine months taking a dental mechanics course so that — in his own words — he might save others from such an agonizing experience. As someone cynically remarked, 'Now he can save others from pain as well as from sin.'

His mission was situated in a beautiful site on the Luapula River, which was an excellent source of fish as well as marvellous scenery. The river was much too wide for a cable operated ferry, but there was an excellent pontoon manned by paddlers nearby in Mambalima. The size of the pontoon was such that the crew employed large paddles while in a standing position. It was fascinating to hear the songs they chanted to the rhythm of the paddles. There was no love lost for the Bemba here and one of the songs went as follows:

> *Filembwee, Filembwee*
> *Munani wa ba Bemba*
> *Nshiliyako.*

This translates roughly as:

> Beans, Beans!
> Food for the Bemba
> I can't eat them.

## Kaunda's Gaoler

Kansenga was an important trading centre in the Congo on the opposite bank of the river and, despite being paid for by the Northern Provincial budget, the pontoon was usually referred to as the Kansenga pontoon.

A year or so later when I was stationed in Mporokoso, Frances and I happened to be in Kansenga on the Congo's Independence Day and were invited to join in the celebrations that evening, which became very convivial. My contribution to the cause of international relations was a tuneless rendering of 'Au claire de la lune', though I have to confess that I do not recollect too much else apart from having to leave early rather abruptly. This was officially attributed to my having been mixing my drinks, but I have always had a suspicion that someone (possibly with an ear for music) had thought it would be a joke to doctor one of them.

Kawambwa was a centre for the Lunda tribe with its Senior Chief Mwata Kasembe (the title of *mwata* approximates that of king). The history of the Lunda is interesting as they were part of a vast empire that had been centred in what is now Zaire and the bulk of them still lived there under Paramount Chief Mwata Yamvwa. Those around Mporokoso were the remaining descendants of those to the east of the Luapula River.

Mwata Kasembe was an imposing figure, especially when encountered being carried on a huge litter borne on the shoulders of a large number of Kawambwa bearers, all shouting and stamping their feet to the accompaniment of drums hammering out a noisy refrain to announce the imminent arrival of a very important person.

On ceremonial occasions such as these the procession was by no means as wild and unmanaged as it appeared, but was in fact controlled by the chief himself using a talking drum. This was much smaller than the regular drums and was carried on the litter to enable the chief to communicate his instructions to the bearers.

From the tribal point of view, Mwata Kasembe was nowhere near as important as the present Mwata Yamvwa who ruled many more people in the Congo. I had the opportunity to meet Yamvwa some years later when I was at Kabompo. He was a living legend. One of Mwata Yamvwa's more spectacular hallmarks was his remarkable armlet, 12 inches wide and the girth of a man's thigh. The armlet was supposedly made entirely of human foreskins.

## Kawambwa

Ceremonial circumcision was an important part of Lunda rituals and presumably the *mwata* had first call on the by-product.

In many ways 1945 was a landmark year. I was by now well established in the office and gaining much useful experience. There was V-E Day and our first child was due. We were not to be together for V-E Day; Frances had been invited to return to Kasama a few weeks before the impending event and, while waiting there patiently, she stayed with the government medical officer and his family.

I was on temporary assignment to Fort Rosebery where Tony Heath, the local DC, was very short staffed and had asked the powers that be if I could be posted to assist him for a short period. This assignment was agreed and thus it came about that I found myself in sole charge of the *boma* at Fort Rosebery when the stirring news of victory in Europe arrived. Tony was away conferring with Arthur Benson, the DC Luwingu in Samfya, a port on Lake Bangweulu. They had no radio and the only way to get the message to them was to take the *boma* lorry, which was suitably decorated before setting off.

We celebrated the event by dining in style. A favourite local dish was known to the European residents as stuffed frog, although it was in fact a chicken that had been completely filleted before stuffing it and sewing it back together again. Over the meal there was a great deal of reminiscing, mostly on the part of an old-timer who claimed to have been present at the Battle of Majuba Hill in 1881. This would have made him about 83 years of age, which seemed rather unlikely. Nevertheless, Arthur, who had made a study of that campaign, listened very carefully and subsequently pronounced that the details recounted all appeared to fit with the facts. So, there we sat for our convivial evening, ex-officers of the RE and NRR plus a former member of Churchill's cabinet office, together with a supposed veteran of Majuba Hill.

The following day we returned to our respective *boma*s to set in train preparations for more elaborate festivities, which were to include representatives of all the local chiefs at a victory dance on the recreation ground.

Victory celebrations apart, my time at Fort Rosebery was enlivened by Tony also being an old Cliftonian, having been captain of both the cricket and rugby teams at the time when I first arrived there and subsequently distinguishing himself in the sporting field by getting his blue at Cambridge for rugger. He was single at the time and invited me to share his house, which was very much appreciated. Apart from being an honoured guest, I was able, from casual conversations in the evenings, to pick up a great deal of the sort of on-the-spot training that was very useful to a cadet.

Going on tours together also provided much experience of the practical side of a DC's job. On one occasion, he sat politely watching in silence while I made a fool of myself when cutting up the carcass of an antelope. Somehow, despite the advice of the head messenger on how it should be done, none had been allocated to the messengers and, as a result, I was forced to pay the price by surrendering a particularly tasty joint that I had selected for my own table. The utter embarrassment was totally unforgettable.

I now awaited the weekly mail lorry from Kasama with redoubled interest as, in addition to the family mail from London, there was always another affectionate and entertaining letter from Frances, still biding her time.

Frances had a difficult pregnancy and it was a considerable relief when our daughter, Vivian, was born on 1 August 1945 and I managed to obtain a few days' leave to visit them. As it was, two months were to elapse before she was sufficiently recovered to make the journey back to Kawambwa.

Her stay in Kasama provided a convenient opportunity for her to resolve a longstanding domestic problem — what to do with Size? I had originally hired him in good faith before Frances arrived and initially he had been a perfectly acceptable cook. Needless to say she did not feel like becoming the proverbial new broom as soon as she reached Kasama, but there had been a steady deterioration in his standards ever since. This fast approached a crisis point shortly after we arrived in Kawambwa.

His views on hygiene did not coincide with ours. Size clearly believed that there was no point in washing saucepans, baking tins and the sieve for straining soup if there was any likelihood of them being used again the following day. I, of course, with army days behind me, was nowhere near as fussed as Frances, but even I had enough when he came with me on tour and roasted a chicken

## Kawambwa

without bothering to gut it first. His excuse being that he knew that I liked 'eggies'.

In due course he accompanied Frances to Kasama (accompanied by his wife and son) where he was supposed to provide whatever assistance might be needed. When asked one day if he would cook the dinner he answered that he had forgotten how to but was willing to try. The meal was a disaster and when our hostess asked, 'Size, do you want to help me or not?' he replied with disarming honesty, 'No'.

The time duly came for Frances to return and numerous packing cases needed to be nailed up. It soon became apparent that his idea was to pass Frances the nails while she did the crating. Clearly the thought of work was an affront to his dignity and Frances informed him that under the circumstances he could return to Lusaka. It was a great relief to us as we already had suspicions that his wife pursued the oldest of professions, presumably with his blessing.

\* \* \*

By the time of their arrival, I had already returned to Kawambwa and reopened the house so that everything was ready for them. My happiness was complete; my family was back with me in our own house with its pretty garden together with new and sufficient staff and a gardener to make life easy.

The agreeable sunny weather of the long dry season with which Northern Rhodesia was blessed made for a very pleasant existence. No doubt, in the lower lying southern and western regions it could have been very oppressive but up on the high plateau the humidity was low.

Some of the essential services, such as the provision of water and sanitation, were provided by the prison service, which, as mentioned was run by the district messengers. This would involve two convicts carrying five-gallon cans of water up from the river to fill the two large drums (one of which had a fire underneath it) that we used to provide domestic hot and cold water. Needless to say, anything intended for consumption had to be boiled and filtered. The prisoners were also responsible for removing and disposing of the buckets from the latrine, this being done after dark.

## Kaunda's Gaoler

The white population of Kawambwa comprised four families, including the DC and us. We had a nine-hole golf course of sorts, laid out by a previous enthusiast, but did not enjoy the facilities of Kasama where the Gymkhana Club had tennis and squash courts together with a swimming pool. We were located on some high ground, together with the *boma* offices and messengers' lines. A mile or so away was Munkanta, the village where the eponymous chief resided.

There was an elderly lion that lived nearby and one evening after dark it decided to take a stroll around the township, roaring its head off. The Andersons and I promptly piled into the front seat of the *boma* pick-up truck (universally referred to as the vanette) and set out to look for it. We found it ahead of us in the road far more quickly than we expected, indeed before we had any opportunity to discuss what we were going to do. I knew that in Kasama any such disturber of the peace would have got short shrift and accordingly had brought my Rigby with me. Leaping out of the vanette so that the bonnet of the vehicle was strategically located between us, I pointed my rifle towards the beast, which was only about ten yards away. However, before I had even had time to take aim, a commanding voice bellowed in my ear, 'Get back! Get back,' which I obeyed with some reluctance. Then I realized that the same voice was now addressing the lion, 'Go home! Go back to your wife.' This was repeated several times before the lion, half dazzled by the headlights, turned on its tail and slunk off into the darkness. I was then told that the lion was supposed to be a reincarnation of one of the chief's predecessors and that had it met its demise in the way I had planned there would have been an almighty crisis among the superstitious villagers.

It was about this time that the Colonial Office began to look at the possibilities of providing some experience for the local population in the practice of government. Their approach to this can best be described as a series of electoral colleges. At the lowest tier, an African District Council was set up for each district; typically this would have fewer than a dozen members, most of them representatives of the chiefs, selected by Mwata Kasembe in the case of Kawambwa. With them to help guide the proceedings would be the DC and the provincial commissioner, if he were available. At a higher level there would also be a white member

## Kawambwa

(nominated by the governor) representing African interests for the Northern Province on LegCo (the Legislative Council), together with an elected member of the local African Welfare Association.

The latter body had been created in the early 1940s to represent those Africans who lived in the townships such as teachers and local townspeople who were more educated and whose link with the tribal chieftains was rather tenuous. This was an opportunity that had been eagerly seized upon, especially by the teachers, as the start of a political organization. They could discuss the future evolution of the colony and specifically seek election to the African District Council under some kind of political label. At that time, the formation of the ANC (African National Congress) and UNIP (United National Independence Party), which would ultimately take the colony down the road to independence, was still a long way in the future.

The African District Council, composed in this fashion, would select one or two of its members to sit on the African Provincial Council, which in its turn would nominate members to the Territorial Council. These were the beginning of the first and very shaky steps towards native government and it is obvious that the colonial service attached great importance to the preservation of the influence of the chiefs at grass roots level.

By a happy coincidence the inaugural meeting of the local African District Council coincided with V-J Day. Frances had already made plans for a celebratory dinner party for the British residents complete with miniature Union flags on the table. Honoured as we were with the presence of Gilbert Howe, the PC and Sir Stewart Gore-Browne one of the members from LegCo representing African interests, we were able to do it in style. Sir Stewart Gore-Browne was in every way a remarkable character, a 'one-off' in every sense of the word and merits some introduction. Because of his deep involvement in the political scene for much of the time that I was in NR, he reappears in this book from time to time.

\* \* \*

He had come out originally in 1911 as an army subaltern with the Anglo–Belgian Border Commission and quickly demonstrated his concern over justice for the native population by getting himself into trouble for having written a letter complaining that the senior officer pocketed part of the bearers' pay. At the conclusion of the work he went off on his own with a handful of porters (each paid 25p a month) to explore. His ambition was to have an English country mansion and the necessary staff to run a large estate, while having only limited resources to fund it. He quickly reached the conclusion that NR was the place where he might be able to realize this dream and, after serving in the First World War, he set about achieving his goal. He started by buying 23,000 acres of land at Shiwa Ngandu near Chinsali, not so far from Kasama, in the Northern Province. With the aid of a book on building construction and using only native labour and locally available materials, he had built himself a magnificent house where he could live 'like a lord'. Indeed, lord he was to the local population, for though they recognized the benefits that he brought to them (such as a local hospital), they christened him *Chipembele* meaning rhinoceros, which said something about his attitude and temper. In his efforts to make the estate self-supporting, he pioneered the production of essential oils in NR, learning about the processes from scratch as he went along.

It was, however, his involvement in politics that marked him out as more than just an eccentric. At a time when few but the missionaries took an interest in furthering the wellbeing of the natives, he clearly espoused the cause of better education. This he maintained was a prerequisite for the time, which he foresaw coming, when they would be able to rule themselves.

He was originally elected to the Legislative Council in 1935 and appointed by the governor as one of the members representing African interests in the legislature as early as 1938. Coincidentally, this appointment led to his vacating his seat of Broken Hill — the new member that replaced him being Roy Welensky. Gore-Browne later became very friendly with Kenneth Kaunda and Harry Nkumbula. The latter benefited at first hand from his generosity and was the recipient of a scholarship he provided to study in London. Much later, during the troubles of 1960–62, Gore-Browne joined the United National Independence Party (UNIP) and ran for election on its ticket.

# 6
# Mporokoso: An Idyllic Interlude

Early in 1946, I was made a district commissioner, two months before my probationary period as a cadet was due to expire. The occasion for this slightly premature happening was that Julian Evetts, the DC at Mporokoso, was going on leave and I was appointed to go and relieve him. We duly upped sticks and prepared to transport ourselves to the new assignment. Once more this involved packing all our worldly possessions into the back of a lorry that set off with the household staff perched on top of the baggage and kept fully occupied with holding everything on despite the bouncing around on the dirt roads; Frances and I, plus the baby, travelled in much greater comfort in a hired car. The habit of taking along one's staff was fairly general. From our point of view relocating them was no great problem and infinitely more desirable than trying to get used to the ideas and habits and indeed even the names of new staff. Of course the other side of the coin meant that it was also a convenient moment if one wanted to get rid of them as we had done previously with Size.

Upon our arrival, Evetts handed over the district together with a liver coloured spaniel that we had agreed to adopt pro tem. Our accommodation was greatly superior to what we had been used to. The bungalow came complete with a swimming pool at the bottom of the garden, which had been dug out by some of the local prison population. It was fed by an underground spring and remained miraculously full for the entire seven or eight months that we were to remain there.

Almost before we had unpacked, a signal was received to say that I was due to receive as an assistant a DA who would be arriving the next day from Kenya with his wife. With less than 24 hours to go it was panic stations. The house in which they were going to live had not been occupied since the start of the war and to say that it was run down was a masterpiece of understatement. We all turned out, together with a large number of native helpers in an attempt to make it somewhat less dreary. We had visions of a newly married wife fresh from England dissolving into tears at the depressing sight. Nothing could have been further from the truth.

Bunny Isaac had been in the RFC during the First World War and had subsequently seen service with the RAF in Cairo in the second. It was there that he had met and fallen for Mary, the lady who accompanied him. Mary was a former matron in the Queen Alexandra's Nursing Service who had been in Africa for quite a number of years and, knowing her way around, was not in the least put out at the sight of her home to be.

As we discovered some time later they were not in fact married. This was not so uncommon in parts of Africa and had given rise to a much-used question 'Are you married, or are you from Kenya?' A good few years later a long delayed divorce ultimately arrived and they were belatedly able to get married in Lusaka.

In point of fact I was not too familiar with the post of DA (district assistant), which was a fairly recent creation that enabled the colonial service to bring its depleted staff up to numbers by taking on comparatively mature but experienced people who would not be expected to remain in post for too many years.

In many ways Mporokoso was one of the great experiences of my career and even now it has the power to evoke the strongest feelings of nostalgia. I was a district commissioner. For practical purposes this meant that, at the age of 26 I was the lord and master of all I surveyed. The sensations washed over and coloured the images of all that went on around me. I was intoxicated with excitement.

The countryside around Mporokoso was especially conducive to this euphoria, being genuinely beautiful and lusher than many other parts of Northern Rhodesia. There was a great deal of wildlife — antelope, jackals, hyenas, wild pig and so on. The district covered almost 10,000 square miles and had hardly been toured since the outbreak of war. The northern boundary faced the Belgian Congo with Lakes Tanganyika and Mweru at either end, while to the west was Kawambwa. Lake Mweru was

## Mporokoso: An Idyllic Interlude

particularly attractive as it contained a number of beautiful islands such as Kilwa. At the core of the district there was an enormous game reserve teeming with elephant, hippopotamus and other species that enjoyed the watery conditions. To the south was Bangweulu, another large lake and swamp system, which drained into the Luapula River bordering the Congo.

It was also an historical area with the district notebooks carrying stories and information about early explorers from the earliest times, before colonization. Bodies such as the African Lakes Corporation had come in those days, thinly disguised as missions, but managed by agents of whom it was cynically remarked that they carried a Bible in one hand and a bag of beads in the other. Those days had long vanished but when one was on *ulendo* in some of the less accessible areas of the bush there were still plenty of beads to be seen, sometimes as just about the only item of clothing worn by some of the teenagers.

One of the first matters to demand my attention was the state of the *boma* stores. To my army trained mind these were far from orderly. Later during my stay I was to discover that my passion for cleanliness and tidiness had led to my acquiring the sobriquet of 'Bwana Cleanall'. In my initial burst of enthusiasm, I even embarked on a programme of sheep dipping until I realized, to my horror, that there were living quarters downstream. There were many unforgettable experiences in Mporokoso that were a part of my new responsibilities, not all of them so pleasant.

\* \* \*

All district officers were required to spend at least 90 days a year on *ulendo*, which entailed sleeping under canvas. I was a great enthusiast for tours with their added possibilities for hunting, and made plans for several. First, however, I decided to take a brief tour with the family to see whether Frances would be able to stand up to the vicissitudes. She had completely recovered from the pregnancy and Vivian at nine months was at a manageable stage, so it seemed a perfect opportunity for a test tour with the whole family together. What was originally planned as a simple *ulendo* became quite involved when it was taken *en famille*; we had no less than 37 carriers and three houseboys who together with Chief Mporokoso made up quite a picturesque entourage. Part of our baggage was a white toilet seat and yellow enamel chamber pot, which swung to and fro as the carrier walked along.

The most popular load was the *mwana*, Vivian, who travelled in something that resembled a meat safe slung from four bamboo poles and carried by four bearers. The meat safe was highly practical because the pierced metal sides were perfect for her to look out of while being impenetrable to mosquitoes. She soon discovered that if she waved her chubby little hands as we paraded through the villages this was a source of great delight to the locals — they adored babies and a more endearing representative of the crown could not have been found. The tour, however, was not to be completed because, despite all of our precautions, Frances succumbed to malaria after a day or so and had to be carried back to the Luangwa River on the proverbial litter; in practice a camp bed borne on poles was used. At the river it was necessary to cross in stages using dugout canoes; Frances had to leave her bed and crossed wearing my dressing gown as well as her own; fortunately, despite feeling wretched, she could see the funny side of it, which she described as her attempt to emulate Livingstone's last journey. This was to be her first and last time on tour.

Undoubtedly, Frances had been infected some time before and it was particularly unfortunate that it made its presence felt during our trip. Like so much of southern Africa, NR was plagued with insects, which included both mosquitoes and tsetse fly. All domestic arrangements were dominated by the need to try to exclude them. At the end of the day, precautions had to be taken against the insect life. Wire netting surrounded all the verandas and one slept under a mosquito net that was tucked into the mattress at the time that the bed was made. Particular care had to be taken when changing clothes or undressing, for the evenings were the time of highest risk. It was also common practice to wear so-called mosquito boots, into which trousers were tucked, provided the heat did not make them too uncomfortable. Babies and children slept in a cot under a device that looked rather like a large sized version of the old-fashioned screen that was used to cover meat in a larder in older times. Attempts were also made to minimize the risks by building houses as high as was practical and away from any trees that might provide shelter for the insect.

## Mporokoso: An Idyllic Interlude

Both of us took quinine regularly, usually at the same time as having sundowners, and I had started this immediately on arrival in Lusaka. In retrospect, I feel that the prophylaxis was quite effective provided it did not get forgotten and also provided one did not get too much exposure to the mosquitoes, something that was almost impossible to avoid when on tour. I had probably contracted the disease during our stay in Kasama, but it was in Mporokoso that it really made itself felt.

Chimpempe, one of the nearest missions, was on the Luapula River at Kafulwe, near to a pontoon crossing. The missionaries there were of a particularly extreme variety to whom imbibing tea or coffee was only slightly less sinful than strong drink. The residents appeared to exist on a concoction of instant Postum. It was interesting to observe that whenever Africans became converts they always seemed to be particularly devout and, one could say, enthusiastic Christians. Nevertheless, despite the comparatively large number of missions and the obvious benefits they brought, such as education and local medicine, the majority of the native population continued secretly to be animists and intensely superstitious.

One of the better-known characters at the mission was an American generally known as 'Chimpempe Robinson'. No doubt he was extremely devout as were most of the Seventh Day Adventists, but he or one of his colleagues had taken a very cavalier view of the restrictions imposed by the local customs and excise department and the agricultural authorities. The local pineapples were not particularly succulent and he considered them to be very inferior to those available in the Americas. Thus, it was to my considerable astonishment when I was offered a remarkably enjoyable pineapple drink one day. It transpired that it had been made from fruit grown on plants from Hawaii that had been brought back and imported when he returned after a spell of spiritual refreshment in the USA. Clearly he had not been over scrupulous about observing the plant quarantine regulations. I can only say that the fruit was greatly superior to that locally grown.

Among my new acquaintances that stood the test of time was Pambi Mukula who, I met on a visit to Chimpempe mission where he worked as a kitchen boy in exchange for his schooling. He first came to our attention when this extremely short and rather comical boy brought the delicious drinks made for us from the mission's pineapples. Later in his life that schoolboy was to merit two inches in *Who's Who in the Commonwealth*.

In common with many of the mission taught boys he became a teacher so as to pass on his rudiments of education. Clearly I made an impression on him — this may sound improbable, but in the eyes of the young a DC was not far removed from God and definitely a great deal closer. Consequently, around 1962 when a crash programme was initiated to get mature students into university, he wrote to me in Ndola Rural and, having reminded me of the time we first met, enquired whether I was able to help with a temporary job to assist him with the costs. Fortunately, I was able to be of some assistance and he was ultimately to become the director of the National Archives of Zambia before he retired not so long ago with a large and prosperous family. In his post he travelled much of the world and visited us several times in the UK subsequent to my retirement. Numerous letters prior to his sad death provided a rich insight into the rapidly changing times in Zambia over more recent years.

I also went to visit Chiengi, which was in a scenic spot on the banks of Lake Mweru. It had formerly been the headquarters of a district and several *boma*s had existed there (possibly including the very first in NR). Despite the scenery, the place seemed to have had a depressing effect on many officers posted there and it had been abandoned after one committed suicide by shooting himself. It struck me that the depression could have been caused by loneliness, for it was a one-man station. Only two buildings were left. One was the gaol, which was a most impressive building in burnt brick with great heavy doors sporting villainous looking bars, bolts and locks. It was of standard nineteenth-century design and I doubt if anybody could have escaped from there — it gave me the willies. The other building was the DC's house that appeared to me to be in a sad state of disrepair; nevertheless, I was to hear later that our friends the Macraes were in the habit of using it as a weekend retreat because of its lakeside location — obviously the atmosphere did not affect them.

During the same trip I was able to meet my opposite number from the other side of the Luapula River, the *chef de poste* of the Kilwa district in the Belgian Congo, who took me for a ride in a

## Mporokoso: An Idyllic Interlude

splendid launch that had been provided by his governor as a part of a programme to encourage the development of fishing in the region. There was already a quite substantial fishing industry, apparently organized on the Congo side by Greeks resident in Kasenga. The fish that were caught were packed in ice before being trucked to Elizabethville.

The only problem was that the fishermen were competing with the crocodiles and as a result the *chef de poste* had organized a campaign against them. His campaign took the form of offering a bounty equivalent of about £1 for a tail or half-a-crown for an egg. We had a very pleasant time chatting, interspersed with the arrival of natives with eggs and looking for their reward. The anti-crocodile campaign had substantially reduced the number of saurians in the Luapula River, but did not appear to have had any effect in Lake Mweru.

Many of the local missionaries felt strongly about the evils of drink and took a very jaundiced view of officials who enjoyed the occasional libation. As a consequence, my new friend the *chef de poste* had a dreadful reputation with the missionaries who had previously regaled me with stories of how much he consumed. Since he did not appear to be drinking in my presence I ventured to enquire about his habits and in the end nearly reduced him to hysterics — '*Moi*, a bottle of brandy before lunch, *mon Dieu*!'

It was at Mporokoso that we celebrated the first anniversary of V-E Day. The word had gone out that 8 June was to be a public holiday in the territory, which made plans for a party easier. Invitations were sent to the seven chiefs in the district and to all the nearby missionaries. The chiefs were especially asked to make sure that any ex-*askari*s in their villages should come too.

It was fascinating to observe the diversity of garb in which the various chiefs arrived. One was wrapped in a kind of toga and wore what appeared to be a paper hat from a Christmas cracker on his head, while another had on the standard government issue uniform for a chief, which looked rather like an academic gown but he had crowned it with a priest's biretta. Surprisingly, despite their musical-comedy outfits, the chiefs invariably had a great deal of dignity about them that commanded respect, not only from their own people but from the Europeans as well.

In the morning there was an open air-service on the golf course

## Kaunda's Gaoler

preceded by a parade of *askaris*, some wearing North West Africa service uniforms and others in Burma green. The service was taken by a newly ordained African preacher whose sermon would have made Churchill proud 'Why did we win the war? Because we had the best guns! Why did we lick the Germans? Because we had the best tanks! How did we finish the Japanese? Because Kingie George had the best soldiers!' and similar uplifting thoughts for the occasion declaimed in Bemba. All went well until the end when he had a problem deciding which way the V for Victory sign should be given.

To complete the service I felt we needed to sound the last post and had sent a messenger to the police-training centre where he had been taught how to blow a bugle. He returned just in time to perform, but unfortunately our spaniel clearly disliked the rendition for he disgraced himself by promptly starting to howl in a manner that was not calculated to enhance the dignity of the moment. Fortunately, the day was saved when one of my colleagues grabbed him and proceeded to clamp his jaws closed until the bugler had finished. Later that day there was a football match followed by elephant meat and roasted ox for our guests.

\* \* \*

One particularly significant difference about Mporokoso was that the district contained the *Mweru wa Ntipa* (Mweru marsh) which was one of the two breeding grounds of the dreaded red locust (the other being just over the border in Tanganyika). The arrival of a swarm of red locusts spells totally devastated crops and local starvation; as a result, there is a full-time international red locust control programme and inspectors regularly wanted to check the area. The director was a Dr Bredo of whom we saw a great deal as a consequence of his not believing in delegating inspections when he was himself available.

The marsh was a remarkable place, rarely visited other than by natives who lived nearby and who fished there. It covered an area of nearly 800 square miles of lake containing some islands and surrounded by marsh and dense, lush vegetation. Only two species of fish were found there, probably as a result of the very high salinity because there was no water flowing out from the lake.

## Mporokoso: An Idyllic Interlude

There were also plentiful crocodiles, which appeared to be frightened of human beings and existed on a diet consisting solely of fish. Depending on the rainfall in any given year, the lake either existed or almost dried out, killing fish and crocodiles with equal impartiality. The swarms of red locusts were intermittent and did not occur every year by any means. At the time I was there, no one was quite sure what precise conditions gave rise to the swarms; they were generally believed to be related to low rainfall but it was nowhere near that simple. Various plans had been contemplated to divert one of the local rivers in order to keep the lake always full, but the cost was prohibitive.

Of course, with two major lakes and the rivers, fishing was a major industry on the NR side as well as in the Belgian Congo. The catches generally were sun dried and then shipped to wherever there was a demand, especially to the line of rail around the copper mines where the native miners were comparatively well paid and could afford to pay a good price in the local markets. Nobody, however, seemed to have thought of salting the fish as an alternative method of preservation until the Macraes (who had entertained us *en route* to Kawambwa) were stationed in Mporokoso. Macrae noted that the district had salt flats on the eastern side of Lake Mweru, which was remarkable since the lake was fresh; obviously there must have been some leaching of a salt deposit nearby. Salt was produced and sold locally to the other nearby villages that could be reached readily by bicycle transport. In the days before there was adequate transport to bring refined 'sea-salt' to the interior, the 'salt' from Lake Mweru was of great importance to the whole of the north and at one time production was estimated to have been as high as 800 tons a year. The process of making it was very primitive and it tasted extremely strong, possibly because it contained a high level of potassium chloride and because of the presence of other minerals.

He set up a simple local cooperative for any fishermen who were interested and the salt collectors. Initially, the *boma* lorry was used to provide transport to get the product to markets; the local European population greatly appreciated the salted tilapia and this gave the providers a good financial return.

The agricultural department made every effort to encourage the production of cereals, rice, sweet potatoes and groundnuts, where possible, for the local market. Food-buying depots were established locally in the most productive areas to try to stimulate production above existing subsistence levels. Goods were purchased for cash and kept in grass shelters until sufficient had accumulated to justify transporting them back to the *boma* by truck. The crops thus collected would be stored in the *boma* warehouse from where they could be sold on to local markets for the townspeople or used to provide foodstuffs for government employees.

One problem when living in the bush is the absence of a dentist. We had both realized the need to visit one for some time and, indeed, had travelled a considerable distance to call on the one in Johnstone Falls only to find that he was away. Now our problems had become more pressing and we again set off in the hope of finding Willie Lammond at home.

It was a journey fraught with problems because for practical purposes the road was non-existent and we had two punctures on the way there. The second occurred while we were still about 45 miles short of Kawambwa and the sun was setting. Changing the wheel while it rapidly darkened was an unnerving experience, as there seemed to be rustlings in the undergrowth that could have been anything; it certainly lent speed to our efforts. Finally, we were ready to start again and the source of the noise became clear; we had taken some chickens with us in the back as peace offerings to our hosts in Kawambwa and Johnstone Falls and they were scratching around while they prepared to settle for the night.

After a night in Kawambwa, we drove on to Johnstone Falls and were relieved to find Willie at home. He devoted the afternoon to sorting out our problems and then showed us the other facilities he had to help him with his work at the mission. These included lathes for turning ivory and workshops in which he endeavoured to train the locals in cabinet making. An unusual sideline he had developed was the manufacture of artificial legs. He was vastly amused at our complaints over the punctures we had sustained *en route*; he had arrived at the mission nearly 40 years before, having walked the entire way from the east coast. This story and his departing good wishes did not prevent us having yet another puncture when we were almost home.

We had only been home a couple of days when we had a visit

## Mporokoso: An Idyllic Interlude

from a man who claimed to be making an inspection on behalf of the secretary of state for the colonies.

Our visitor, whom we nicknamed 'the Nark', asked Frances a great many questions over lunch, which was a great irritation because he had addressed exactly the same questions to me earlier during his visit to the *boma* office. He seemed very disappointed when I made do with water for my lunchtime drink. We were not sorry to see him leave.

Then we received another visitor, this time with open arms. He was Professor Debenham with whom I had studied at Cambridge. This was the first of several visits sponsored by the government, which resulted in some major works when I was stationed at Luwingu some years later.

# 7
# The Secretariat

My stay in Mporokoso was disappointingly brief and it was only a comparatively short time before I was transferred to the Secretariat at Lusaka. The transfer was primarily with the objective of expanding my administrative skills and there were various tricks of the trade to be absorbed. For a while I was put in charge of a substantial section of the registry files headed 'development'. After the hiatus of the war years the government was anxious to bring up to date and implement various schemes that had lain dormant for that period. These included various topics dealing with such things as agriculture, forestry and communications, but the biggest and most important question mark by far hung over 'air'.

I have already referred to the existence of the airfield at Kasama, but there were several others around the colony that had been run very efficiently by the South African Air Force (SAAF) during the war as part of the backup to the Middle East forces. Various communications facilities such as radar had been installed and the impending departure of the SAAF looked as if it would leave a vacuum. With just two or three months grace we had to familiarize ourselves with and take over all the facilities, including radio communication systems, radar and fuel storage, and prepare for the NRG to operate them.

The chief postmaster, himself a South African, was dispatched to Cape Town with instructions to track down and hire ex-servicemen with radio transmitter experience. In the meantime the establishment officer set out to recruit a director of civil aviation and a number of officers with experience in running airports.

Group Captain Muspratt-Williams, who became the director, epitomized the standard caricature of a wartime RAF officer with all the mannerisms and exaggerated language of the time. He was

## The Secretariat

to educate me in such tricks as how to land an aircraft when the undercarriage would not descend by coming down on a bridle path in a wood, saying quite airily that it was a cinch, 'It's easy old boy you just have to line it up down the path, and when you come down the trees simply shear the wings off and act as a brake, leaving the fuselage to skid along the path' — I was convinced that he was not talking about something he had not done himself. When the NRG decided to buy its own aircraft, he hitched a ride back to the UK, picked up the plane and flew it back to Lusaka. Many people found working in the Secretariat tedious but this never bothered Muspratt; he invariably managed to find things to do that took him away from the office.

Frances was able get a Polish nanny for Vivian from a refugee camp and then got herself a job as the business manager of a small African newspaper called *Mutende* (the standard Bemba greeting meaning 'peace'). The government information department, whose director was Harry Franklin, published this. He was another of those larger than life characters who seemed to turn up in NR. Like Sir Stewart Gore-Browne, he supported the concept that the African population should be ruling itself. His principal claim to fame was the short-wave radio station that broadcast news in numerous languages. Although this idea was fine, it became bogged down with the problem that very few people in the African population could afford a receiver. Harry canvassed far and wide for a manufacturer who was willing to produce a cheap receiver. In the end he hit on the ingenious idea of approaching EverReady and convinced them that a receiver could be made and sold at cost, with profits to be made through the sales of the batteries to power it. It was a great success.

It was about this time that we had our first visitors. Initially there was Frances's mother, Mrs Knight, together with a friend. My mother-in-law's husband had been commodore of the Union Castle Line so they had plenty of introductions when they got to Cape Town and had been very well received there. I had bought an old Buick with which we were able to chauffeur them around. To say that it was 'clapped out' was probably a flattering description, for it had at one time been rolled before I acquired it and still showed some of the bruises. Later on my mother came and we were able to take her to see the fantastic splendour of the

## Kaunda's Gaoler

Victoria Falls. It was probably just as well that we went, for it was to be almost the only time I got to visit them.

Subsequently, she spent a lot of time with our friends the Isaacs who had also been moved to Lusaka. They were her contemporaries and she delighted in trying to solve the problem of how to progress their efforts to get divorced from their previous partners.

On one occasion when they were temporarily camped out on a large farm to the south of the Kafue River, we were invited down for the weekend and set out in high spirits. Unfortunately, we took a wrong turning on the dirt roads and finally ended up nearly 100 miles out of our way at the Otto Beit Bridge on the Zambezi, overlooking Southern Rhodesia. We turned around and set off to retrace our steps feeling that this was all quite hilarious. However, by the time we finally arrived around midnight the joke was falling a little bit flat and we were quite relieved to have got there.

During my stay in Lusaka, King George and Queen Elizabeth visited NR as part of their tour of southern Africa. They had with them the young Princess Elizabeth as she then was, and it was while she was in Southern Rhodesia that she stood by Rhodes's tomb in the Matopo Hills and made her speech dedicating herself to the service of the commonwealth; it was broadcast all over the area and made a profound impression.

There were two other matters in which I became seriously involved during my stay in the Secretariat. One was the creation of a new Department of Forestry and the other the groundnut scheme. The latter, of course was one of the great postwar scandals and became a standing joke since everyone knew that groundnuts really ought to be called monkey nuts. These nuts were successfully grown in West Africa where there was plenty of rich soil and it appeared to the British government of the day, egged on by Unilever, that a similarly rich crop could be grown in many other places including much of East Africa. In its heyday the scheme was widely extolled on the basis that it would solve all Britain's postwar problems. Northern Rhodesia was one of the areas that had been selected as suitable for this great development.

The development secretary and I were both working late one evening when an office orderly came in bearing an imposing file much garlanded with red flags. After a few minutes of study I leaped from my chair, my eyes popping, and headed off at a rate

## The Secretariat

of knots to see the secretary. It was a comprehensive and damning report from the Department of Agriculture, which could (and probably should) have killed the project stone dead as far as NR was concerned. As I recall, it pointed out that the statistics on which the projections were based had been absurdly exaggerated and the only way in which this could have been done was through the selective use of the yields on the experimental plots rather than by averaging them. Further, not only did it suggest that the yields had been selected but also the plots from which they had been culled. The report looked like dynamite and to me had a ring of truth. The secretary, however, did not want to believe these suggestions and stalled on giving it his approval. As it turned out, it was already too late to do anything as the various colonial governments had already given the scheme their approval and allocated the necessary finance several months before.

# 8
# Leave

Normally, leave did not come until one had been in post for three years. It accumulated at a rate of 60 days a year. However, shortage of staff combined with the war meant that many officers had substantial accumulations of leave due to them. To overcome this problem, newer members, myself included, were offered early leave, namely after just two years, provided we were willing to take it locally and forego the home leave that would have been due the following year. The proposal that we could go and enjoy ourselves in the flesh pots of South Africa at places like Cape Town seemed wonderful and we eagerly accepted the opportunity to stay over Christmas at the Mount Nelson, then the Premier Hotel in Cape Town.

Shortly before we departed from Lusaka for the Cape we had moved into what was considered to be a relatively modern two-bedroom bungalow built of 'Kimberly brick', the name given to locally manufactured bricks made from sun-dried mud. However, by the time we returned from leave it had already been expropriated for another family and we had to wait a while for another lot of bricks to come off the local production line. It could be that the inconvenience was well worth it, as the new bungalow turned out to have three bedrooms. The toilet, of course, was outside and one night it was necessary for Frances to pay a visit. Hardly had she opened the door from our bedroom to the garden when there was the piercing sound of police whistles. It transpired that there was a fugitive from justice in the area and the police were in hot pursuit; the miscreant had elected to hide himself in our loo where fortunately the police found him just before Frances got there.

Four years were to elapse after my arrival in NR before I became due for home leave and this announcement coincided with our fifth wedding anniversary. Although basically the time could be spent however we liked, there were a number of business matters with which to deal.

There was the so-called second Devonshire Course. Before the war it had been standard practice for recruits to spend a whole year in Cambridge under the aegis of Professor Debenham on a course of training and indoctrination. This had been named after the eponymous duke who had originated it while permanent secretary at the Colonial Office. Others and I should have gone through it at the time of joining the service, but due to the hostilities and urgency it had not taken place. Of course, the practical experience that we had gained rendered it largely unnecessary, butced it largely unnecessary, but the powers felt that we should not escape entirely and a second Devonshire Course had been devised. There were also a number of colonial service examinations that needed to be taken in order to make progress in my career. The examination in elementary Bemba had already been passed in Kawambwa and I had decided in my own mind that it would be a good idea for the other courses that I took to be advanced Bemba and law.

The year that we spent at home was to be the most carefree in my life. The reunion included so many friends and relations, including several that had not even existed when we departed.

I had interviews for the course, which was to take place at the London School of Economics (LSE), and at the London School of Oriental and African Studies (SOAS) rather than Cambridge. Despite some objections from my amiable but lofty tutor, I finally got my way on the courses and it was agreed that I could study Chi Bemba, as they preferred to call it. For law, I signed up with Gibson and Weldon, a firm of law tutors in Chancery Lane. I also joined the Inns of Court with a view to taking the bar exams over the long leaves that could be anticipated in the future. The preliminary test was the dinners; it soon became apparent that it was quite true to suggest that one literally ate one's way to the English Bar with a requirement to participate in six dinners per year as a minimum.

The lectures we received on constitutional law and legal history were very interesting and it was subsequently possible to continue with the studies on criminal law and common law by correspondence while I was in Luwingu. Roman law is normally a dry as dust subject but one of the lecturers endeavoured to inject some life into it by involving the students as if in a game: 'You Mr Jones! You are the wealthy son of a Roman senator, and you Miss Smith! You are an attractive slave of another senator. The two of you have a romp together. When the child of your union is born, to whom does it belong?' — Miss Smith: 'I object to the question!'

The main course was to be carried out at the LSE, which had become rather notorious as a left-wing institution since the advent to power of a Labour government. As a result, most of the participants were rather suspicious that lectures would be heavily politically biased. It was a pleasant surprise to realize that they were not and that, despite the opportunities there were for brainwashing, it did not take place. Overall, there was a very pleasing atmosphere about the lectures and seminars. It was ironic that the Colonial Office did not seem to attract socialists, despite the fact that a colony was almost a socialist institution insofar as its government was intended to be unbiased and for the benefit of all. All in all, the course was very beneficial and provided many valuable insights into how the commonwealth operated.

A special course had been arranged for me at the SOAS where I learnt how to write Bemba so as to show all the tones. Professor Guthrie claimed to be able to write English the same way. I was quite young then and had no real problems, although in my experience as one gets older it becomes very difficult to hear tonal variations.

Cars were still in very short supply at the time and it was particularly pleasing to be able to take delivery in the UK of a Ford Popular, free of purchase tax, for export to Africa. Upon our arrival back in Cape Town, I set off to drive the car back to Lusaka on my own apart from the company of Harvey, our Siamese cat. Frances, who was again pregnant, decided to stay with friends for a few days before proceeding to Lusaka by the relative comfort of rail before going on to Ndola to take a plane for the remaining hop to Kasama.

I had already had some intimations before going on leave that my next tour was likely to be at Luwingu and my stay in Lusaka was just sufficiently long to receive official notification of my appointment and to be properly briefed.

# 9

# Luwingu

Shortly before arriving at Luwingu, while I was mentally congratulating myself on the perfect way in which the Ford had behaved, it stopped abruptly with a stripped bearing. Pride suffered a grievous fall at the necessity of having to accept a lift with a local trader for the last few miles rather than being able to stage a triumphal entry. The car was subsequently towed in for the necessary repairs.

Upon arrival I discovered that my predecessor in Luwingu, Derek Goodfellow, had completed his tour of duty some while previously and had already departed, leaving his DO, Micky Chittenden, in charge. He and his wife Cecile made me very welcome while we awaited Frances's arrival. They had begun the redecoration of the DC's house; however, it was not yet complete so they very kindly offered to accommodate all of us until it was finished.

Micky had been part of the army's establishment in Nairobi before joining the colonial service as part of the postwar intake. I had already been briefed on his supposed eccentricities in Lusaka. Consequently, we were not too taken aback when this large portly man told us that it was his family's custom to dine in their pyjamas whether or not they had guests. He was an accomplished raconteur and this turned out be rather like a very camp send-up of the life of the proconsul in the jungle and would have been perfectly suited to a *Carry On* film.

Progress in the colonial service was to some extent governed by the need to prove that one was suited for higher posts. The easiest way to do this was to demonstrate progressively improved knowledge of the matters in which one was involved and while I was in Luwingu various opportunities arose.

The first thing I needed to do was to reach the highest standard in Bemba. The White Fathers mission was nearby in Ipusikilo and Father Etienne was a noted Bemba scholar, so each Sunday afternoon, if it were practical, I would go over and spend some time with him studying the Bemba language and customs. About a year later this led to my passing a test in higher Bemba. Around the same time I was also able to sit the law exam for which I had been studying in London. After a period of feverish revision with my notes, this too was passed and left me with only the need for another, lower language, as the remaining hurdle to clear before I became a fully qualified administrative officer. This I was subsequently able to do by learning sufficient of the Lovale language in 1958 while posted in Kabompo.

My actual takeover did not get off to the most auspicious start. As far as the district was concerned, everything appeared to be in apple pie order, much as I had expected, as Luwingu was a prized posting. The fly in the ointment, however, was that the current district notebook appeared to be missing from the large collection in the *boma* office and Micky declared that he had never even seen it. After an exhaustive search that went on for the better part of a week, I prepared a catalogue of the existing notebooks. I finally endorsed the taking over certificate to the effect that one was missing and informed the PC of my concerns, as it was a serious breach of colonial regulations. I always supposed that it would turn up in the end as mysteriously as it had disappeared but it was not to be; indeed a year or so later all the district notebooks were withdrawn.

To the casual reader this may appear to be a great deal of fuss about nothing, but in those days it was no small matter and the disappearance of a district notebook was greeted with the same degree of incredulity as if I had announced that the crown jewels were missing. The notebooks were about the size of a Victorian family Bible, so simple disappearance was hardly feasible. Not surprisingly, suspicion fell on Micky Chittenden, though I maintained that it was out of character. His attitude to things was generally humorous or preposterous but invariably light hearted. Some years later he confided to me that he had once produced a counterfeit *boma* date stamp with the words 'District Commissioner' replaced by 'District Kommissar'. This he had subsequently used on some document that had gone on to the holy of holies, namely the

## Luwingu

Secretariat Accountant General's Department. When queried about the matter he compounded the send-up by saying that he must have accidentally used one required by him for use 'in some other capacity'.

The particular significance of the district notebook was that it contained the most authentic record of the history of the district from its very first days. Sometimes a district messenger would be instructed to go out to visit a village or chief and to try to piece together some matters that had occurred in the past. Subsequent discussion with the messenger of his report by the DC meant, it was hoped, that it could be interpreted so that a reasonably accurate record was available. This was needed to understand fully the report while it was still fresh in everyone's mind. An example of such a report is included as Appendix 3 — 50 years on it makes for interesting reading.

In Luwingu (as in most of the Northern Province), the district messengers did all the police work and it was a part of my job to carry out inspections on a Saturday morning, first of the messengers and then of the gaol. Complaints by the inmates were invited and investigated before being recorded in the visiting justice's book. At the same time, any complaints by the head warder against any of the prisoners would be investigated and summarily dealt with.

At this time Northern Rhodesia was going through something of a boom based on the revenues from the copper mines around Ndola. The war, coupled with the enormous expansion associated with the rebuilding of Europe's shattered economies, had led to a surge in demand for base metals and good prices were to be expected. The lack of local finance had in the past always had an inhibiting effect on the best-intentioned schemes that were contemplated by the government. Now things had taken a turn for the better and the post of development secretary was created as a measure of the determination of the authorities to improve the infrastructure. Reference has already been made to the development of a nascent internal air service. In addition, an aerial survey was undertaken and plans made for an enhanced trunk road system. In some places the construction of these roads had already begun.

The improved roads were of enormous benefit to the people of the Northern Province, especially now that one could travel from places such as Luwingu and Mporokoso, via Fort Rosebery and the Kapalala ferry, directly to Ndola across a section of the Belgian Congo. The pedicule, as it was known, projected like a finger into the middle of Northern Rhodesia. Government stores for the *boma* were regularly carried over this direct route by the district lorry.

I soon discovered that Luwingu was an important focal point. Among the items that we carried in the stores were cement, tools and equipment for the construction of new roads and buildings together with considerable quantities of fuel for the district lorry. The fuel was also required to keep going the tugs and launches used on Lake Bangweulu and the various waterways through its swamps.

We had two tugs, eponymously named *Maizie* and *Beans* after their two principal cargoes, and it was hoped that they could be used to pull barges, having a capacity of 30 tons, along the Luapula River to markets in the Copper Belt when the river was high enough.

To provide the traction to cope with this load it was necessary to replace the *Maizie*'s existing engine. This did not go off as smoothly as planned. First, the old engine was dismantled so that it could be removed and then the hull was dragged out of the swamps onto a suitable piece of land. A marine engineer, who had come up especially from Port Elizabeth, supervised the installation of the new engine, which weighed about two tons. What with the weight of the new engine, returning *Maizie* to the water presented unexpected difficulties and, after one week of 100 men tugging and straining, next to no progress had been made. At last someone suggested that 'since it is the African women who always do all the heavy work we should hire the women'. Messengers were sent to all the local villages to request that all women not actually in childbirth come and earn a shilling for towing the good ship down the slipway. Come they did and it was an incredible sight to see them heaving on the ropes, some in advanced stages of pregnancy and others actually suckling their babies. The boat promptly started to move off down the improvised slipway and the job was finished in an afternoon.

As in other districts, tours were one of the most important

## Luwingu

activities, but around Luwingu where the *boma* owned a flotilla of small craft, the experience became much more varied.

One of these craft was known locally as the 'Governor's Launch' and had presumably been acquired sometime when HE came on a visit. Using this, I had myself transported to Chilubi Island to visit the Santa Maria medical mission, which was run by the White Fathers. The doctor in charge was a dedicated lady, Dr Cunningham as I recall. From Chilubi Island it was possible to travel across the lake to another medical mission at Kasaba on the Lupososhi estuary, run by English nurses from their Franciscan headquarters near Guildford together with a priest in charge. My visit to the latter mission had an ulterior motive, for, with Frances pregnant and recalling the difficult first accouchement she had experienced with Vivian, I was anxious for her to be able to get nursing help when she arrived in Luwingu. It was a happy little community that I found, including two priests and a lay brother, their proud boast being that their combined ages amounted to 180 years, which was quite a feat in those parts at that time. I was particularly pleased as Mother Carmel herself offered to come with one of the sisters. Indeed, she remembered Vivian from a visit to Mporokoso and particularly recalled that she used to sit outside in the 'meat safe', as we generally referred to her wire-netted cot.

\* \* \*

The possibility of hunting continued to fire my enthusiasm and the presence of an emergency landing ground at Mofu close to the large Isangano game reserve was the only excuse needed. My intention was to be off very early, but around midnight there was a great hullabaloo from the direction of the African suburb and I arrived just in time to see the house of the forest ranger and his family burnt to the ground. They had been asleep and woken to find the roof blazing above their heads, but fortunately had managed to escape unscathed.

In the end I got to bed at 1.00 and arose again at about 4.00 a.m., heading off with the head messenger and one other. Upon our arrival we left the van and started to follow some tracks, finally catching up with a vast herd of eland. These scented us and promptly took off at a gentle trot. After a short while we managed to catch up with them again without being spotted and I was able to shoot a likely looking animal. The next thing to happen was that the herd stampeded and was heading straight for me. I recall attempting to reload and thinking to myself that it was a good job that they were not buffalo, though at close to 1000 lb. each in weight, standing as if paralysed in their way was not a clever move. Fortunately, Mulenga, the head messenger, had the good sense to grab me and pull me behind a thicket. The herd thundered past us so close that we could have reached out and touched them. I was pleased to find that the beast I had shot was lying there and must have died instantaneously as the bullet entered its neck.

\* \* \*

The most significant event of our stay in Luwingu was undoubtedly the Debenham expedition to make a comprehensive study of the Bangweulu swamp. It was hoped that as a result of his investigations it would be possible to put forward new proposals for works that would drain some of the swampy land, turning it into a fertile and prosperous area with properly navigable waterways.

Lake Bangweulu is famous because of its association with David Livingstone who discovered it in 1868. It was on his second visit when he came from the north that he made the mistake of turning to the west, as a result of which he died (in the village of Chief Chitambo) while trying to traverse the area. Had he turned to the east, as the chief had advised him to do, he would have made his escape from the swamp quite rapidly. Unfortunately, however, he did not follow the advice of the chief whom he did not trust.

The lake itself is as picturesque as its name, which in Bemba means 'where the sky and water meet'. It covers an area of 400–500 square miles and with neighbouring Lake Walilupo a further 140 square miles, though neither are more than around 20 feet deep. In the rainy season, the total area, including the swamps, is at least 3500 square miles. These lakes and the vast swamps make a huge and fascinating area lying between the Chambeshi and Luapula rivers. The former runs just a short distance from the lake without actually running into it. The numerous waterways through the swamps between the two lakes were connected naturally by flooding in the rainy season.

## Luwingu

Fishing was a major local industry and in the lake and waterways it was excellent, the best catch being *mpende*, the local name for a type of tilapia that is quite delicious. There were also other fish of up to 14 kilograms in weight. The largest of all was *sampa*, the giant catfish (heterebranchus), which was reputed to reach as much as 100 kilograms or more, though it was not caught very often, possibly because of its size. All the diverse tribal people living around the lake indulge in fishing to a greater or lesser degree using a variety of techniques. Baskets and crudely made screens of papyrus rushes were used by the womenfolk, while in the dry season, as the water became progressively more shallow, many fish were trapped in small lagoons and could literally be lifted out by hand. Nets and occasionally lines were used by the menfolk from canoes. The lake was also home to several unique species, including the lungfish, which survives the drought by burying itself at the outset of the dry season. An unusual very large wading bird in the shape of the shoebill, which is supposedly unrelated to any other species, could sometimes be seen.

Around 500–600 tons of fish were caught each year, which, after having been cleaned and dried or smoked in the villages, were carried in large packages to Kapalala for transhipment to Ndola. Some were also taken to the small settlement of Samfya in the Fort Rosebery district. Getting there was quite an expedition as it could take up to three days to paddle a dugout canoe from some of the more remote parts of the swamps. A large part of the journey was across the open lake where conditions could change abruptly, with considerable danger to heavily laden canoes. After I had left Luwingu the trade via Samfya ultimately became greater than that through Kapalala.

In general, the main type of boat used on the lake was a dugout, which could be easily paddled, whereas in the swamps, which were very shallow, the canoes were poled. Certain villages were known to specialize in the art of making canoes and they sold them to the surrounding people. They preferred to use a tree known as *mofu* and as a result it was becoming quite rare in the locality. The advantage of this particular type of wood was that the dugouts made from it would last for up to ten years; on the other hand the wood was denser than water, which meant that if the boat capsized it was quite likely to sink. Because of its size the lake was sometimes quite rough and, as a consequence, some tribes that were inherently fearful of the water would not venture out very far for fishing. One or two tribes, however, had become far more expert in managing their primitive craft and had no such fear, venturing way out onto the lake. Like many large lakes around the world, Bangweulu had a monster, which existed in the minds of the local population. Considering how shallow the lake was I think that its existence can safely be discounted. Certainly, it had nowhere near the notoriety of Kangomato, which was supposed to inhabit the swamps in the Congo not so far away.

The whole area together with a lot of surrounding land was prone to flooding to a greater or lesser extent during the rainy season. In former times, prior to 1940, there were numerous islands that were above the water line, the largest being the Lunga Bank of some 150 square miles and noted for its comparative fertility. Even further back in time, during the world war campaigns, the Chambeshi River had been sufficiently navigable during the wet season that troops and supplies were moved to the front via the river. This however had all changed.

Over a period of time there had been great growths of various weeds, which had effectively blocked the waterways. The resultant slow flow of water meant that any natural scouring action that might have kept the channels clear had ceased and drainage downstream had deteriorated. There has never been an adequate explanation for this comparatively rapid change in the ecosystem. The only one that had some plausibility (however improbable it may sound) was that hippopotamuses had formerly kept the weeds down and the channels clear when they walked along the bottom of the waterways and that they had been hunted to the point that they had ceased to act as natural dredgers. The Chambeshi ceased to flow freely and its not inconsiderable volume formed a number of minor lakes and ultimately reached the Luapula through a maze of small waterways and by permeation through the dense reeds of the swamps.

The consequence of this was that during the rainy season the Chambeshi and its local tributaries burst their banks and the lakes overflowed, flooding vast areas of the surrounding countryside and effectively transforming all of it into a swamp; parts, such as the Lunga Bank mentioned above, had become uninhabitable several years before. At one time the Lunga Bank had been home to as many as 6000 people living on the cassava and maize they grew but the land had become useless. For many years the colonial government had harboured the notion that this land could be returned to its former state by better drainage and that it could produce considerable amounts of economically attractive crops, particularly rice. Various DCs had made several attempts to drain the area without any permanent success. One result of their efforts had been to move the point at which the Chambeshi 'officially' flowed into the Luapula some miles further south. This was navigable but only to very small craft such as the motorboats used by some traders when visiting the islands that were permanently above the swamps.

The advent of some degree of financial flexibility meant that these proposals could be taken down off their shelves and dusted off. There was, however, no action until matters finally came to a head when the Kapitabane, the only navigable channel of the Chambeshi River, became blocked; this catalysed some action.

A decision was made to invite Professor Debenham of Cambridge University to come out with a team from his own department to make a comprehensive study of the Bangweulu swamp during the long college vacation of 1949.

With his party, he made the most complete survey of the area to date. It was a very arduous task, for camps had to be relocated regularly and the swampy conditions were hardly appropriate for accurate surveying. Matters became even more complicated when Professor Debenham had a minor heart attack. Fortunately, he soon recovered and considered himself well enough to carry on, while being transported in a *machila* rather like a hammock suspended from poles, worryingly reminiscent of Livingstone's last trip. Despite these problems the job was completed more or less on time and a report prepared with various recommendations for cutting a channel.

After the departure of the Debenham party for a last visit to the lake, the Chittendens and Greenalls thought they could relax and take what they felt to be a well-deserved breather while awaiting decisions to be made on high on what do about the recommendations. Relaxation, however, was not to be. I had made plans to take Frances into Kasama where she would stay pending the arrival of our second baby, but the day before we were due to leave the baby decided to pre-empt our decision. I promptly headed off in a panic to the medical mission 30 miles away in the hope of getting the midwife while Micky was asked to drive posthaste in his jeep to Kasama for the medical officer. Fortunately for my peace of mind, I was not to know that the previous evening he had stripped down the engine and that the first stage of 'posthaste' was to reassemble it. Incredibly, when one considered the distance and state of the road, the medical officer arrived only seven hours after the first signs of labour. Lydia was ultimately born on the veranda of our house, the same one where Philip Jelf, a previous DC, had been mauled by a lion back in the 1920s.

\* \* \*

The attack showed how unspoiled the district had been at that time. A detailed account written by the victim was published in the *Northern Rhodesia Journal* in 1960 and from it I have extracted a summary. He was asleep in his bed in the early hours when he was woken by a blow and realized that some animal was on top of him. He managed to get free and screamed to a friend for help while trying to get away from the lion, which eventually caught him when he collapsed on the floor of another room. The lion was actually chewing on his shoulder when shots were fired and the lion bolted, the friend having had to run to the nearby gaol to get the warders who were armed. The following night the lion was back and, having smashed a pane of glass in the dining room, stuck its head in. It took, in those times, two days for a doctor to get to Jelf to dress the wound properly and, incidentally, to remove one of the bullets that had been fired at the lion. Sometime later the lion took some poisoned bait and it turned out to be an old lioness with teeth that were much worn down, which was probably very fortunate for Jelf.

Lions were still plentiful in the district though they were not usually a great problem, although ones that could no longer hunt sometimes turned to human prey. My daughter Vivian has reminded me of the occasion when she was out for an afternoon walk with one of our staff and the native drums started to beat rather fast, which was the local equivalent of an air raid alarm and signified that there was a lion wandering around the vicinity. The maid with a protesting Vivian in tow promptly rushed back to the house to be greeted by an anxious Frances. In nearby Chiengi on Lake Mweru there had been a notorious man-eater, 'Chiengi Charlie', which was reputed to have killed and eaten at least 90 people.

\* \* \*

A short time later, the formal authorization and financial approval arrived from the PC for work on a diversionary cut at Nsalushi Island, as recommended by Professor Debenham, to be commenced. The PC was, of course, well aware that the rains were only about six weeks away, although the letter of instruction blithely ignored this lack of consideration on the part of mother nature until the last sentence, which I still recall — 'In haste, but not, I hope, in such a hurry as you will be when you receive this!'

The work involved digging out a canal through the swamp about 3000 yards long and 40 feet wide to a depth of four to five feet. Indeed, it could hardly be described as digging since the whole of the route was already under a couple of feet or so of water. A great many people were involved. Vernon Brelsford, the Kasama DC, had overall responsibility for the professional and technical side of matters. On site, James Pook (one of the Cambridge team) was to look after the practical aspects of the dig while, as the area DC, I was responsible for finding, hiring and generally looking after the workforce. We hoped to be able to recruit the necessary labourers locally, but as a precaution the neighbouring district of Mpika was alerted to be ready to provide additional labour if it appeared necessary.

The timing of the start was critical; during the dry season the water level was falling at nearly half an inch a day and it was necessary for the waters to be at the lowest practical level to enable the surveyors to enter the swamp and to make the necessary observations. It was also important because lower water levels would facilitate the digging, which would all have to be done by hand. The big worry was that although the rainy season was officially six weeks away, the coming of the rains was notoriously unpredictable and could easily vary by a week or two. It was to be a race against time.

## Kaunda's Gaoler

I hoped that a workforce could be drawn from the villages on Nsalushi Island because those people were well used to working in and around the swamps, so district messengers were sent out to do the recruiting. Initially, they had come in slowly, for they were suspicious about what we really wanted to do, but ultimately a labour force of about 400 was assembled on Nsalushi Island. James and I pitched our tent under the only tree. The same tree also served as my office where I paid out the workers. The people of the swamps and flood plains had no equals when it came to the backbreaking task of digging the cut, armed only with the most primitive tools because they preferred to use their own hoes rather than the *boma* shovels that could have been provided. They seemed to have no problems working up to their knees in mud or indeed up to their waists in water. They also worked together in groups, which appeared to be very dangerous because they wielded their hoes over their heads; nevertheless, this was what they seemed to prefer, but it was a great relief when the task was finished without more than one or two injuries, all of which were treatable. The rains held off and the work was completed with a comfortable amount of time to spare. On the great day the small retaining bank of mud and weeds was breached to great cheers and water swept down through the cut. The river now dropped eight feet over a couple of miles and the speed with which the current flowed was spectacular. We were counting on this speed to keep the cut open and at the same time further erode the channel to a greater depth.

I had hoped to share part of the glory by joining Pook on a ride down the cut to christen it. He, however, got to his canoe well ahead of me and was borne along at great speed, followed behind at a little distance by myself. When I got down to the outflow end of the cut I was tremendously elated at the apparent success of our efforts. The workers were obviously very delighted, showing their approval by leaping into the cut. The provision of a rudimentary fence some way back from the sides of the cut completed the work. It was hoped that during the flood season the fence would trap debris that overflowed the banks and thereby ultimately create an artificial levee.

The only contretemps in the entire operation occurred as we were preparing to leave. Unbeknown to us, a number of buffalo had been living on Nsalushi Island, which our workforce had driven off with the exception of the bull. This now decided to put in an appearance, encouraged at a considerable distance by some of the workers, the rest of them having taken to the branches of my tree the moment it was seen. From their post of safety every encouragement was wildly shouted for the DC to shoot the bull to provide a welcome change to the regular diet. James yelled at them to get down from the tree in a voice that would have done a sergeant major proud and, confronted by a small crowd, the buffalo stopped and we eyed each other. I took a shot at the bull, followed immediately by James, at which point the animal dropped dead. Encouraged by my past research on the conventions of big-game hunting, I am afraid I very unsportingly claimed the head. He, not surprisingly, felt put out and promptly suggested that my shot had in fact missed, which was very galling as I considered myself a crack shot. It was the only time in 25 years that I actually got a shot at one of the big-five dangerous game animals.

Apart from the improved drainage the cut also turned out to be useful in another way as it gave direct access from Kasama (the provincial capital) to Kasoma, the village of the senior Unga chief.

The onset of the rains shortly after was sufficient to keep me away from the swamps, for it was altogether more pleasant during the wet season to make tours in the upland areas where, as was subsequently to become apparent, there was trouble brewing.

\* \* \*

Some time earlier I had visited the Bemba area of Chief Tungati. It had been a rather unusual experience as it was the first time that I had visited an area where the chief had a reasonable education and a good knowledge of English. He insisted that his villages were kept swept, with the huts properly thatched and paths hoed. It was surprising how much more prosperous they appeared when properly maintained. My feeling of wellbeing on this tour was also helped by the fact that I managed to shoot a couple of reedbuck, which provided a welcome addition to our diet.

There were indeed comparatively few chiefs with much by way of an education, though DCs made every effort behind the scenes to encourage the paramount chief and tribal elders to appoint someone literate whenever an opportunity presented itself. This, for example, could occur whenever a situation arose in which there appeared to be two or more candidates in the running.

A second chief in the area whom I needed to visit was also educated to a higher than usual level. Chief Shimumbi turned out to be a very pleasant and cultivated individual speaking excellent English; he too maintained high standards in his villages with the people looking both fitter and apparently happier than was generally the case elsewhere. Looked back on from a distance of many years it seemed to be generally the case that where the leaders were educated there was invariably a better atmosphere.

It may be that following these two pleasant experiences on tour and with the cut under my belt that I felt slightly euphoric about local affairs. Be that as it may, but back at the *boma*, I received a letter from Chief Nsamba, the leader of the people on the island where we had recruited our labourers. In it he asked for permission to visit the area of another chief and, seeing nothing untoward in the request, I gave my approval without bothering to consult the head messenger.

Of course I was not to know that, despite being of the same tribe, the two chiefs were hostile, not at all well disposed to each other and verging on outright hostility. Consequently, when Nsamba appeared at the other village it nearly provoked a riot, especially as he paraded around with a banner of some sort. The local protestors not only flung mud at him but also contrived to upset his canoe and tip him into the swampy water.

When this news reached the ears of the PC, George Billing, he reacted angrily and directed the senior chief of the Unga to summon an *ndaba* or tribal conclave to be held at the village of Kasoma, where the wretched Chief Nsamba could be accused before all his fellow Unga chiefs.

Holding an *ndaba* at Kasoma, which was on the Lunga Bank, provided a welcome opportunity for many people to make a firsthand inspection of the Nsalushi channel for the first time.

The *ndaba* was held on a nearby island that was large enough for the entire concourse of chiefs and people who had assembled to attend the meeting. It was presided over by the PC and started with a speech that was read out by the Unga court clerk on behalf of the senior chief, welcoming the PC to their country. After he had made a formal reply thanking them for the welcome he had been given, the PC came straight to the main point of the meeting. News, he said, had come to his ears that a serious complaint had been levelled against one of the young chiefs and he was there in person to deal with it.

Chief Nsamba was requested to stand up, on his own, isolated from his supporters and where all could see his embarrassment. There were no formal charges, but the offended chief who felt that he had been insulted when Nsamba paraded his banner through his territory gave a detailed description of what had occurred. The three other Unga chiefs were then invited to comment and they were uniformly critical. Finally, the PC rose to his feet and began a scathing criticism of Nsamba, 'This young man ... scarcely left his mother's breast' and much more in the same vein that would be well understood by the crowd. Finally, he turned to the other chiefs and demanded, 'And what will the Bwana Governor say? What will happen next time the Bwana Governor comes here? And how are you going to explain to him why one of your young men has been behaving in this disgraceful fashion?' And with these words he swept out of the meeting followed by myself and the other DCs present, together with our various retinues of messengers and interpreters. I was most impressed by the way he handled the matter — I had been taught nothing like this in my various training courses.

Nsamba wound up being suspended for a month. Out of context this may not sound very significant but to a chief it was a dreadful humiliation. Maybe the loss of his powers and emoluments for a month was no big deal, but the fact that all the members of his tribe knew, made it a disaster in terms of prestige.

Shortly after my return from the *ndaba*, the Secretary for Native Affairs (SNA), accompanied needless to say by the PC, came to Luwingu where he wanted to see the swamps. We were most anxious to make a good impression because the SNA was a very important person. I had no doubts that he would be entirely satisfied with what he saw of Bangweulu and during his contacts with the villagers, however, it was equally desirable that he should be entertained in a manner that he would recall at a later date. This part of the proceedings could safely be deputed to Frances and she decided that it would be a good idea to have a lunch party where he would have the opportunity to meet some of the local notables.

The guest invitations had been sent out and all of the preparations were completed, but something was lacking. There was a dearth of fresh flowers at that season with which to decorate the table. Naturally this simply served as a challenge to Frances and one that was easily overcome by going out and gathering an armful of greenery. The lunch was a great success and we were mentally congratulating ourselves on the way it had gone when Father Etienne, my Bemba teacher, leaned forward and, after thanking Frances for an excellent repast, remarked on what an original idea it was to decorate the table with fronds of cannabis. Fortunately, the SNA was as much of a botanical ignoramus as we were.

It was a particularly successful tour for the SNA and he was able to take a look at the new channel. On one occasion we came across a group of women basket fishing. This was done with a wicker basket of much the same shape as the regular baskets but much bigger, being about seven feet long. It took two women to manipulate a single basket but it only took a small group with their baskets to close off completely a channel 30 feet wide. These fish baskets are known as *ubwamba*, which is the vernacular name for naked or nakedness. Consequently, when the secretary asked them to show him *ubwamba* and how they did it, there was general hilarity and I did not have to over strain my recently acquired pass in higher Bemba to explain the joke to him.

My rapid translation clearly impressed him. He complimented me on having passed my examination in advanced Bemba and then went on to encourage me to take the law exams too, as soon as they could conveniently be arranged. I duly put in for the exams and from then on paid strict attention to office hours and reserved time for study until the worst was over, which was a cause for considerable relief.

\* \* \*

Later that year I received instructions to extend the cut from Nsalushi Island as far as Matongo Island and I was able to put into practice my observations and the practical experience gained on the first occasion. This work took me away from Luwingu for the best part of five weeks, so it was a great relief when Frances and our two daughters got an invitation to go and stay with friends at Fort Rosebery during my absence.

Our medical problems did not go away when we were reunited. Frances had been suffering for some time with a grumbling appendix and it had been decided that the next time we had local leave she would have it attended to. We planned to spend the leave with old friends of ours, the Naylors who were both in the NR Department of Health and whom we had not seen for some time. Fortunately, Kasama had quite a good air service to Ndola that was of great value. Frances was duly admitted to the Roan Antelope Mine Hospital and was operated on by Charles Fisher. The Fisher family had, in the past, provided several famous medical missionaries whose exploits have been celebrated in two books — *Ndotulu* and *Nswana*. The operation itself was complicated by Frances being four months' pregnant at the time, but everything passed off successfully.

Our third daughter, Cynthia, was born in Kitwe hospital later that May. The family was able to stay with the DC Kitwe, Tony Heath, while awaiting the event. I had previously worked with him when he was DC Fort Rosebery and Frances and our daughters were able to stay with him. The problem of looking after our enlarged family was solved for the time being when the Ndola convent school accepted Vivian as a primary boarder. Much to our surprise, the nuns also agreed to oblige us by taking care of Lydia for a short while, even although she was under two. Sadly, Cynthia was not to be with us for very long as she succumbed to gastroenteritis at five months.

\* \* \*

I had by now been stationed in Luwingu for well over two years and should by rights have been transferred to another district; however, a gubernatorial visit was looming. Normally, when the governor HE Sir Gilbert Rennie came visiting it was with a considerable retinue, including his staff and, needless to say, the PC. Very often an *ndaba* would be held to present the chiefs to the Queen's official representative. On this occasion, however, it was decided to dispense with it since an *ndaba* had been held for the

Chief Nsamba affair the previous year. There would just be a simple inspection of the district; at least that is what I had supposed would be the case, but I had failed to take account of Sir Gilbert's interest in roads.

In Luwingu, the *boma* offices, the courthouse and houses occupied by the white residents were located on an escarpment that overlooked the township and messengers' lines and was connected to them by a steep road. As we were walking down this road as part of the inspection, Sir Gilbert drew me aside and whispered confidentially, 'You know Greenall, I am rather concerned that you will have serious trouble with this road during the rains — you can see that there is no drainage worth talking about and the surface will get seriously eroded. If you would allow me to make a suggestion,' which was to the effect that I should have constructed a series of low bumps as he termed them every 20 or 30 yards, which would not only slow the traffic but also provide a means of channeling off surface water.

Needless to say, I reacted predictably and promised that it would be attended to at once, all the time wondering how he could bother himself with such a small detail to which I would have expected the road *capitao* or district messengers to attend. On reflection, however, I realized that he was right and there was no reason just because one was important (as I believed myself to be) not to make sure that all jobs got done properly. I was far from being the only DC to feel suitably chastened by being on the receiving end of some whispered advice.

When the governor was expected, endless pains were taken to find out his likes and dislikes, which could usually be ascertained from his private secretary. By convention, the resident DC and his family made their house available for the duration of the visit and moved into the guesthouse. The governor also expected, as of right, to sit at the head of the table at meal times.

This normally did not lead to any problems as everyone considered it his rightful place. At least that was the case until he went to visit Fort Rosebery where Macrae was the DC. Surprisingly, since he was a very experienced officer, he decided that he would avoid yielding the honour. As the story went, he said to himself, 'Nobody else is going to sit at the head of my table. I will have a round table made.'

Accordingly, Macrae got the *boma* carpenter to make him a splendid table out of *mulombwa* or Rhodesian rosewood, which was easy to work with and took a magnificent polish.

Once the visit to Luwingu had come to an end and everyone had made their farewells, HE and his party duly set off for Fort Rosebery, a distance of about 100 miles. They arrived at about midday and when the houseboy announced lunch the governor took Mrs Macrae by the arm and went in to the dining room. Taking in the situation at a glance he reacted remarkably quickly and said, 'No formality, just sit in your usual places.' It was, however, not quite the same that night at dinner as HE had noted where Macrae sat and proceeded carefully to take that place.

A few months before I was due to leave Luwingu, staff at the *boma* rose to an all-time high. Denis Frost and his wife came to commence the takeover and at the same time a cadet, John Waddington, came to assist with sorting out a problem of demarcation with Mpika district. John was of great assistance as a draughtsman in the preparation of the revised map and his splendid humorous sketches greatly enlivened the proceedings, which lasted for about five weeks. Unfortunately, he appeared to be particularly prone to malaria and had to leave us for treatment in Kasama hospital.

The demarcation sounds simple, for it followed the centre of the Chambeshi River leaving Mpika to the west and the Bangweulu swamp in Luwingu to the east. When, however, one took into account that this was in the flood plain, which contained no trees or rocks or solid ground to use as reference points, it was not quite that straightforward.

This was almost my last tour in Luwingu, and a very pleasant one as Gordon Tredwell (DC Mpika) and I paddled slowly down the river observing all manner of game and birds. This seemingly pointless exercise also led to the totally unexpected discovery of a village where almost every woman was dressed in the skin of a black lechwe, a species of large antelope that existed solely in the Bangweulu swamp. Many years before, huge herds had been so plentiful that they were regarded as a prime source of meat for the growing number of native workers in the Copper Belt. They were snared or else trapped by driving whole herds of them into nets. The meat was then taken by canoe to Kapalala and then on to

Ndola. Such wholesale slaughter clearly could not be supported and within a few years the lechwe were reduced to a few herds and an attempt was made to protect the survivors. When he left, Gordon took with him the entire village to stand trial in the Mpika *boma*; but for his perseverance it is quite possible that there would not be a single black lechwe left in the swamps today. Not too long afterwards the black lechwe was declared a protected species.

# 10
## Broken Hill (1952–55)

My sojourn in Luwingu had lasted for three years so we were entitled to substantial home leave. This provided a very welcome break and family reunion. It was August 1952 when we arrived back in NR where I was due to take up an entirely different type of posting at Broken Hill urban district.

Although it was a matter of regret no longer being in the bush and being confined to an office, there was a great compensation in the new job as we were for practical purposes next door to the Dominican school where the children could now attend on a daily basis.

Our neighbour on the other side was a former engine driver, the charismatic Mr Roy Welensky. Originally from Southern Rhodesia he had originally been christened Raphael but had changed his name. He was a man who always seemed larger than life; a trade union leader for the railway men, he had formerly been the heavyweight boxing champion of Northern and Southern Rhodesia and was a member of LegCo. He had been elected to that body as an 'unofficial member' in 1938 following the resignation of Sir Stewart Gore-Browne.

Welensky's organizing ability and capacity for hard work had quickly been recognized and he was made director of Manpower during the war, a post he retained until 1948. I was also aware that he had founded the NR Labour Party in 1941. For some years he had also been on the Executive Council, but from the remoteness of an outstation posting like Luwingu, one had no idea how deeply involved he was in the local political scene. He was to figure very largely in the future development of the federation.

The transition itself to urban surroundings was quite considerable after the quietness and semi-tropical location of Luwingu. Broken Hill in itself was a pleasant town with many shady tree-

## Kaunda's Gaoler

lined streets. The local soil was quite fertile and it had become the centre of an extensive farming area, devoted mainly to maize and cattle. Because of this, much of the scrub had been cleared and the town was surrounded by relatively open countryside. Apart from a passing resemblance to the Secretariat in Lusaka, the whole setup of Broken Hill was different from anything I had experienced before. There were two administrative areas, each with its own *boma*. The urban district comprised all the townships together with the crown lands surrounding them, which were entirely farms. The native reserves and trust lands were the responsibility of Broken Hill rural district.

Being much more populous than most other areas, Broken Hill had its own urban native court that was supervised by the native courts adviser. This was a senior post and filled by a qualified barrister or magistrate who was well acquainted with the native laws and customs. He was responsible not only for Broken Hill but also for the native courts located at other urban centres in the territory. In consultation with the paramount or senior chiefs, he undertook the appointment of assessors and ensured that there was a proper tribal mix.

All cases were reviewed by a DC or DO in the presence of the court clerk or assessor. It was policy not to interfere. Very rarely, if it were felt that there had been a miscarriage of justice, they had the power to revise the sentence or even to order a retrial. There was no other recourse or appeal, for it was not provided for by native custom. Nevertheless, it seemed a considerable improvement when compared with the system of trial by ordeal previously practised by the Africans.

The black population sought justice from the local native court. On one occasion I had to review a case in which there had been a complaint from a maidservant — the houseboy had stolen some material from her. The piece of fabric in question was of great importance as she kept it especially for her own personal use each month. The houseboy belatedly admitted that it was in his possession but said that he could not have stolen it for he had not taken it out of the house but used it for drying the washing up.

The European population also got involved in minor litigation, but usually their problems had to be addressed to the police. Many of these complaints were of the 'master and servant' variety. Some

## Broken Hill (1952–55)

of them were outlandish in the extreme, such as the occasion when Mrs Welensky filed a formal complaint with the police that one of her 'houseboys' had stolen a slice of Christmas cake.

The rural district *boma* had a particularly interesting dining room that was used for formal entertaining. It had previously been the old courtroom and when I had the opportunity to dine there I always delighted in telling the guests that in the 1920s it had been the site of a famous trial. A notorious witch doctor who had been responsible for more than 120 deaths was tried there and subsequently sentenced to death. Native justice at the time relied heavily on trial by ordeal, the general principle being that if someone survived then they could not be guilty. This witch doctor's particular speciality was holding suspects under water, almost invariably with fatal consequences. Possibly it was not really a suitable topic for polite dinner-table conversation, but I found that it always seemed to go down well with a coffee and glass of brandy after the meal.

One significant benefit of the concentration of population at Broken Hill was the simplification of tax gathering. It was a comparatively simple matter to go along to the mines or the railway depot on paydays accompanied by a few messengers to collect it.

While these mundane matters took up much of the working day, the great question that was on everybody's mind was the potential outcome of the consultations that were leading to the creation of the Central African Federation from Southern and Northern Rhodesia and Nyasaland. It was discussed in the bush districts where we had previously been stationed, of course, but very much within the family. It had seemed quite remote, not something with which one had any personal involvement and, of course, I had been on leave during a major part of the debate. It was very different when we arrived in Broken Hill with its comparatively large population of white settlers and was a subject of many heated debates.

Amalgamation with Southern Rhodesia, a pet project of Prime Minister Sir Godfrey Huggins (later Viscount Malvern), had been brewing for a while. The problem was tied up with the future of Southern Rhodesia, which some people considered to be economically vulnerable and where there was also a small but vocal minority that wanted to become part of South Africa. There had indeed been a referendum on that subject long before in 1922. The possibility of union with NR first arose seriously in the 1930s when Huggins was already prime minister of Southern Rhodesia and it had been discussed at a conference at the Victoria Falls in the mid-1930s. A resolution calling for amalgamation had been passed along with a call for complete self-government as the basis of a new constitution. At that time the matter was simply brushed aside by the then governor. By the late 1940s the settlers of Northern Rhodesia led by Roy Welensky were becoming increasingly strident in their demands and actually threatened to bring the protectorate to a standstill if there were no progress in meeting their requests. The so-called first Victoria Falls Conference had taken place in 1949 without the presence of representatives from London or of the NR government, both of which declined to attend. Not surprisingly, everybody had his or her own agenda to follow. The local white politicians of NR perceived that they would achieve real decision-making powers and a wider sphere of influence. The white settlers of Southern Rhodesia, on the other hand, perceived union and self-government as a means of permanently preserving their status, although they did not say so as succinctly. They also took an approving look at what appeared to be a particularly docile (for want of a better word) native population in Northern Rhodesia. Even more importantly, Southern Rhodesia was also extremely short of money, presumably because a great deal had been spent on the infrastructure over the years. Its politicians perceived the cash flow from the copper mines in the northern territories as a solution to the shortage. Further, being easily the most populous region, they realized that they would have the controlling number of votes. This would be important when deciding policies. In the end, and with the knowledge that the British government opposed direct union of the two Rhodesias, a motion was put forward urging the creation of a federation.

That same year in London the then colonial secretary, Mr A. Creech Jones, made it clear that British policy was committed to the development of the local population to the point where it could govern itself. He also stated that union would merely serve to entrench white supremacy without any obvious benefit to the natives and was therefore unacceptable. Despite these words he was very conscious of the problems that the whites could create and worried about what the Colonial Office regarded as the baleful influence of South Africa. Creech Jones pointed to the

## Broken Hill (1952-55)

existence of the Central African Council that had been set up some time before, though it had not been a great success. Despite his reasoned objections, he agreed to examine the possibility of federation provided that Nyasaland was also included to reduce the overall influence of Southern Rhodesia.

Sir Godfrey and Welensky could recognize a white flag when they saw one, no matter how small, and the latter submitted a resolution to the NR Legislative Council (LegCo), requesting federation. Naturally, the African members voted against it but the official members who could have voted it down abstained by leaving the chamber, saying that the time was not right. Matters came to a head at the Close Association Conference at Victoria Falls in 1951 when all the governments concerned participated.

Although the British government was emphatically not in favour of direct union, it perceived the background reasons for what they were. It was also concerned at the upsurge of rampant white nationalism in South Africa and noted that many South Africans were being attracted to Rhodesia because of opportunities in the mining industry The Colonial Office was anxious that apartheid and its more pernicious manifestations should not penetrate the colonies to the north along with the immigrants. London was also well aware of the local nationalist movements, such as the African National Congress, and wanted to adopt policies that would ensure that matters should not get out of hand. Unfortunately, it believed that the African nationalist politicians were only concerned with their own personal interests and that they lacked grass roots support among the mass of the population. This tragic misconception was to persist for a long time, presumably because most of the advice reaching London was based on the reliance placed on local chiefs as sources of information. In Kaunda's own words: 'The Colonial Office's perpetual reliance upon information from the traditional rulers ... led to the British government being hopelessly ill-informed.'

The conference also came up with the expression 'partnership' and the settlers suggested that a union was the way to address the problem of ensuring that development was for the benefit of the African population. In short, over a period of time, partnership would pave the way to a multicultural society. The white settlers' real views were better summed up in an off-the-cuff remark by Sir

Godfrey Huggins when he said, 'Yes, it will be a partnership — such as exists between a horse and its rider'.

Thoughts of 'partnership' and a 'multicultural society', however, sounded attractive, especially to the Labour Party politicians in London and the terms were much bandied around in Parliament. To the majority of people in NR and London the question of when a multicultural nation would develop was too remote to be seriously discussed. No one was willing to speculate on what precisely was meant by 'a period of time'. Off-the-cuff estimates varied from 50 years to the length of one's career. If the question of what was needed to move positively in this direction had been asked, the answer would invariably have been that it was necessary to raise the standard of native education as fast as possible. This idea had indeed been clearly enunciated as policy over the years in a number of Colonial Office statements, although lack of funds was cited as the reason why it had not been implemented.

British participation in the Close Association Conference was abruptly abandoned when the UK politicians dashed for home following Mr Attlee's call for a general election. The Conservatives were returned to power and Oliver Lyttelton, the new colonial secretary, clearly came to the conclusion that the problem needed to be resolved and decided that some sort of federation would have to take place. In the spring of 1952 he called a further conference in London at Lancaster House, which he chaired jointly with Lord Salisbury. The purpose of the conference was to investigate and prepare recommendations for the implementation of federation. Agreement on a constitution was finally reached, though not without a great deal of argument. For practical purposes the local population was totally excluded from the debate because the black politicians boycotted most of the meetings as a protest against any consideration of federation.

The British government did, however, insist on a trial period in which to see how the federation developed, with provision for constitutional reviews after seven and ten years. At the last moment, in early 1953, it also insisted on adding a section that mandated the creation of an African Affairs Board, intended to ensure that any legislation the proposed federal government passed was equitable and not discriminatory. This almost proved to be a breaking point, for the federalists were adamantly against it and in

## Broken Hill (1952–55)

the end its powers were significantly watered down. A referendum on federation was undertaken in April and somewhat more than 60 per cent of those voting came out in favour of federation, which was a smaller majority than one might have expected considering that virtually all the electors were white settlers.

We were told to advise the chiefs of developments. Towards the end of my stay in Luwingu, I attended a DCs' conference in Kasama. When the subject of federation came up, the PC told us that 'we might as well do what the government asks and throw our weight behind it. It won't make the slightest difference to the African view, which is immovable.' Politically aware natives of course realized they were being left out. The chiefs were all opposed but in a muted fashion, apart from one paramount chief. The exception, King Lewanika, agreed to vote in favour, having been told that it was what HM the Queen would like him to do.

The Northern Rhodesia African Congress (NRAC), which had been formed four or five years previously by uniting the various native welfare societies, provided the most vocal opposition, perceiving that its goals of 'one man one vote' and independence would recede. Lack of organization and experience, however, meant that its campaign was not particularly effective even though almost to a man the native population was opposed to the proposed new constitution. Shortly before federation took place the NRAC appeared to have accepted defeat and called a meeting at which Harry Nkumbula became its president (replacing Mr Mbikusita who subsequently joined the Federal Party) and Kenneth Kaunda was elected to the post of secretary general. The new president's first action was to rename the group the African National Congress (ANC). However, the meeting's primary purpose was to try to determine future policy after federation. As a result, over the years that immediately followed federation, the ANC* pursued a course that concentrated on

---

* Nationalist bodies throughout Africa used the name African National Congress. No doubt there was contact between them, but the organizations in different countries were all distinct. The name African National Congress of Northern Rhodesia was probably its official title. In *Zambia Shall be Free*, Kenneth Kaunda uses all the names. For simplicity ANC has been used throughout this book.

recruitment and political education throughout the rural communities.

Explaining the change to a federation to the natives was a hopeless task. They believed that their links were with the Queen through various treaties made many years before. They also believed that these treaties made it the responsibility of the British monarchy to protect them. They could not understand the purpose of the new constitution since it appeared that the link to the crown was to be abandoned and they were to be left to the tender mercies of the settlers who were usually the source of precisely the type of abuse from which they needed protection. They did not expect the settlers to change their ways unless forced to. It was reported, possibly apocryphally, that when Mr Bush, the caring secretary for Native Affairs, went to visit some native authorities and was asked 'Why?' he replied 'Because if it doesn't happen, Southern Rhodesia will go bankrupt, which might make it vulnerable to a South African takeover.'

The colonial officers were told in no uncertain terms that we were to go about our business as if nothing were happening and under no circumstances were we to discuss our own views. I do not think that those persons in London who subsequently set out to revile us for our attitude were aware of this ban. It was a fact that in private discussions most of us believed that the constitution was unsatisfactory because it was so manifestly unfair.

About this time I had a conversation with a DC who was strongly in favour of federation and heard that some of them had been told privately that they would be well looked after when it came about. This came as a rather rude shock as my views were not kept particularly secret and it appeared obvious that I was not one of the potentially favoured few. I was sufficiently concerned to consider resignation seriously and to embark on a new career by joining a cousin in Canada. In the event I decided to do nothing at the time but discuss it the next time I was on leave.

The royal assent to federation was signed in July. The timing was rather unfortunate coming, as it did, so close to the date of the coronation and it came as no particular surprise to us when the ANC called for a boycott of the local celebrations. The ANC was very influential among the workforce in Broken Hill and the boycott was almost completely successful, casting a baleful shadow

1. RIGHT. Wartime wedding, 1943

2. BELOW. The District Commissioner's house, Luwingu

3. Fisherman, Mpulungu, Lake Tanganyika

4. The family, Kabompo

5. ABOVE. *Boma* staff, Kabompo

6. BELOW. The bluff, overlooking the Kabompo river

7. ABOVE. The Kabompo river in flood

8. BELOW. Some of Mwata Yamvwa's entourage outside Kabompo courthouse

9. RIGHT. Mwata Yamvwa

10. BELOW. Lunda gathering to welcome Mwata Yamvwa at Kabompo

11. Members of the Lunda royal family

12. ABOVE. Kabompo football team

13. BELOW. Local Lunda craftwork

14. LEFT. Carved guardian spirit by DC's office

15. BELOW. Installation of the *ngambela* at Manyinga

## Broken Hill (1952–55)

over what should have been a happy occasion. The local ceremonies involved the PC in full regalia presiding over a parade with the local police and army units; a visitor who had been in India during the run-up to indepedence there remarked that these were exactly the same methods that had been used by the Congress in India. Later, of course Kaunda was to confirm that the ANC had copied them.

The Central African Federation officially came into existence on 23 October 1953 with Sir Godfrey Huggins as its first prime minister. He had been prime minister of Southern Rhodesia ever since 1933 and before that had enjoyed a career as a well thought of surgeon. Roy Welensky became Minister of Transport and was to retain that portfolio until he became prime minister in 1956.

At the time of the elections to the new federal assembly, I was a returning officer and noted that the number of persons voting was less than 1000, which was about a 65 per cent turnout. The elections passed off as peacefully as could be hoped. The requirements for being on the electoral register were so tight that few natives were actually able to cast votes. The qualifying requirements included owning a property worth a certain minimum amount, an ability to read and write English, or an account of the order of £250 in the bank. Naturally, this embraced most people of European origin, both settlers and expatriates, so they were eligible to vote. The discrimination between the two classes is of some importance as there were very few true settlers in NR. There were, however, quite a number of expatriate workers associated with the mines and railways, for example, and they would probably have been happy to become true settlers if the conditions had been right and they had felt sure of continuing white domination.

The new constitution resulted in some changes to the administration of NR with the creation of a new federal parliament. Until then there were two responsible bodies in existence. One, the African Representative Council, represented native opinion and consisted mainly of African chiefs or their representatives. These in turn had been selected by the African provincial councils, which were chaired by the PCs.

The second was the Legislative Council, usually referred to as LegCo, a far more significant body. Subsequent to federation this was made up of several groups of people. There were the eight colonial civil servants the governor nominated and who, because of their official status, were known as the 'official representatives'. The second group comprised four African members nominated by the African Representative Council, together with two additional white members nominated by the governor — people like Sir Stewart Gore-Browne, who were responsible for looking after native interests. The third grouping consisted of elected white members such as Mr Welensky. In a peculiar misuse of the English language these were always referred to locally as the 'unofficial representatives'.

Roy Welensky, who had founded the NR Labour Party some years before, was already the leader of the white settlers. He was outspoken and charismatic, a natural leader. Later he was knighted and, as leader of the Federal Party, became prime minister. Amazingly, he and Gore-Browne were great friends in private even though their political views on the future of Northern Rhodesia were diametrically opposed.

With the arrival of federation came an increase in interracial tension and crime. For some of it the cause was easy to find. The prospect of relatively good pay brought in large numbers of Africans from all over the country, but many of them could not find work. As a result they tended to hang around in the streets and were ready for any sort of trouble. They were colloquially known as 'loafers'. Periodically, a 'loafer drive' would be organized with a view to rounding up some of them for return to their tribal territories. These sweeps were invariably intensified after any form of violence.

In August 1954 there were a number of cases of assault on white women on their own at home in Broken Hill, which was often the case with railway men's families. Not surprisingly, the husbands were incensed and hellbent on some form of retribution. Fortunately, Superintendent Coton of the local police was able to defuse the situation, pointing out that any escalation was likely to put all local people in jeopardy. Mr Coton remarked that violence did not achieve anything useful and he had seen enough of it to last anyone a lifetime in the 11 years he had spent in the Palestine police.

The immediate outcome was that the police and I, as the senior administrative officer on the spot, organized another roundup of

## Broken Hill (1952–55)

loafers and circulated a recommendation to residents to fit burglar bars to their downstairs windows.

The white residents did not behave a great deal better, the majority adopting an arrogant and bullying attitude towards natives who worked for them. Officially discrimination and segregation did not exist, but in practice it did. It was especially noticeable in shops where one door for whites and another for coloureds was fairly common.

Quite apart from racial problems, Broken Hill seemed to be an unhealthy place in which to be living because of the dust produced from the mining operations. It was very unusual to have every member of the family fit all at the same time.

Sometimes one wondered who was responsible for appointing some of the people who received jobs following the elections. The new NR government decided that it needed a member with a portfolio to represent Native interests and appointed Harry Franklin, the former director of the Department of Information, Frances's former boss in fact. Harry had something of a reputation as a man who enjoyed a drink with the best of them, coupled with a roving eye.

\* \* \*

At first life in Broken Hill was not particularly easy; out in the bush stations it had always seemed to be very convenient to order goods on account and we were rather horrified to discover that we were considerably overdrawn. The conclusion that we reluctantly came to was that Frances should seek some employment, which of necessity had to be with the federal government. They were very helpful and decided there was a need for immigration officers and promptly elevated her to that status. The first task that fell to her and another lady appointed at the same time was to create for themselves a suitable uniform.

With Frances working things became considerably easier and by the time my tour of Broken Hill was complete in 1954, the debts we had previously accumulated had all been repaid, which was a great relief.

In 1955, the prime minister became the first Viscount Malvern. Sir Godfrey's ennoblement created quite a stir. The story that did the rounds at the time was that when the Queen Mother had arrived shortly before, the plane she had flown in was the brand new Vickers Viscount. Shortly after being introduced to the prime minister, she is supposed to have said to him, 'And how do you like the new Viscount?' to which he allegedly replied 'Ma'am it is such a signal honour that I am quite overwhelmed.'

# 11
## Ndola and Kitwe (1956–58)

When we returned from a spell of leave it was to find that I had been appointed to the Department of Labour in Ndola, which, despite some initial reservations, turned out to be quite interesting because of the extensive unrest caused by the political upheavals of the time.

With a population at that time of around 70,000, Ndola was one of the largest towns in NR. The huge spreading 'Slave Tree' near its centre had traditionally marked the site of an Arab slave market in the nineteenth century. Like Broken Hill, Ndola was mainly surrounded by farmland, but one did not have to go far to find scrubby forest and relatively uninhabited country, which could have its own unexpected consequences.

One of the amenities the British settlers had brought to Ndola was a golf club. The course was considered to be one of the best in NR, so good in fact that some of its annual tournaments (such as the Cock of the North competition) drew competitors from other parts of the world. During one particular mixed doubles tournament, a lion wandering onto the course rudely interrupted proceedings. Needless to say, the participants hastily decamped to the clubhouse — that is all but one game that had only two holes left to play and, more importantly, both pairs fancied their chances of winning. They went ahead and finished the round and turned their cards in only to be told that the match had been cancelled because the lion had interrupted play. 'But', said the one with lowest score, 'we finished the round and if a round has been started you must finish; the other players all withdrew.' The putative winner was so upset at the cancellation that she insisted that the matter be referred to the Royal and Ancient for a ruling. In due course, this was received and stated that there was no precedent regarding the presence of lions on the course to help

## Kaunda's Gaoler

guide them and therefore the matter had been considered by the committee, which had voted that, under circumstances such as these, the tournament should be rescheduled. Ultimately, justice was seen to be done when the first-time winners proceeded to win the rematch.

I had barely been a month in Ndola and had spent the time getting to know various personnel officers and employers when the ANC organized a boycott of European and Asian shops, especially those that practised any form of segregation of their customers. The troubles began initially in Livingstone, Lusaka and Broken Hill, while Ndola and the Copper Belt were not affected, though this did not last long.

Although there was no official discrimination in NR as it was practised in South Africa, its existence was nevertheless pretty widespread and the Africans had plenty to complain about. Sometimes they were not allowed into shops and were served through a hatch and where they were admitted European customers received preferential treatment. According to Kaunda's book, the boycott was also organized as a device to try to boost sales at African-owned shops, many of which operated on a knife-edge.

The boycott caused a certain amount of trouble and at least one of its leaders was imprisoned as a result. Nkumbula and Kaunda also found themselves on the wrong side of bars for a couple of months for 'possessing seditious literature'. I was not involved in the proceedings in any way but the magazine in question, which was a 'prohibited publication', was called *Africa and the Colonial World* and had been published in the UK.

The government took a very negative view of the ANC and, rightly or wrongly, considered that the African advisory councils (an outgrowth of the native authority) should be the representatives of native opinion. On the one hand they would not accept that the ANC was a 'representative body of educated native opinion', but then proceeded to set that view on its head by suggesting that educated natives were not representative of the masses.

The practical means that were taken to counter the ANC sometimes verged on the ludicrous. On one occasion the secretary for Native Affairs met with the chiefs to urge them not to subscribe money to the ANC because the money would be used to buy

## Ndola and Kitwe (1956–58)

motorcars. The chiefs' reply was that the money they paid in taxes was used by the government to buy cars and they could not see the difference. Later the government put it to the chiefs that anyone seeking to address a meeting should first have to get permission from the chief. In a surprising display of independence, the chiefs refused, pointing out that white people did not have to get permission from anybody.

At the time, a strike at McAlpines, a major local building contractor, complicated matters. I became secretary to the conciliation proceedings and met with some of the strikers. Shortly afterwards, the strikers went back to work quite amiably. I received brief notoriety when the *Northern News* gave me a line saying, 'The Labour Officer spoke to the strikers and they went back to work.'

It was too much to hope that the boycott of white-owned shops would not spread and it duly reached Ndola and the Copper Belt where it was very successful. To compound the problem, the African Mineworkers' Union decided to support the boycott by intermittent striking. To appreciate the chaos that this caused it is necessary to appreciate the sequence of copper production.

The vast smelters that were used to produce the metal from the ore take three days to heat up to the right temperature for smelting before production can be commenced. These three days are totally unproductive and if for any reason production has to be stopped, the process also takes three days to shut down.

It follows that even a very brief strike must result in prolonged shutdown and a lot of lost production. With the African workers employed on a daily basis, a three-day strike only lost them three days' pay but the value of the lost production was huge. With eight or nine mines in the area, the union simply rotated the strikes so that as fast as one mine started up again, another one would be shut down. It was a while before the government realized that they had a full-blown economic crisis on their hands and were forced to invoke emergency legislation that had recently been passed. The trade union leaders were arrested and sent off to rural areas until the troubles subsided. I was obliged to accompany one of the groups of police, for it was essential for a magistrate to be present; fortunately the arrests went off without any serious trouble. I recall that one of the minor officials of the union made a big issue of the matter because he was not on the 'list'; he was most upset and demanded to be arrested, for without it he felt that he would lose a lot of face — needless to say his protests were ignored.

Frances was convinced of the benefits of federation and was exasperated at what she perceived as the shilly-shallying going on in London. In one letter home she remarked that it did not appear as if the UK had 'enough money to maintain an empire as well as a welfare state'.

Reaching an agreement with the African Mineworkers' Union was every bit as difficult as settling with the more militant British trade unions of the time and it was not long before they found something else to complain about. The Chamber of Mines was anxious to be seen to be promoting the wellbeing of the Africans and consequently proposed to move a number of them into staff supervisory posts, which meant that they would go onto a monthly salary instead of daily shift work. While this sounded all very well it also meant that they would have to resign from the union and become members of the African Staff Association. The mining companies said that they could not possibly have a situation in which the same body was representing both supervisors and the supervised. The African Mineworkers' Union, however, saw the move as an attempt to weaken its position by deliberately promoting some of its most influential members — a view that was also heard in the UK some years ago.

Further strikes took place in mid-September and a state of emergency was again proclaimed as a result. Troops were brought in to control the situation. An operations room manned by members of the police and military together with myself was set up — all of us were there before dawn waiting for something to happen. It never did and the following morning the workers on the morning shift all turned up for work. Riots in Southern Rhodesia quickly supplanted non-existent strikes in the newspaper headlines. The governor, Sir Arthur Benson, initiated an ingenious scheme to bring outside influence to bear on the strikers. This was to be achieved by bringing the chiefs together with their DCs to visit the troubled areas. It was quite effective but it was also expensive from the government's point of view because the visits became very popular with the chiefs.

\* \* \*

## Ndola and Kitwe (1956–58)

Shortly after becoming labour officer I was offered a transfer to Mongu, the notoriously unhealthy provincial capital of Barotseland. I was to go initially as a DO but with the prospect of taking over there as DC when the then incumbent went on leave. This should have been considered a plum posting, for it was generally supposed that the DC of a provincial capital was the presumptive PC. In my eyes, however, it was fatally flawed and a poisoned chalice. The reason behind the proposed transfer was that the present DO had to be moved away as his wife was showing signs of excessive stress. Thus, the proposal that we, who had just lost one child to a tropical disease, should move to one of the least healthy posts in the protectorate showed a breathtaking degree of insensitivity on the part of the administration.

The only possible justification that existed was that the colonial service worked very closely on the basis of 'Buggins's turn', whereby the person with the most seniority was automatically nominated; of course, they also had on their side the principle that one accepted at the time of joining that one would automatically accept where one was sent.

It was an awkward moment from my point of view. Outright refusal was out of the question, so I set out in the best of bureaucratic tradition to sabotage it by seeking the advice of the Department of Health, which not surprisingly intervened on the grounds that medically it was an unsuitable posting for the Greenalls.

So the moment passed and the post was subsequently offered to a colleague in the Department of Labour who had a grown-up family. He took it up, while I remained an interested spectator, for by watching someone else's career one sometimes obtains a fairly accurate idea of what might have happened to oneself.

Some years subsequently, he was moved to Kasama (where my career had started) as DC, just before the Northern Province erupted like a bush fire. In response to the troubles, a district commissioners' meeting was held at which the options of a softly-softly or hard-line approach were discussed. The group decided to take a hard line and this was subsequently acted upon until word came from Lusaka that this was contrary to policy and that the officers were at fault. The PC promptly notified the various DCs, but at the same time distanced himself from any criticism by stating that he had taken no part in the decision and personally disagreed with it. This was despite the fact that he had been present at the meeting and offered no word of objection — what it is to know that one can rely on the support of one's superior! My erstwhile colleague ultimately returned to the Department of Labour and when we met in Ndola many years later his opening words were, 'The wheel has gone full circle.'

\* \* \*

As a result of the state of emergency, my tour of Ndola was cut very short. I returned to the administration and was posted to Kitwe, where my tour continued uneventfully.

It was about that time or shortly afterwards that Lennox-Boyd, the then colonial secretary, arrived on a visit. We met at a social gathering where I think that he must have taken me for someone on the staff of one of the mines as he told me a totally unrepeatable story about a conversation he supposedly had with the Archbishop of Canterbury.

# 12
# Kabompo:
# The Garden of Eden

We were happily enjoying my leave in a cottage in Suffolk on the banks of the Orwell when I received a letter advising me that I could expect to be posted to Kabompo on my return. The letter went on to suggest that I would find it a most interesting posting and that, although there was no obvious overt political activity in the area, there were, however, one or two potentially tricky tribal matters that might be waiting for me.

After two successive tours on the line of rail I was delighted at the prospect of returning to the rural areas and this took a prominent place in my thinking as I prepared to fly back from our leave in the UK. Frances had already left some while before, making a leisurely journey on the Union Castle Line's *Athlone Castle*. She planned to have a short visit with her cousins who farmed in the Paarl wine-growing district near Cape Town before going on to Salisbury to pick up the children from school *en route* to rejoining me back in Ndola.

Amazingly, as it seemed to me at the time, we were all reunited as planned towards the middle of December 1958 and spent a hectic few days arranging transport, picking up stores for our personal use, getting the children first to the clinic and then to a dentist, which all had to be fitted in with some much valued briefing from the DO Balovale who happened to be in Kitwe at the time. It was not the best time of the year to be travelling and I was greatly relieved when the Public Works Department offered me the use of a Land Rover, for without a four-wheel drive vehicle, traversing the route from Solwezi to Kabompo might have been very fraught.

## Kaunda's Gaoler

At last the Greenalls, plus Harvey the cat, set off for Solwezi where we were able to spend a night in the PC's guesthouse. The following day, feeling somewhat refreshed, we began the leg of the journey to Kabompo — bump, bump, bump all the way. Finally, after about 100 miles of this, we arrived at about 6.00 p.m. totally worn out.

The following day, however, the arduous journey suddenly seemed enormously worthwhile. When the sun rose we were able to see the view from the *boma*, which was as usual situated on the high ground. In Kabompo it was sited on a bluff some 170 feet above a bend in the river below; it was truly magnificent and from the DC's house one could see for almost 40 miles. The countryside around was so much more luxuriant than the scrubby brush of the Northern Province and below the bluff the spray from the cascades created the feeling that one was looking into a fountain of diamonds.

Unlike the previous outstations where I had been posted, Kabompo had a moderate resident European population. Their houses all tended to be along the same side of the *boma* where they could share the view. Needless to say, the DC's house occupied the prime position, with the others arranged in some sort of pecking order reflecting their position or seniority.

Roland Hill, the outgoing DC, was there for a while after we arrived. His wife had a remarkable artistic talent and it is her drawings that have been used to illustrate the chapter ends. The two of them were to become lifelong friends.

The undoubted doyen of the establishment was Charlie White – an old-timer. He was an academic and former DC who now undertook various specialized studies in fields in which the government might be interested. At that time he was looking in detail at the subject of native land tenure, but he had previously distinguished himself with the preparation of a number of books such as one on the birds of Northern Rhodesia.

Another of the local residents was Tony Lander, the assistant DC who was my right-hand man for most of my time in Kabompo. Over that period there were also a couple of cadets. The first was named McInnes and I recall him as having a flair for finance and taking a considerable interest in horseracing. He was of enormous assistance to me when Kaunda was with us. The

## Kabompo: The Garden of Eden

other, John Hart, was a self-styled Geordie who was to prove his worth during a nasty moment to be recounted later.

There were several people from other government departments, such as Agriculture, Forestry and Game, and at times a number of community development officers. All in all, we were a very happy little community.

We soon discovered that there was a beautiful spot for picnics by the river during the dry season. The river had fallen to a comparatively low level and the falls were fairly small, but nearby there was a pool of clear shallow water. Even if it was not deep enough for proper swimming it was still perfect for the children. At some time someone had built a low mud wall to separate the pool from the river, so it was quite safe. We were not the only ones to enjoy the pool, as the area above it was crowded with flocks of small brightly coloured birds that filled the air with song.

It was handy when the children were home on holiday from school and we were also able to put it to very good use when my mother came for a visit. Since we always left the spot well before sundown, midges or mosquitoes did not bother us there.

Initially it was necessary for us to stay for a few weeks in the Kabompo rest house, which was rather tedious but it could not be avoided. Being nearly ten years since I had last served on an outstation, it was going to take a little while for me to get my hand in and to assist the takeover. I had arrived five or six weeks before Roland Hill, the incumbent DC, was due to depart on home leave. The overlap also provided me with an opportunity to pick up the rudiments of the Lovale language — higher Bemba cut no ice with the locals at all.

Fortunately, Charlie White was a great expert on the Lovale language and customs and he kindly agreed to give me an hour of his time every day for tuition. Charlie was a character, what these days would be termed a 'one off'; Frances and I were fascinated by his novel approach to learning languages and he gave me a first rate introduction to Lovale, which was quite different from Bemba. He also made available to me as an assistant a *boma* 'super clerk' named James Chinjavata, a very well educated local with whom I tried to speak Lovale most of the time, especially when on tour. It was about this time that I realized that to become proficient one really needed to think in the language. Of course, nowadays, some 40 years later, this is the norm but no one had suggested it to me before. I tried to do this by thinking through all my actions as I got up in the morning: 'It is dawn', 'I am getting up', 'I am washing my face' and so on; I found this somewhat elementary device of considerable assistance.

The weeks of transition before I formally took over from Roland Hill included Christmas and we were able to make the most of it. On Christmas Eve we were invited to a party at Roland's house where the guests included several prominent local Africans. Kabompo, as I was rapidly to discover, was one of the few remaining stations that had not fallen under the influence of the ANC, whose tentacles could always be found following on any attempts to achieve social and welfare advancement for the natives. The following day we attended a service at the *boma*, which was also attended by a multiracial congregation and conducted by a newly ordained African priest.

Later at dinner we were entertained right royally to a typical English Christmas dinner with turkey and all the trimmings, liberally washed down with excellent Portuguese wine obtained from Angola. I say liberally because I see from old correspondence that I was obliged shortly thereafter to order a supply of liver pills from home.

\* \* \*

January and the New Year meant that we had to get Vivian and Lydia to school back in Salisbury where they were enrolled at the Dominican convent. There were regular flights from Balovale to Salisbury, but the former was 100 miles away across territory with which we were unacquainted. Fortunately, Charlie White stepped into the breach and offered to take the children along with Frances to see them off.

This was an unexpected offer because Charlie was a well-known misogynist. He did, however, provide Frances with a delightful trip when she was able to get over the border briefly into Angola. Besides Charlie and Frances, the entourage that set off was a very mixed bag with a pregnant native woman and the black driver who was a wine importer with a goat and a demijohn of his merchandise hidden by his seat. There were also two other native

## Kabompo: The Garden of Eden

male passengers whose function was never clear; the one, with long hair and willowy hips, looked like an African send-up of effeminancy; the other was nondescript. Besides all this and the luggage, there were of course Vivian and Lydia.

A few weeks, or indeed months, at Kabompo were to do nothing to detract from our first delighted impression that we had arrived in an offshoot of the Garden of Eden. In letters home, which were all saved, again and again Frances came back to the loveliness of the surrounding country and the delightful climate:

> I am hoping to get my colour snaps soon so you will see how simply lovely Kabompo is. It is really quite out of this world and makes any other *boma* I've seen look just a dump. We have thick ground mists just now, and the river in the early morning is blanketed in woolly clouds, which we look down on from our windows. It is quite a wonderful sight. It only warms up at midday and then I can take off my cardigan and only wear a short-sleeved dress. The fishing season is almost upon us and there are already a number of fishermen out in canoes at night, with lights hanging from their bows. The fish eagles are busy too; they are beautiful birds standing nearly two and half feet tall and with a beautiful white feathered chest; we are rather frightened for Sheila [our Pekinese] who likes to sit out of doors watching the world go by. Experts say a fish eagle could easily take her as they go off with far heavier fish or small buck. Cyril says that we ought to fasten her lead to an anchor.

And again a few weeks later:

> Although this is our hot season, we are astonished and amazed to find that except at midday when the wind drops, it's lovely and cool here. At night I still have two blankets. This house, right up on the bluff, catches all of the wind and it's rather like being on the deck of a ship. If the year continues as it has been, the climate here is money for jam ... infinitely cooler than Broken Hill or Kitwe at this time of year. This is the most wonderful district for wild flowers,

and the bush at this moment is carpeted in small pink orchids, which smell simply lovely — they almost overdo the scent. Later on, as we noticed when we first got here, there are hundreds of flowering trees, and the woods are filled with small, peach coloured gladioli. We gathered them by the armful when we first got here in December — like bluebells in England. I've never seen such lovely wild flowers in the bush before, something in flower all the year round.

The profusion of flowers that grew around Kabompo also meant that honey was a potentially marketable resource and was sufficiently valuable for some of the more adventurous locals to go in search of the nests of wild bees. Although it was at considerable risk to the collectors, the combs were not too hard to find, for a small bird with a loud chirrup was equally fond of honey and could be relied on to give away the nest's location. The community development officer suggested to the government that it should help promote this trade. One of our friends, a forestry officer named Abe Gow, was assigned to the task and given special responsibility for the 'honey 'industry'. He was at first unwilling to do the job because he was not a trained apiarist, but finally accepted on the understanding that all the operations would be done with locally available utensils that could readily be found in the natives' huts. As a result, a Kabompo honey cooperative was set up, though I believe that it was disbanded subsequent to my departure from the district. Nevertheless, it is a considerable testimony to the product's excellence that many, many years later Kabompo honey is available at some branches of Waitrose stores.

Of course, the exploitation of the honey also meant that there was beeswax available. This was quite a valuable commodity for export, especially when it was of good enough quality for cosmetics. It was unfortunate that attempts to produce superior beeswax were not a success despite Abe demonstrating that it was possible to produce top-quality material with minimal facilities. The crude solid wax originally obtained did not command a good price and had to be sold comparatively cheaply because it was full of dead bees and dirt. To convert this to the more highly valued commodity it was necessary to boil up the crude material. This

## Kabompo: The Garden of Eden

was a process that had to be got just right and cooked 'to a turn', which meant heating for neither too long nor too short a period of time. Unfortunately for the local population, the traders preferred to do the cooking themselves and only wanted to buy the cheap low-quality material. This apparent deprivation of the poor population of a higher price was at first sight deplorable; however, they had brought it upon themselves. The lure of potential wealth overcame any honest scruples that the local Africans might have had, for they found it all too easy to secrete a large stone in the centre of the wax to make it nice and heavy. As a second cooking tended to degrade the wax, leaving it only suitable for polishes, it was not really practical for the traders to melt it down again to determine the true weight.

The Department of Agriculture was also attempting to encourage farmers to cultivate Turkish tobacco locally for sun drying, for the variety had been found to grow well around Kabompo.

\* \* \*

The matters about which I had been forewarned back in England had arisen as a result of the death of Chief Sikufele, the senior chief of the district. In essence, the difficulty was that he had been an Mbunda/Lozi while the majority of his subjects were Luchazi, Chokwe and Lunda. These problems had already impacted badly on one of my predecessors, Robin Short, who in his book *African Sunset* devoted a chapter to the region titled 'Kabompo: The Bad River'. He claims that there was 'a peculiar atmosphere of violence that infected the place, born of all of the hatreds around it', and devotes part of his chapter to suicides and murder. It is probably fortunate that I was ignorant of his prejudices at the time, as they would undoubtedly have influenced me. As it was, my impressions were totally the reverse of those he described. He even complained about the river with 'the dull ceaseless boom of the water over the rapids'. The only explanation that I can offer is that some of the DCs preceding me had diametrically different views about the desirability of trees. One had refused to cut down any, which had undoubtedly given rise to a very gloomy atmosphere. In contrast, his successor had a team cutting them down non-stop for practically his entire tenure of the post — an activity that was very popular as it provided a great deal of firewood. We benefited greatly from the impression of spaciousness and our feeling towards the river was that it was a place of beauty.

The anticipated problems had become pressing. Upon my arrival I discovered that a new senior chief had already been installed as the successor to the deceased Sikufele. In fairness, he had been chosen perfectly properly by a democratic vote but then, following the advice of his *ngambela* (head councillor), he had paid a formal visit to the Lozi paramount chief, Lewanika. This had been a singularly inept move politically, as the various tribes around Kabompo all hated the Lozi whom Lewanika epitomized. Many of the local tribes also hated each other, but this was not nearly as significant as their dislike of the Lozi who had dominated them just a few generations before.

Nevertheless, being the centre for several different tribes had its compensations, as I was soon to discover when I found that my predecessors had succeeded in putting into place a very efficient intelligence system that had as its basis the general mistrust of one tribe for another.

I was fed a surprising amount of information coupled with remarkably accurate forecasts of what might be expected to happen. Consequently, I was able to forestall potential problems by convening a special meeting of the Manyinga native authority to listen to various protest groups.

The name Manyinga means 'bloody', probably a reference to some past battle, and in view of its history I alerted the various authorities and the Balovale branch of the NR police decided to send along some reserves who remained discretely in the background.

The meeting was intended to be a session of 'listening to the voice of the people', something that seemed to have been ignored for far too long. I had hoped that when he heard the innumerable complaints, the senior chief would accept them and abdicate. Unfortunately, he did nothing of the sort but produced a sulky version of the divine right of kings that would have done credit to a Bourbon. Even when the native authority passed a resolution rejecting him, he failed to react at once and the meeting broke up. This left me with a very lengthy report to write, suggesting that there was only one course of action possible, which was that we

## Kabompo: The Garden of Eden

should endorse the views of the native authority. The governor responded rapidly, confirming that both the chief and the *ngambela* should be replaced.

The new chief was chosen by acclamation. He was a nephew of the dead Sikufele and turned out to be a senior district messenger at the time employed as the head warder of Kabompo prison. He in turn chose a well-educated and cultured man, John Munyaka of the Lunda tribe, as his new *ngambela*.

Having chosen the *ngambela* from a tribe other than the Lozi meant that there was no more nonsense about kowtowing to Lewanika. The Lunda were subjects of the very important Paramount Chief Mwata Yamvwa who figures later in this story. When the latter paid a visit to the district two years later it was a revelation to see John Munyaka in his smart city suit on his hands and knees leading the procession of greeting.

Sikufele's chieftainship had only recently been created. It was at the time when Kabompo became an official administrative district, which was well within memory. However, the office of *ngambela* for any tribe was an old one and much respected. The Manyinga native authority also clearly had a sense of style and newness had nothing to do with the councillors' notions that the installation of a new *ngambela* should be an occasion for colourful pageantry. There was considerable excitement and anticipation in the district as the date approached and I had a particular interest, for in 14 years I had never witnessed such ceremonies. John Munyaka was rather unusual in that he was considered to be a 'model husband' — he had three wives — and was most scrupulous about treating them all in exactly the same way. If one were given a new blanket, the other two also received new blankets and, reputedly, even the time he devoted to conjugal pleasures was apportioned so that no one would be jealous. John was a particularly handsome African who was also extremely popular with the locals and I suspected that there was a major photo opportunity coming, as indeed it turned out.

The core of the ceremony was the senior chief's acceptance of his *ngambela* and officially confirming him in the post. He in turn then avowed his loyalty and dedicated himself to furthering the interests of the people he served regardless of their tribal allegiance.

The most spectacular part of the ceremony took place before the installation. The prospective *ngambela* had to undergo ritual humiliation. He was required to sit on the ground like a commoner in the centre of Manyinga facing towards the DC and other members of the government party. Either side of the candidate sat the chieftain and his councillors on benches while behind him and out of sight sat the ordinary members of the tribe. The head *kapasu* then approached carrying a splendid new brightly coloured blanket, which he passed over to one of the councillors who carefully wrapped it around John Munyaka over his smart Western suit, so that apart from his head he was completely covered. His semi-reclining pose on the ground was one of humility, to be maintained until the conclusion of the proceedings.

An invitation was then extended to all those in the district who had any complaint against him, real or imagined and over the course of his entire life, to remind him of his past failings. The people making these accusations did so anonymously, standing behind him while he was obliged to sit looking straight ahead and making no comment while listening to this litany. No matter how provoked, he was not allowed to turn around lest he identify his accusers and possibly seek revenge when he was in power — a salutary process I sometimes feel we could do well to adopt with some of our own public figures.

After two or three hours of this the councillor who had robed him raised him to his feet and formally presented him to the chieftain who had advanced to meet him. They both then turned to face the populace to receive their greeting.

\* \* \*

Several tribes lived in the area around Kabompo and they had quite different traditions from the Bemba with whom I was familiar. The principal tribes were the Lovale and the Lunda. For many of their rituals and ceremonies they employed masked dancers or *makishi* who would perform on different occasions but were an essential part of the run-up to ritual circumcision.

These dancers' art was highly traditional and tended to be passed down from father to son. Some of them could almost have been regarded as professional, for they certainly were in great demand and went wherever they were required. There appeared to

## Kabompo: The Garden of Eden

be two distinct types of dance, the one basically a mimicry of various types of animals and the other more of a slapstick comedy routine with a lot of coarse humour. Somewhere in between these extremes were acrobatic routines that could involve 'dancing' on a tightrope stretched between two poles or on a crosspiece at the top of a pole.

On one occasion as I came to the end of a tour, Frances was able to join me and a performance was staged especially for us. I suspect that with my wife present the show had been somewhat censored although the natives were not usually particularly shy about their performances. Initially, the senior dancer came to us and apologized because he was going to have to use his 'second best' mask as he had left the other in the Congo — one-upmanship of the highest order! The letter in which Frances described the scene to my mother and her description, which is still vivid after all these years, cannot be bettered:

> We had finished our dinner and were seated before a large camp fire with our cups of coffee before anything really began to happen. Women started to gather, a few at a time and clustered towards the fire. They would provide the chanted and clapped chorus, which was to be the background to the dancer's acrobatics. On the other side the men all stood together. They laughed and chatted but did not sing or clap, this being the women's contribution to the entertainment. The African male is very loth to take any part in what might be considered female work!
>
> While we waited for the great man to arrive, the huge log fire burnt brightly, lighting the chorus of women and the collection of male spectators. Children sat around in the sand, at the feet of their elders. It was very cold indeed. I had on four jerseys and Cyril's old Burberry raincoat on top to keep the wind from slicing through.
>
> The hand clapping grew more enthusiastic, there was an air of expectancy and things began to warm up (even if the temperature didn't). On the left among the men were four large drums, quite different from those usually to be seen in the Northern Province. The drums were about four feet tall and shaped exactly like an Express Dairy milk bottle. They

stood on the 'neck' end of the bottle with the skin stretched over the other end. People held the drums towards the fires, presumably to alter the tension of the skin in the cold. There were two drummers to the four drums, sometimes they used their hands and at other times sticks. The drumming, clapping and chanting seemed interminable, then suddenly the crowd at the end parted and the *makishi* bounced like a mediaeval tumbler into the circle of light cast from the sparkling fire, a hurricane lamp and a few flaming torches.

I examined his costume carefully. His mask was a fine affair with a simpering expression and black dyed hair of sisal. It was an immensely female expression — rather like that of the old dears who used to sell tapes and ribbons in shops where the price was always something and eleven three. He made his greetings to the Bwana DC in an ingratiating falsetto, which I thought matched the expression on his mask to a 'T'. His mask was set rather far back so that when he raised his head he could see through the knitted raffia neckpiece which kept it in place on his shoulders. The knitted raffia skin, which not only covered his neck and shoulders but his body and legs too, was quite a work of art and very intricate — I was told that they were knitted under conditions of great secrecy. Fixed coyly across his front the *makishi* wore a cheap looking satin square, gaily printed and no doubt made in India, which was fixed across his back by a piece of string. But what really held it up was a massive pair of Marilyn Monroe's best. It looked as if he had a couple of handsome gourds fixed in. Every now and again while he was prancing around, the square would slip and he would jerk it back over the obstructions with an apologetic titter.

But it was the bustle that really absorbed my interest. This was a pretty solid affair, with various yellow dusters and other ragbag odds and ends fixed to it, including the halves of two bicycle bells with outsize clappers, and dancing cheek to cheek. The whole ensemble was topped off by a couple of zebra-tail flywhisks, stuck into the bustle above the bells. On his legs he wore rattles made of small dried gourds, looking rather like a Morris dancer's leg bells.

## Kabompo: The Garden of Eden

The whole effect was of Widow Twankey, as I recalled her from the somewhat rude environment of the Wolverhampton Hippodrome.

We then had an hour or so of close dancing with bicycle bells, bosom, stomach muscles and bustle all working overtime. Every so often the *makishi* would pause for breath and take the opportunity to hold his palm for offerings. I noted that it appeared to be a silver collection and so had to put away the handful of pennies I'd been provided with and fumble around for my second line of defence, threepennies and sixpences. As he received each coin he held up his head and poured it into some secret hiding place beneath his chin. It gave the effect of swallowing the money.

The second part of the performance was a trapeze act performed on a length of bark rope hung between two 18-foot poles. Before commencing this, the *makishi* carefully removed his bustle and replaced it with a thick loincloth. The bosom remained and caused considerable amusement when he hung upside down from the rope and it slipped and hit him very indecently on the chin. The only remarkable thing about the trapeze act as such was its totally uninhibited vulgarity. When it was over, there was a thin piping conversation from the top of the pole — rather like the voice used in Punch and Judy shows. This was translated to mean that he couldn't come down from the pole until the Bwana DC had made descent possible by placing £1 at the foot of the pole. A very dignified haggle then took place, translated step by step by the interpreter, between Cyril and Falsetto. Finally it was agreed that the sum of 12/6 (62½ p) might, just, bring the *makishi* back from the skies, as indeed was the case when he crept down the pole head first, giving a very clever imitation of a caterpillar.

So in clouds of dust, belchings of wood smoke from the fire and the chatter of happy Africans, we returned somewhat stunned and definitely poorer to our tents for the night.

We struck camp about ten in the morning. The tents and equipment were loaded into the *boma* truck while we travelled in the Land Rover to a level plain some 15 miles away. This was part of the flood plain of the Mombeshi River but at this time of the year it is covered with yellow, dried grass. There were no trees or scrub for several hundred yards. In the centre of this plain was a kind of grass gazebo, perhaps 25-feet long and ten wide and somewhat more than shoulder high but with no roof. This was the instruction camp for the boys awaiting circumcision and at each corner both inside and outside were figurines and phallic symbols made of grass, twigs and leaves, which were perched on bamboo poles. The artists were of the school of realism though the effects tended to be rather surrealistic. I took some photographs, which I shall try to commercialize whenever I'm in Port Said.

Having looked at the palisade, we went over to a clearing where there was to be further dancing by the *makishi*. As at the dancing the night before, the women stood on one side providing the rhythmic chorus, while the men and the drums were on the other. Having been caught out the previous night, the Bwana DC first enquired whether the dancers were professional or local and was told that one was professional, while the rest were not. So, before anyone climbed up poles and began haggling, he fixed for £1 all in, as it were, apart from any largesse that might be scattered at intervals through the performance — our sightseeing was becoming expensive and I calculated that for what we had spent in total we could have had quite good seats for *My Fair Lady*.

The dancing was not so very different from the previous night, a lot of shuffling, stomach wriggling and raising of dust. But this time there were six of them; they all had a knitted raffia skin covering their entire body, to which was fastened the trappings appropriate to their characterizations. I gathered that these characters are very traditional and do not vary a great deal.

There were a pregnant woman (nine months); a fool — pure folly with a yard long dunce's hat built into his mask; two lions, which were great fun, for not only were their masks surrounded by a beard of ginger whiskers, but a red-white-and-blue Union Jack was painted between eyes and

## Kabompo: The Garden of Eden

ears rather like tricolour eyelashes and producing a look of great ferocity. They were excellent and cavorted round the place frightening everybody. Then there was the traditional fool of the circumcision ceremony who wore a knitted, three dimensional, miniature phallus fixed to his navel. Finally there was the professional with gaudy knitted breasts, which projected at least nine inches from the wearer. They had been most lovingly knitted in purple and orange spiral stripes. Like all of the others he wore a bustle but his had the distinction of having dozens and dozens of metal bottle tops hanging from strings. If only Donald Swan and Michael Flanders could have seen him. He also did the caterpillar imitation and, with the lions, were the only ones that I thought really funny.

One begins to feel that with their preoccupation with these matters, so many anthropologists are just a lot of dirty old men pretending to be scientists. After some further reflection I said to Cyril 'Can it be that like beauty, vulgarity is something in the eyes of the beholder?'

The actual circumcision ceremony was always held in secret, and strangers who were not members of the tribe were excluded. The *boma* chief clerk, Chanda was a Bemba and needless to say not permitted to be present; nevertheless, on one occasion his curiosity got the better of him and he decided to audition for the role of an African Peeping Tom by trying to look through the surrounding palisade. Unfortunately, the Lunda were not as tolerant as the people of Coventry and did not take kindly to this infringement of their privacy. Chanda was promptly chased away and only escaped from his pursuers, who were threatening to remove more than his foreskin, with the aid of a bicycle.

Shortly after we got back home, Sheila, our dog, rushed over to her basket and then back to us; this was repeated several times until finally Frances went to investigate. At first nothing could be seen but, on lifting the basket to shake it out, there, was a spitting cobra; fortunately in a somnolent mood.

Meanwhile, in the greater area of Northern Rhodesia trouble was developing on more than one front.

# 13
# Distant Thunder

It has been said many times that hindsight can be amazingly prophetic and much of the ensuing history of Northern Rhodesia seems quite foreseeable at this distance in time. However, in 1958 a typical rural DC's life was so filled with the minutiae of local administration that the momentous events in the rest of colonial Africa seemed far away. The thought that the sands had nearly run out for the federation simply never entered one's mind. Part of the argument that had been put forward in justification was that it had been set up with the express purpose of accelerating the rate of progress towards a self-governing union in which the local population and immigrant settlers would be equals. At least this was the suggestion and what everyone had been told, although few of the people living in NR believed it.

We knew, of course, that it had been deeply unpopular with the natives and chiefs. Many of us also recognized the inequitable representation of the two groups, but assumed it was a problem that would recede as fast as finances would permit the educational system to be improved. When one was living in the bush, the fact that the federation was not developing in the way the Colonial Office had envisaged and that there were deep undercurrents running in the nationalist groups were not contemplated. If anyone had pointed this out then, it would simply have been regarded as a joke in the worst possible taste.

The first of the colonies to go had been the Gold Coast, reborn as Ghana. There had been a peaceful and relatively planned transition. The highly educated Kwame Nkrumah who was originally imprisoned in 1952 had been released and then made prime minister of the colony when his supporters, the Convention Peoples' Party, were swept to power following elections the following year. Independence had come in March 1957 and

## Distant Thunder

Nigeria was due to follow in 1960; though it had not yet taken place. The horrors of the fratricidal civil war between Nigeria and the secessionist Ibo state of Biafra were a long way off into the future (1967). The French approach to the dismemberment of their African empire had proceeded on somewhat different lines in the hope that their influence would remain in being and indeed they were remarkably successful in achieving their objective.

Not far to the north in Kenya, the Mau Mau, the secret society of the Kikuyu tribe, still existed, although the revolt that had begun in 1952 had been quashed and its leader, Jomo Kenyatta, imprisoned. The Belgian Congo was also to become independent in 1960, but to the average DC on an outstation in Northern Rhodesia all appeared to be relatively peaceful.

It may well have been that back in the rarefied atmosphere of the Colonial Office in London, or in the secret advice given to the governor by Special Branch, the possibility of serious trouble in NR was actively considered, but, if so, such thoughts were kept remarkably secret from those who would have to cope with it at first hand.

As was said much earlier, I went to Africa imbued with the romantic notion that the empire's destiny was to bring to the benighted natives the civilizing benefits of Pax Britannica. Some 13 years later the basic tenet was still accepted although I had long since realized that these goals could not be attained too quickly. The standard view of the average DC of the time was frequently expressed in the view that 'they are making progress very nicely and will be ready for self government *about the time that I retire.*'

In truth, the Northern Province and rural areas simply did not seem to provide an environment that was conducive to the heady brew of nationalism. Sparsely populated and almost entirely tribal, with many tribes having no great love of their neighbours, there were for practical purposes no urban areas in which prospective revolutionaries could gather to plot in comparative secrecy. In most districts, education of the majority for practical purposes stopped after a maximum of four years. Some of the brighter pupils with the benefit of two years' extra schooling plus maybe a year's 'training' might well return to the school as the next generation of teachers to educate their successors. In these circumstances, there could hardly have been an 'intelligentsia' in the sense

## Kaunda's Gaoler

that it is usually understood, with people likely to have ideas and aspirations for independence, let alone the means for propagating such concepts.

Although this is retrospective thinking, I am convinced that it is what I would have said at the time had the question been asked and of course it could not have been further from the truth. As Kenneth Kaunda revealed in his book *Zambia Shall Be Free*, during much of this period he was working in the Northern Province either teaching or farming. He spent every moment of his spare time busy cycling around the district, covering up to 200 miles in a weekend, and spreading the gospel about the ANC with a fair degree of success.

Despite this, the thought remains with me to this day that, left to their own devices and following the guidance of their own chiefs, the tribes of the sparsely populated Northern Province would probably have thought that the rule of the *bwana*s was reasonably benevolent. In an area where the land was generally too poor for anything but subsistence farming, unlike Nyasaland and Kenya, there were too few white farmers visibly getting rich to excite jealousy.

Matters were, of course, different in the Copper Belt and along the line of rail. There, much greater concentrations of natives were being thrown into close proximity with one another. As a result, tribal prejudices tended to become eroded and, probably, loyalties to their traditional chiefs weakened. With more money in their pockets and ready access to beer in their free time, the right conditions for seditious discussion existed. There were also greater numbers of white settlers, mining engineers and so on who obviously lived a much more visible and enviable life style, as distinct from the DOs and DCs who were not just fewer in numbers but simply received insufficient pay to live flamboyantly.

For those who may doubt the latter statement it can be firmly stated that looking back from a distance of 40 years one sometimes wonders how one managed; certainly at times it seemed like a struggle. At the time of my appointment in 1943, I was offered the magnificent salary of £350 per annum from which I had to provide all my kit and uniform. In the course of writing this book I have had occasion to refresh my memory of the Colonial Office regulations. These had been carefully explained to me before leaving and we were obliged to sign a document in which we gave an undertaking not to embark on any additional work. The regulations were strictly enforced to avoid any suggestion of exploitation and effectively prevented officers from indulging in any entrepreneurial activities to supplement their income. Involvement with any of the local businesses and even buying shares in the copper mines was not permitted. It is true that wives could become local employees of the administration, but any idea of their entering into a business venture of their own was frowned upon, especially if there were any potential for overlap with her husband's work.

These days one hears so much about 'conflict of interest' that everyone understands its significance, but in those days it was not a term in use and many of the restrictions seemed petty and pointless.

# 14
# Confined in the Garden of Eden

To most of the white settlers the federation looked like a success story, even if there did appear to have been a systematic transfer of money from Northern Rhodesia and Nyasaland to the much more affluent Southern Rhodesia. The government in London had belatedly become aware of the deep-seated dissatisfaction of the African population at the way in which the federation had been established. Further, it was not happy at the lack of progress being made toward a multicultural society and realized that the federal government showed no interest in change. In an attempt to increase the participation of the native population, the colonial secretary had put forward a proposal to change the federal constitution and this was on everybody's mind, as were the elections that were planned to coincide with its introduction. The elections were expected to create a certain amount of trouble because for the first time it would be possible for Africans to represent Europeans and vice versa, though even so there would still be very few Africans entitled to vote. It was all too little and too late. Despite the supposed increase in representation, the proposal was considered to be totally inadequate by the nationalists.

Leading members of the ANC, including its president Harry Nkumbula and Kenneth Kaunda, had recently returned from the All African Peoples' Conference in Accra where they had learned the meaning of positive non-violent action such as civil disobedience while sitting at the feet of Nkrumah, the acknowledged mastermind of African independence movements. Numerous different organizations in other colonies besides NR were called the ANC and, although they shared the same ideals and general philosophy, their links were fairly tenuous. Among others who attended the conference was Dr Hastings Banda, the talented leader of the Nyasaland African Congress, who had recently returned to that country from exile in Britain.

Kaunda subsequently went on an extended visit to India where he met with Gandhi. Shortly after his return in October 1958 and on the same day as Nkumbula was re-elected the leader of the ANC unopposed, Kaunda, Simon Kapepwe and some other leading members of the ANC resigned and formed their own party, the Zambia African National Congress (ZANC).

Discontent had been simmering in the ANC for some while, as it appeared to have lost its sense of direction. Indeed, it was widely believed among white officials that at least one of its senior members was in the pay of the security forces. The precise explanations for the split in the ANC were never entirely clear. There were several reasons advanced that were generally held to be contributory but none seemed likely to have caused the break to occur as abruptly as it did. Nkumbula had already aroused resentment in the ANC by using party funds to enjoy 'the high life' and he was known for his partiality for drink. It had not improved matters when he set out to consolidate his position as president in a manner that would make it difficult to replace him. Suspicions that he had begun to consider a compromise with the government were fuelled when he called off some boycotts on his return from a visit to London, which suggested that he was trying to make the new and unpopular constitutional changes work. Also, he seemed to be paying more attention to the advice of Harry Franklin than to his own executive and was becoming involved with the Constitution Party, a small group of rather woolly headed liberals. Whatever the reasons, the break was sudden and the animosity it generated very long lasting.

The elections planned for March 1959 under the latest constitution were for the parliament of the federation and rumours were rife. One of these was that the first African to cast a vote, be it a man or woman, would have their hand cut off; this rumour was apparently based on a report by Special Branch. The government was jarred into action. Although the country appeared to all intents comparatively peaceful and law abiding, the central government was taking no chances and prepared a list of the top officials of ZANC. In the parlance of the time they were referred to as the First and Second XI to reflect the two stages in which it was proposed, first to detain, and then exile them to rural areas well removed from the zones of noticeable political activity. The North Western Province was perfect for this purpose. This scheme, which was worked out in the greatest secrecy, was known as Operation Longjump.

In my isolated outpost of empire we knew little or nothing of the above or even what was going on in the overall context. Our first intimation of trouble was when, in early March less than three months after my arrival in Kabompo all the DCs were summoned to an emergency meeting in Solwezi. It was so secret and hush-hush that we were not given the slightest inkling of what it was all about. The DC Balovale and I agreed that we would travel together from Kabompo to Solwezi; it was the wet season, the roads were in a dreadful state and driving was a bit like swimming in oil.

Upon our arrival we were taken to a sit together around a conference table with the PC and other DCs, all of us in complete ignorance of what was going on. All we knew was that our secret instructions were to be flown in by air. The airstrip at Solwezi was located about a couple of miles from the township and, under normal circumstances, was totally unmanned because the sound of any incoming aircraft's engines would announce its impending arrival, at which point the duty officer would hightail it down to the field. On this occasion, however, an estimated time of arrival had been advised and everyone assumed that someone else was looking after the plane's reception. The plane, however, arrived well ahead of the schedule and the pilot must have been rather taken aback by there being no welcoming committee waiting to relieve him of his precious bundle of papers. He resolved the problem of how to attract attention to his arrival by 'buzzing' the provincial offices repeatedly until he could see that someone had taken note of his existence and was piling into a car to make all possible speed to the airport.

We were given full details of the planned roundup and arrest of the First XI and the new safeguard of elections regulations authorizing this. These days the term 'gob-smacked' seems the most appropriate way to describe our reactions to the draconian

16. RIGHT. Makishi dancer

17. BELOW. Makishi dancers

18. ABOVE. Ndaba of Kabompo district chiefs to meet the PC

19. OPPOSITE. Preparing an *al fresco* meeting with Chief Nkana and his council

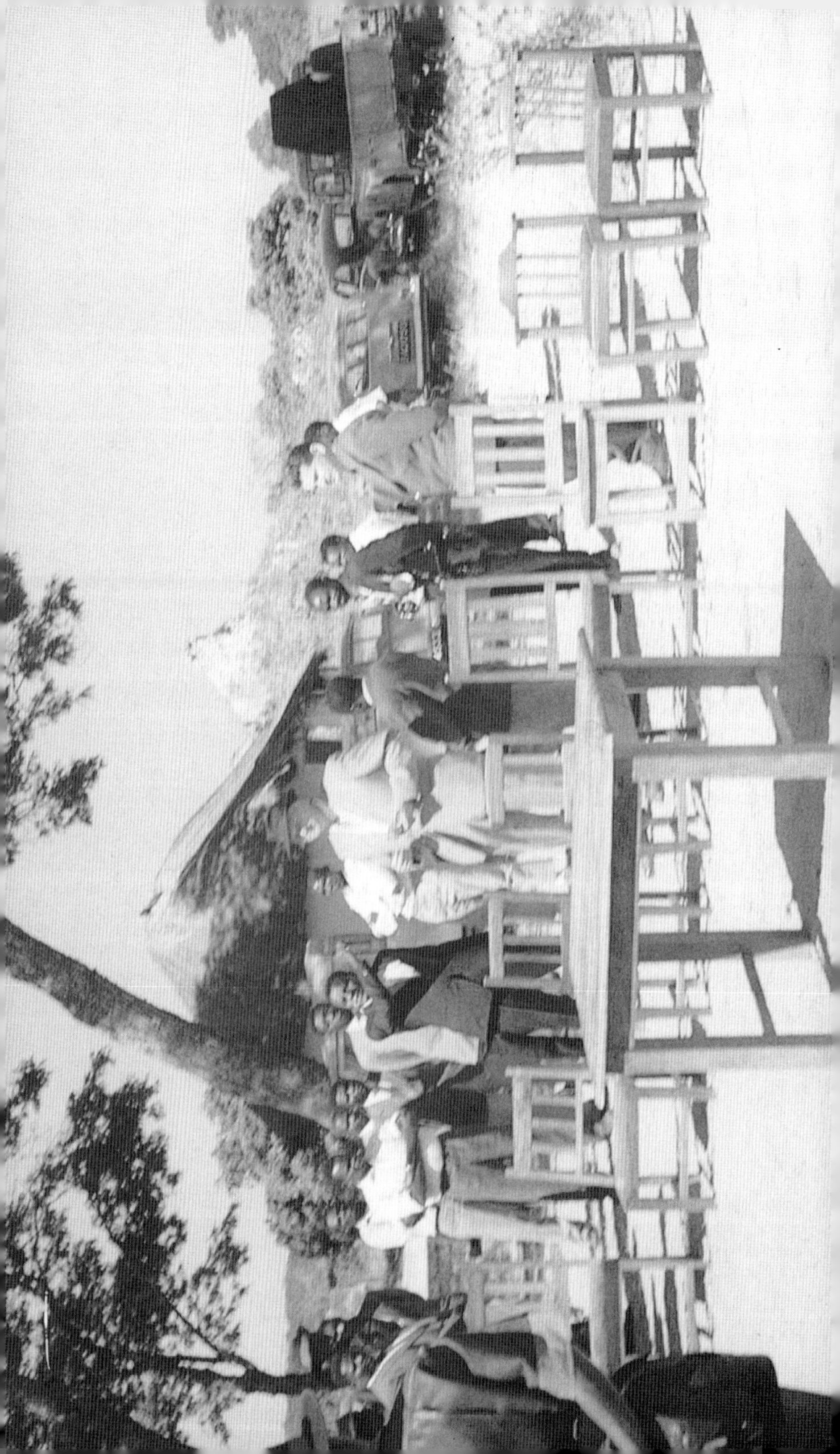

20. ABOVE. Kapasus parade for opening of Mushili courthouse, Masaiti

21. BELOW. PC Ewen Thompson, with his wife, and VIPs attend opening celebrations, Mushili courthouse

22. ABOVE. Light-hearted moment with Kaunda at Luanshya airport

23. BELOW. Buttering up the press

24. LEFT. 'It's just a simple lunch ' — Luanshya

25. RIGHT. Messenger in the newly-designed uniform, 1954

26. OPPOSITE. The splendour of Victoria Falls and its rainbow

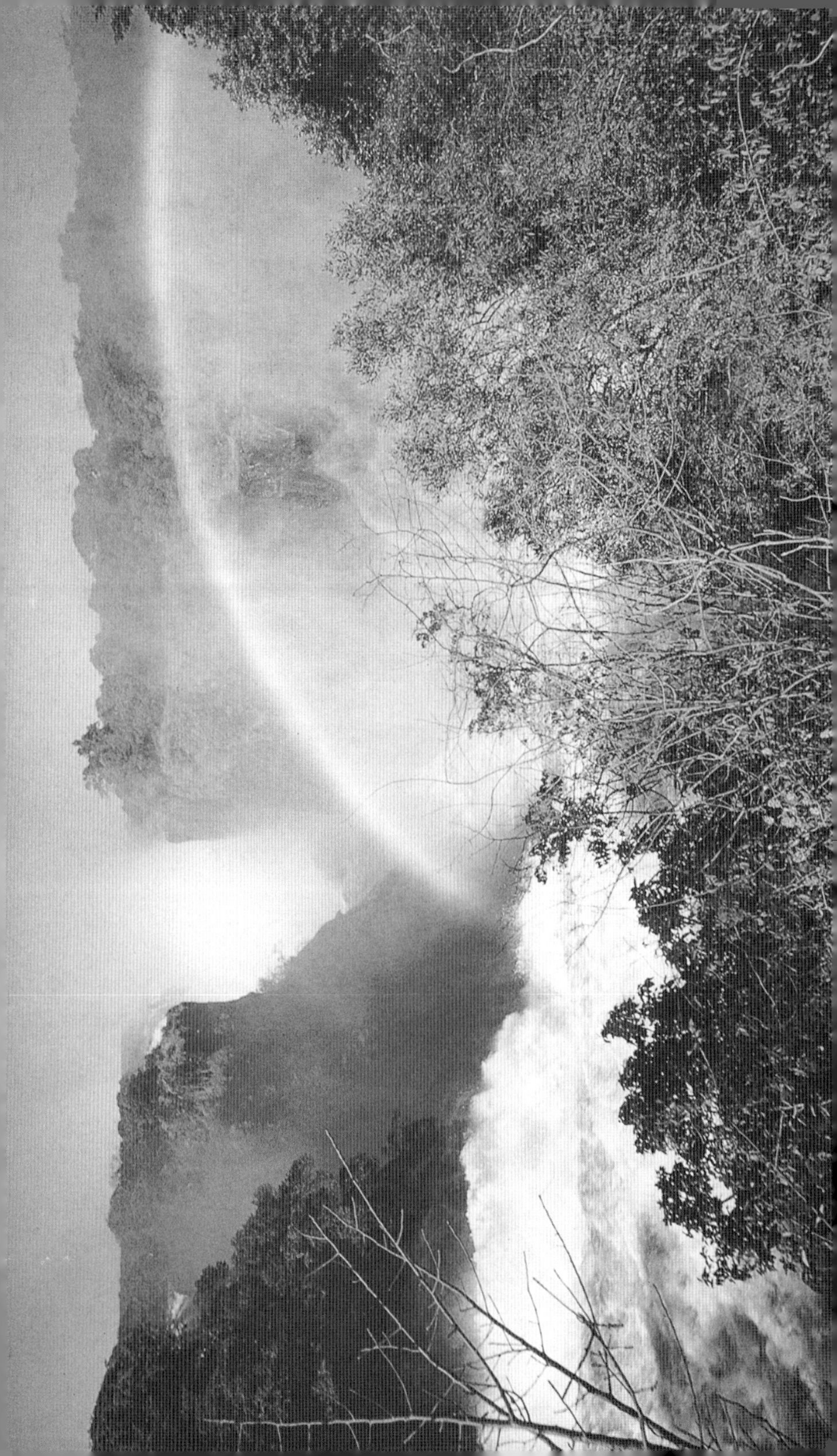

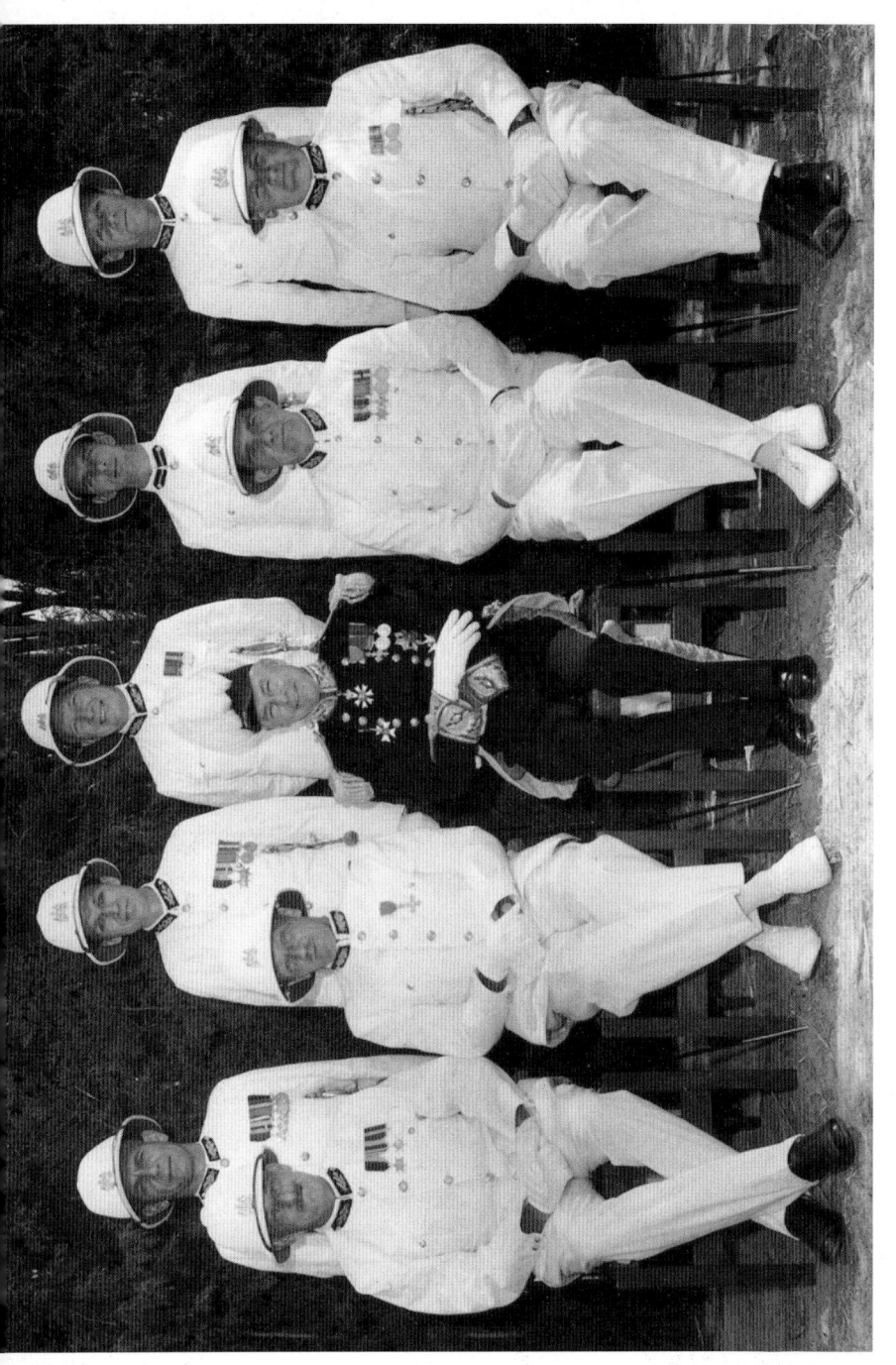

27. The governor, Sir Evelyn Hone, with DCs of the Western Province

measures that were being proposed. Very specific instructions had been worked out on where people were to be detained, how the restrictions were to be enforced and the legal status of the restricted persons. We were also given forewarning of probable action against the Second XI.

The government's actions had been kept remarkably secret and, when the arrests were made, they went very smoothly and without any trouble. To explain them, the governor (Sir Arthur Benson) made a speech the following morning. He prorogued the new party by invoking his powers under the recently passed NR emergency legislation. The grounds he gave for his action were that the new party intended to sabotage the upcoming elections by violence and murder. In his speech he said that the ZANC employed witchcraft and unmentionable curses; finally he wound up by comparing them to Al Capone's gang, which had earned itself the sobriquet of 'murder incorporated'.

By any standards it sounded intemperate and the reasons for his choice of language were queried when a commission subsequently investigated the ensuing problems. When asked to provide the evidence for his allegations, the best the governor could do was to say that because the meetings at which these matters were discussed took place in private at night there were no witnesses.

It is a reflection on the extent to which the DCs were kept in the dark about the larger picture that it was only on reading *State of Emergency: Crisis in Central Africa, Nyasaland* that I realized that the rumours referred to earlier corresponded to the information garnered by Special Branch in Nyasaland following a secret meeting of the Nyasaland African Congress (NAC) earlier that year in January. On the basis of the intelligence gained it was alleged that Dr Banda's followers were planning a campaign involving the assassination of many government officials and white settlers.

This may well have been the background to Sir Arthur's speech. The proscription of the ZANC, and the arrest and detention of Kaunda and other members of the First and Second XI followed about ten days after the proscription of the NAC and the declaration of a state of emergency in Nyasaland on 3 March, just after midnight. By daylight, the authorities had successfully managed the wholesale arrest of members of the NAC and they were subsequently imprisoned in Southern Rhodesia. The government of that colony had introduced a state of emergency on 26 February, presumably so they could feel that the country was completely under control, thus permitting them to provide troops and police as reinforcements to Nyasaland.

My mandate was perfectly clear; Kenneth Kaunda, his private secretary Frank Makarios Chitambala (as he liked to be known) and one Musonda (who did not appear to have any other name) were going to be arrested. They would then be sent to me for safekeeping in the district of Kabompo for the foreseeable future and funds would be voted for their upkeep. In practical terms, this meant that they would be released from arrest into my care and could live where they liked and travel freely provided they remained within the boundaries of the district and reported to me every day of the week except Sundays. Presumably, this dispensation was so that DCs could not complain that they had to be on duty seven days a week. Along with my written instructions I also received a private injunction by word of mouth: 'For the love of God, don't lose them!'

Back in Kabompo, there was barely time to arrange for a house to be prepared for the exiles before they and their escort arrived one evening just as the sun was setting. The handover was quite dramatic, taking place as it did in the *boma* office lit by two flickering oil lamps, for there was insufficient power for electric light. The only power in Kabompo in those days was a small generator that provided sufficient electricity for the police radio (itself a major step towards civilization after Luwingu).

This all took place in the presence of the head messenger and two other senior messengers. I recall how very insistent the escort was that they had to have a receipt for the detainees before they could depart.* I read to the restricted persons a summary of the regulations under which they were being detained and their freedom curtailed. They were then sent off to their house, which had to be in the messenger lines, for the night.

They were told that we would meet again the following day when I proposed to go into detail about the practical aspects of the restrictions on their life in Kabompo. They would also be advised

---

* A standard police procedure.

## Confined in the Garden of Eden

what assistance would be provided by the native labourer who had been allocated to ensure that essential services were looked after.

I had already briefed the district messengers on the situation, which included a full report on the text of the governor's speech about the ZANC and concluded by telling them to ensure that the local people understood what was going on and who the detainees were. It was rather amusing many years later, on reading Kaunda's account of his arrival in Kabompo, to discover how the local people had shunned them as if they were cannibals; I could only put this down to the way the messengers had produced their own over literal translation of 'murder incorporated'.

The following day I met with Kaunda and his fellow detainees and we had a perfectly civilized discussion about how the restrictions would work until we got to the problem of catering (and on such matters the fate of nations may be finely balanced). They provided me with details of their normal diet, which I attempted to cost at the daily rate; however, such basic items as fresh milk, bread, vegetables and meat, which they were obviously accustomed to buying in a market in Lusaka, were unavailable in Kabompo, where every individual family had its own garden and food garnering system. The expatriates regularly ordered goods from afar to come with the mail lorry. The fact that Kaunda was a vegetarian did not make life any easier since he also excluded fish from his diet.

They demanded that they be given rations — clearly they wanted it to become established that they were in fact prisoners as this was what a prisoner in gaol would have. I was having none of this and the argument went back and forth. Ultimately, the problem was solved by the creation of a 'restricted persons canteen' where the restricted persons could draw their allowances and pay for purchases in the canteen. I managed to duck these problems by putting McInnes in charge and provided him with an advance fund of £20 to be replenished as necessary. My long-suffering wife was pressed into cooperating in the provision of cold storage facilities for perishable foodstuffs.

The restrictions that were imposed on them were hardly onerous since they were allowed the freedom of the district, which encompassed some 10,000 square miles. In point of fact they never made any attempt to leave Kabompo township, despite the allegation that appeared in the *Spectator* that Kaunda had to walk 100 miles to get a letter to the outside world. Where they would have gone to had they walked 100 miles is also a mystery. They must have had a fair amount of mail because Frances remarked how she invariably used to meet Kaunda at the post office whenever she went there with her letters. Looking back after all these years it seems incredible if Special Branch made no attempt to check on his correspondence. I certainly was given no instructions on this score and his mail went out with all the other letters. There is no doubt that Kaunda's solicitor thought that it had been examined as he wrote to me remarking in his letter 'No doubt you are already aware of this.'

The government believed that its prompt reaction and the detention of the leaders would effectively crush trouble before it arose and sat back to await developments. Reaction was not long in coming. The Northern Province erupted in strife as the supporters of ZANC sought to bring everything to a standstill. Bridges were destroyed, schools burnt down and some of the *boma* cattle kraals were also torched. On one occasion, the unfortunate cattle were still inside. At least one chief had a narrow escape when his house was torched while he was asleep.

The sabotage appeared to be quite aimless and more concerned with whether or not the target was 'soft'. This is why schools that had done nothing but provide much needed education were targets. The *Northern News* of 19 May contained a letter from an old friend of ours, the Reverend Simms (the father of the young lady who taught me *Bemba*) who was in charge of the mission at Fort Rosebery. The letter and the philosophy it expresses from 40 years ago make interesting reading today:

> Some weeks ago I received a threatening letter from the Zambia African Congress. ... The nature of the threat was not disclosed but I was left in no doubt when I saw the school and all its contents go up in flames at 2.00 a.m. on May the 10th. The loss of thousands of school primers, Bibles, furniture etc. ... It is 52 years since I came to this country and apart from preaching the Gospel I have taught for all of that time. ... How many Africans I have taught to read and write in this time I cannot say. Much of it was

done in the days of the BSAC before the government paid a penny for African education. ... I would like to ask the writer how, with such a record, I have incurred the enmity of Zambia or any other African Congress.

It is also interesting that when the cutting was sent to the *Daily Express* back home, it was returned — 'not interested'.

Nevertheless, the numbers of those participating in the troubles must have been quite small because it did not take long with the aid of the faithful messengers to restore a degree of order. As a result, the elections were able to go ahead as planned without any obvious violence although there was some evidence that people were staying away to boycott them.

Life inevitably became much more exciting with political 'restrictees' on my hands. Somehow or other they managed to persuade the African manager of the local store, which a Greek-Cypriot named Andrew Sardanis owned, to extend some credit to them. With this they purchased for themselves a portable radio together with three white sheets. The trader then presented me with the bill, which, after some consideration, I settled.

It all seemed harmless enough. I saw no reason for them not to be able to keep abreast of what was happening by radio. It seemed infinitely better that they heard the official news rather than the rumours that spread effortlessly throughout the protectorate. The government had already suggested to me that I pass on old copies of newspapers and magazines. This presumably was in the hope of persuading them that basically we were kind and benevolent and maybe they would change their ways.

I was, however, rather taken aback when the three of them turned up to report as usual wearing the sheets over their shoulders like togas. Obviously, I was displeased but it did not strike me as serious and it seemed much easier to laugh it off than make an issue of it. Peaceful political activity from someone supposedly advocating violence seemed a step in the right direction. Later when I heard that Kaunda was denouncing violence (his policy of 'positive non-violent action') and demanding that his followers adopt passive resistance, I felt quite pleased. I did not realize at the time that its practitioners could interpret positive non-violent action in various ways. They considered, for example, that there was nothing wrong with intimidation provided that the violence was only threatened.

Mr Sardanis, the storeowner who provided the sheets, seemed to do well from his support as he later came to occupy a ministerial post in Kaunda's first government; still later it was rumoured that he gave advice to Betty Kaunda on investments in Cyprus.

After he had settled down, the local population presented Kaunda with a most unusual walking stick that, instead of the usual semicircular handle, had one that formed a complete circle. Taken all in all, he was quite an imposing sight as he strolled around in the early evening wearing the sheet and using the cane.

Clearly, he remarked upon the cane very favourably because the local wood carvers produced a number of them for sale. I was therefore somewhat put out when my mother came to visit shortly afterwards and announced that she would like me to buy her one. I had a difficult job explaining that it was inappropriate for the DC to be buying copies of a political detainee's cane. Knowing that mother liked to get her own way, I should not have been surprised when, many years later while tidying up her affairs, I discovered the selfsame cane she had bought without my knowledge.

It soon came to my attention that, although he had made no complaint to me, Kaunda was quite unwell. He was suffering from recurrent malaria and was having serious digestive problems brought on by the local water, a matter on which I was able to sympathize as I had been suffering myself. Since I felt responsible for their wellbeing while under restriction, I made haste to alert the PC (the first time I had encoded a message), drawing his attention to the fact that none of the detainees had been medically examined since their arrest and the potential problems that would arise in the event that one of them became seriously ill.

Almost at once, the medical officer from Balovale arrived in great haste, having received a rocket from on high. After an examination Kaunda was given treatment to which he responded. There was subsequently a further discussion on the subject of his diet in the presence of the MO. Fortunately, he was not taken ill again.

Kaunda, of course, was not the only restricted person. Frank Chitambala managed to get himself into hot water quite rapidly. A letter arrived through the post, addressed to E. C. Greenall, DC, Kabompo. It was very succinct and in essence said, 'You will be very sorry if you find yourself in the wrong country after independence,' signed Frank Chitambala.

A message was of course sent off to Balovale, but in Kabompo we deemed it necessary to act. Within a short while the author of the letter found himself before me, as the magistrate in the local court on a charge of 'threatening violence', with the local police inspector acting as public prosecutor. Kaunda sat at the back of the court taking a keen interest in the proceedings. The accused pleaded not guilty, but on being confronted with the letter admitted having written it but denied that there was any threat of violence. The prosecutor asked what meaning the letter could have other than to warn of future violence and Chitambala was quickly found guilty. The police recommended that he should receive a prison sentence. I realized the potential opportunities for histrionics in a magistrate when the accused was asked if he had anything to say in mitigation and complete silence descended on the court. There was not a sound and with what I thought was a delicate touch I bound him over to keep the peace for three months. This was just as well as two days later I received a telegram from the attorney general instructing us not to prosecute.

It had one benefit, for thereafter the restricted persons treated me with respect until their removal. It was not, however, to be the last I heard of Frank Chitambala. In late 1960, subsequent to his release from prison, he wrote to the governor complaining that the DC, Kabompo was intimidating local members of UNIP. He later applied to go to Moscow University. The impact back home also produced correspondence with letters arriving addressed to 'Mr K. Kaunda, c/o The DC, Commandant, Kabompo Concentration Camp'.

Even at that time, away from a political environment Kaunda could be pleasant and was invariably civil, patting our dog whenever he met Frances *en route* to the post office.

The MO's visit to Kaunda could have been better timed as I was unfortunate enough to go down with an exceedingly bad attack of malaria shortly after he had left. Kabompo was a mosquito infested area and I had been out of these for nearly six years during which time I had been reasonably free of fevers, but now that I was back and on tour I was an easy target for the mosquitoes despite taking my Paludrine prophylaxis. On this occasion I had gone to bed feeling perfectly well but woke up in the middle of the night with a dreadful shivering fit. That it was malaria I had no doubt but it was different from previous bouts — a high temperature had always accompanied them whereas this time I was extremely cold. Fortunately, Frances managed to get the attention of a neighbour who drove to fetch Dr Mc Gibbon from the mission at Loloma. On his arrival he gave me an injection and told me that I had what was known as a 'cold rigor'. It was a great relief when he came because I genuinely believed that I was shaking the life out of myself.

With the enforced disbandment of ZANC, the former members of the ANC no longer had a party. Mainza Chona, who established the United National Independence Party, otherwise known as UNIP, remedied this in 1959. Kaunda was still in detention when this new political entity was formed, but after his release speedily became its leader.

In his book *Zambia Shall Be Free*, Kaunda recounts how he and his companions had great difficulty getting to know the local people since none of the three restricted persons could speak Lovale. They soon picked up enough to get by and overcome the initial suspicions — this done they could get on with spreading their political views.

Their proselytizing must have had some success because it was not long before word of it reached the powers in Lusaka and they took immediate steps to bring it to an end. A directive was issued that the exiles were to be banned from public political activity anywhere. Furthermore, they had to acknowledge that they were cognizant of the fact by signing a copy of the relevant document.

I received the instructions together with the order that had to be served on Kaunda. This led to the only problem I had with him during the period he was in Kabompo. The order was no more than a single side of official stationery so I took it through to my native clerk and instructed him to type it at once thinking that it would take no more than 20 minutes. Kaunda was due to report to the head messenger and would probably still be wearing his toga. I decided that it would do him no harm to be kept waiting while the typing was done. This was standard practice when someone had done something of which one disapproved.

Half an hour passed and I went to collect the letter — it had not been started — nor had anything else come to that. I do not know what species of indolence had come over the clerk, for he was an excellent worker and a competent typist. After a while I could hear a disturbance in the outer office as Kaunda raised his voice demanding to know what was going on and the head clerk trying to calm him down. The noise also affected my typist who seemed quite unable to sit at his typewriter but agitatedly hopped from one leg to another. In the end I did not get my order until nearly the end of the morning and Kaunda had reached boiling point. I was reading the order through and checking it for errors when he burst into my office, closely followed by the head messenger — Kaunda was livid! He describes the incident of how he was kept waiting all morning in his book, but apparently had never been aware of what had gone on while trying to get the order typed.

What followed would have appeared ridiculous in the extreme to any uninformed onlooker but it could have had serious consequences.

I rose to my feet and Kaunda made straight for me, hotly pursued by the messenger. Had he laid his hands on me it would have been a case of assault that I could not have overlooked, particularly with the head messenger present. It was equally out of the question for me to resort to force to keep him at arms length so I had no choice but to beat a tactical retreat around the desk. This had the useful effect, when Kaunda turned around, of interposing the messenger between us and thus restored a degree of sanity.

Words were exchanged with him accusing me of not knowing how to treat him properly and my response 'I will decide how *I* am going to treat you.' Even so, Kaunda had to have the last word when ordered to leave — 'I respect the head messenger more than I do you.'

Later and under protest he signed the order. This was the only time he was with me that Kaunda caused any serious problem. He did not remain in Kabompo for very long afterwards. The restricted persons did not seem to be short of money and I later heard that they had access to substantial funds from Ghana. It was early May and somehow he contrived for a lawyer in Lusaka to arrange for a writ of habeas corpus. This may have been the last straw for the government. About one week later, after he had been with me for only eight weeks, some senior police officers arrived from Lusaka and he was formally charged with sedition.

## Kaunda's Gaoler

I was forewarned of the arrival of the police party and requested to use what they were pleased to call a pretext to ensure that Kaunda and the other restricted persons were at the *boma* when they actually arrived.

I reluctantly consented to do this as being the lesser of two evils. I was persuaded that it was important that the restricted persons were not alerted before the police arrived. If they were, then they would have had an opportunity to destroy any of their papers that might have shown whether they had been engaged in treasonable activity during their period of restriction. If, as turned out to be the case, there were none then they would automatically be free from any such suspicion. Thus it was possible that they might actually benefit from the minor deception to be practised on them.

Accordingly, I wrote a letter to Kaunda inviting them all to come to the office at 4.00 p.m. to discuss matters concerning their terms of restriction. Shortly before they arrived, the two senior police officers came into my office and sat down. The restricted persons were shown in by the head messenger at the appointed time and greeted me politely. Before I could reply, the policemen rose to their feet, one them saying, 'Excuse me Sir! But are you Kenneth Kaunda?' He looked shocked, but eventually replied 'Yes' and then seemed to withdraw into himself on being informed that he was under arrest.

He remained in this trance-like state for the rest of the proceedings, taking little interest in what was going on. The officers explained the basis of their rearrest and then escorted them to their house in the messengers' lines where they were allowed to pack after the quarters had been searched.

We said farewell and I left the police to load up for their drive back to Balovale and then on to Lusaka where he was later transferred to the much more controlled regime of the prison in Salisbury. He was to remain there until early 1960 when he was released in time to meet and talk with Harold Macmillan during his visit to Lusaka, which was just before he made his famous speech in South Africa in which he said 'A wind of change is blowing through this continent whether we like it or not.'

I suspect that while he was actually in gaol Kaunda must have decided that it had not been such a bad time in Kabompo because in 1962, some while after he was released, he sent me a copy of his book, *Zambia Shall Be Free*. Naturally I wrote to thank him for the book and could not resist the temptation to extend an invitation for him to visit me at any time, saying 'My door is always open for you, and you can rely on me to keep to my side of the table.' Later, after he became president, we were to become friends and we remembered the occasion when we again met with a desk between us, but this time with him sitting on the administrative side, but that was some years in the future.

The Bantu have a saying that friendship is sometimes preceded by a violent quarrel, and indeed this may be the case.

# 15
# Tribal Troubles

All in all, the problems in NR passed off peacefully compared with what happened in Nyasaland. There, some 1300 Africans had been detained and during the ensuing disturbances over 50 people were killed. The immediate conesquence of this was the Devlin Enquiry. The report that was published in July was very critical of how the Nyasaland government had handled the troubles and cast doubts on the existence of the murder plot. It was symptomatic of the general tenor of the report that, having promised general anonymity to witnesses, Devlin applied this principle carefully to the Congress witnesses but insisted on publishing the names of members of Special Branch, whose lives depended on their secrecy. The Conservative government in the UK survived the ensuing debate in Parliament, having pointed to various inaccuracies in the report. A few months later the Conservatives also survived a general election. They were returned with an increased majority and Macmillan gave the Colonial Office to Macleod who replaced Lennox-Boyd.

With Kaunda's abrupt departure, life at the *boma* briefly returned to normal, or gave a semblance of it for a few days. The next problem to rear its head, about the same time as Kaunda left me, had nothing to do with independence or any local politics; rather it was the Lumpa Church and its founder Alice Lenshina. Although these troubles were pretty well confined to the Northern Province, their repercussions rumbled around the whole country.

The Lenshina cult was one of those mysterious movements that seem to arise from time to time, especially in Africa. It started around the time of the formation of the federation in 1953 when an otherwise unremarkable villager named Alice, who attended a Presbyterian church, had what appeared to be a profound religious experience. There were cynics who pointed out that it occurred

## Tribal Troubles

while she was picking mushrooms, some of which were well known to have hallucinogenic properties. Be that as it may, she believed that she had received a message that she was to seek further religious instruction and then to spread the news of her enlightenment. She went to the missionaries, convinced them of her sincerity and received a certain amount of instruction before being sent out to 'spread the message'. The part of her message that struck a particularly sensitive note among the local natives was that 'the Lord' would protect all believers from witchcraft. Any native who claimed to have more power than a witch or other practitioner of magic was bound to get attention. The same message from a white man had little impact since it was well known that white people were immune to local magic.

She drew ever-increasing crowds to her preaching, which was centred on Kasomo, a village in the Chinsali area fairly close to Kasama. She was so popular that instances were recorded of families having walked for two or three weeks to hear her. She also composed hymns in Bemba, which were very stirring and popular. She soon fell out with the established churches, for they realized that their members were deserting them in large numbers to join the Lumpa Church, as it came to known. She was particularly antagonistic towards the Catholic Church, for she equated such things as rosaries with fetishes and the celebration of communion with witchcraft. The very name 'Lumpa' was an offence to some missionary groups as it was a local dialect word meaning 'highest'. About this time Alice decided that in future she would add 'Lenshina' (the Bemba word for queen) to her name.

The Lumpa Church had written rules that its members were expected to follow. Bearing in mind Alice Lenshina's comparative lack of formal education, it would be interesting to know who actually wrote the rules, for they had clearly been well thought out. They were both comprehensive and well written, covering such aspects as the status of the church being 'not political' and general behaviour — 'Members will not smoke or chew tobacco in church.' Her support was such that, using only native labour and money raised from her supporters, she was able to have several brick-built churches erected, including one that was about 80 metres long and could hold several hundred worshippers.

The troubles that occurred in 1959 were caused by one of the tenets of the Lumpa Church failing to recognize the authority of any earthly government. It followed from this that its members were not liable for taxes, which immediately put it on a collision course with both the chiefs and the colonial government. With a membership of up to 100,000 this could not be tolerated. Alice, who was about 35 at the time, had arrogant confidence in her rightness. The local chiefs took exception to the residents of their villages simply leaving and starting to build new ones closer to Kasomo, often on another chief's land. Both these acts required their permission and it had neither been requested nor was it forthcoming. One chief sent out his *kapasu*s who got quite badly beaten up. When the same treatment was meted out to the district messengers it was clear that firmer action was needed. A detachment of the NR police was brought in and with a considerable show of brute force crushed the malcontents and arrested some of the instigators who were put in prison for a while.

This might have been the end of the Lumpa Church but Alice Lenshina simply quietened down and concentrated on preaching and church building while her supporters regrouped. A few years later, as will be seen, a major disaster was to take place.

\* \* \*

There followed several crises of more or less importance on the domestic front. Problems with cooks were very common in Northern Rhodesia; however, we seemed to have had more than our fair share while I was in Kabompo.

Shortly after our arrival I had been affected by tummy trouble but had ignored it for as long as possible because experience showed that the changing quality of water took some time getting used to. However, days stretched into weeks and then to months while Frances seemed to be unaffected. Finally, I got permission to take myself off to the health centre in Salisbury for a checkup. I had hardly got there when my problem righted itself and I was shortly afterwards given a clean bill of health. After some discussion we came to the conclusion that the answer had to lie with the cook. This was not easy to explain because we always ate together; finally a germ of suspicion developed; every mid-morning the cook would come over to the *boma* with a cup of tea.

## Tribal Troubles

We set a watch and when, with the aid of an interpreter we challenged him, he broke down. He had done no harm, he said, but had wanted to win my goodwill, so had been adding a love potion to the tea to ensure my happiness. Needless to say he was replaced.

His successor was a reasonable cook but had other aspirations and, after a few months, he walked out on us with the excuse that Frances would not let him have the keys to the store cupboard (which effectively shut off a potential source of extra income). In his place we had hired John Henry who had come from Angola; he spoke virtually no English and communications were restricted to arm waving.

He had not been with us for long when one of us had occasion to go into the kitchen and, on turning on the tap, was greeted with an outpouring of dirty soap-sudsy water. After careful investigation it appeared that he considered it would save both soap and effort for those responsible for keeping our water tank full if the water left after washing up were returned to the tank for recycling.

On another occasion, he was busy mincing meat for one of his dubious concoctions when Lydia decided to give him a hand, literally by putting it into the mincer. Despite her initial yell he continued to turn the handle for a moment. When her hand was finally extricated and he saw the damage done to her thumb, he gave vent to such a loud series of screams that they put Lydia's completely into the shade. She has recently reminded me that while we were eating cottage pie that evening she asked me how it felt to be a cannibal and eat her finger – my hasty departure for the toilet followed by sounds of retching provided her with some compensation for the pain. This was shortly before school recommenced and it was with great apprehension that we saw her off. In the end the school told us that everything seemed to be healing properly but the scars can still be seen to this day.

Little did I know it but Frances was hatching a plot to get rid of him behind my back and when I next set off on tour she told me that she would not dream of my going without someone to cook for me, so I was to take John Henry. The tour had lasted barely 24 hours before I came rushing back requiring more comfort than the inconvenience of a toilet in the jungle. I went back out the following day but decided that, despite the associated problems, I could not face another meal on tour, so drove home again each night for dinner. By the time the tour had finished I had come to the conclusion that there was not room for both John Henry and myself at the *boma* and as a result we were again searching for a cook.

John Henry as a name was itself remarkable in its normality as the work names the natives adopted were a constant source of wonder. Obviously, they were given names at birth, generally based on rather involved principles depending on the tribe and whether or not they were matrilineal (as were the Bemba and most of the local tribes). When they came to be employed by whites, however, they usually adopted a name of their own devising and with a limited knowledge of English the results could be strange, names that I recall included 'Enema', 'Sheeti Bed' and 'Bedi Poti'.

Once when stationed at Kabompo, I was personally involved in the choice of such a name. There was at the *boma* a very good dispensary assistant who wanted to progress and obtain further qualifications, which entailed studying after work by the light of a hurricane lamp. As a part of his duties he was often called upon to help deliver children and would sometimes accompany the prospective mother to the nearest hospital at Loluma about 20 miles away. Whenever it was practical I would help by providing transport in the vanette, though this was very dependent on my own commitments. This particular time, his own wife was the patient and, not realizing that the event was close at hand, I finished off my work before preparing to leave — I was disconcerted to discover that there in the back of the van was the mother plus the baby and the dispensary assistant who had delivered it. Predictably, the new arrival was christened 'Vanetti'.

\* \* \*

Reference has already been made to the troubles at Kabompo over the election of a nephew of a senior chief during Robin Short's regime. This was a few years before I arrived. The disturbances had resulted in the deportation of a number of the more riotously inclined headmen, all members of the Luchazi tribe.

Over the period 1960–61, these problems came back to haunt me. The peaceful installation of the new chief and his *ngambela* appeared to have given the Luchazi the idea that it was now time

## Tribal Troubles

for the exiles to be returned. Whatever the whys and wherefores of the matter, they suddenly erupted from their villages and instituted a series of protest marches and meetings, first at the new native authority headquarters at Manyinga. The native authority's attempts to cool the situation by reasoning with the protesters were unsuccessful and they then resorted to court action, charging the leaders with unlawful processions and assemblies. These too did not defuse the situation but simply transferred the protests to the Kabompo *boma* where they were taken to go to prison.

At this point the Luchazi decided to bring with them their senior chief — Chiwala. This was a strategic error as I recalled the way in which we had dealt with Chief Nsamba when at Luwingu. Since the days when Robin Short had his problems in Kabompo, communications between the administrative centres had been hugely improved and within a short time my security report and recommendation were on the PC's desk and a very terse message of 'strike at the centre' received in reply.

Within a short time I had Chiwala arrested and arraigned before me. I informed him that he had been suspended as chief for a month and left him under no delusions that the suspension could easily be extended. He was dumbfounded. Suspension of a chief was a singularly humiliating matter, for he lost all his powers and privileges and everyone in his tribe would know it. He also suffered from the loss of his subsidy from the government.

As if by magic all the crowds disappeared and by the following day the *boma* and Manyinga were back to normal. After the month had elapsed the chief was restored to his former status. This was the last we were to hear of the Luchazi during my time at Kabompo.

\* \* \*

Matters indeed became so peaceful that I felt that Frances and I deserved a break and would take a couple of days off to visit Kafue Game Park; it was vast, the largest reserve in NR covering more than 9000 square miles. Once again I can do no better than let Frances tell the story:

We left the *boma* shortly after 6.00 a.m. in the second car (a

## Kaunda's Gaoler

Bedford half tonner). At Manyinga we picked up two members of the native authority who had been detailed off by the chief to accompany us. Our two passengers had brought their cook! He was about thirteen and half. Everyone managed to pile into the back of the truck.

We had lunch and a wash at Kasempa. I had not seen this *boma* before and I felt quite curious as everyone who gets posted there seems to resign at the end of their tour — a gloomy place, sitting in a basin of hills. I can quite understand the resignations. It cannot be compared with our beautiful Kabompo, quite apart from the derelict appearance not only of the *boma* but also of the surrounding countryside. The bush had not been properly burnt early in the year so fires had devastated hundreds of miles of bush, and for the first time I saw villagers whose children really looked near to starving. Their eyes looked as though they had built-in spectacles and their cheeks were really hollow.

It was an extremely hot day, so we delayed our departure from Kasempa till about 4 o'clock. We were held up by a bridge that had collapsed so we didn't arrive at Moshi camp around 6.30 as planned. Thus it was well after dark when we entered the game park and almost at once we spotted a pair of bright eyes just ahead. Cyril slowed down and the owner of the eyes moved slowly to the edge of the road, looking for the entire world like a small slice of dappled sunlight in the dark. We turned so that the headlamps showed us our friendly leopard. The leopard sat down and had a good look at us, running his tongue across his whiskers once or twice to show that he was real. After he had looked us over carefully and noted our many peculiarities for future reference, he unfolded himself and sauntered off as though he were saying 'Oh dear, they let anybody into game parks these days.'

When we arrived at Moshi camp and told the warden, Johnny Uys, that we had seen the leopard he was quite impressed and said that we had been lucky as they are hard to find around here. Moshi is a cluster of about six rondavels on the edge of the Kafue River, on a slight incline and well shaded by trees. Like all the government rest

## Tribal Troubles

houses, beds and bedding were provided and there was a kitchen and cook to prepare one's food.

We extracted our passengers and all the frightful luggage that seems to go with this sort of excursion, cardboard boxes, broken tins and bottles of water. Chikoti, the driver, expressed his intention to sleep for the night in the back of the truck. 'You'd better watch out,' Johnny told him, 'the hippos come up here to play in the early morning.' I don't think that Chikoti believed him.

He had been recruited by Cyril on a recent Copper Belt trip and has the most frightful squint. Naturally, Cyril enquired after his eyesight. 'It's nothing *Bwana*,' said Chikoti, 'I'm a driver Class I, and eye is quite all right — it's only bent!'

One of the most interesting fauna in the park was Johnny. Lean, fair-haired and with bright blue eyes he is apparently the heir to a fortune. But he worships mammals rather than mammon. When he talks of animals and birds he looks and sounds like an evangelist; mention poachers and he becomes an avenging angel. He told us that he is buying himself a plane when he goes on leave shortly so that he can spot them from the air. It appears that the government has generously offered him one [shilling] and three pence [about 7p] a mile allowance when he uses the plane for game patrols. At one time he was a great hunter but he never kills animals now, not even shooting for the pot.

Johnny is a lion enthusiast; he claims to know how they think and to be quite friendly with them. 'I know lions — man — once you've had a lion as a pet, you never want any other animal around the house.'

Sadly, he appeared to have lost sight of the basic premise that wild animals are always wild and therefore unpredictable — and he was always taking what most people would have considered to be unacceptable risks. He later died, the way that he had lived, when he was trampled by an elephant while trying to save the life of a tourist who had ventured too close and then tripped and fallen.

By the time we woke up next morning the gamboling hippo

had returned to the river; it was still only 5.30, but I could not possibly have slept any more for the tooting, cawing, hooting, yelling and shouting of hundreds of weird birds. It was a rerun of the Pulborough nightingales played with a worn out stylus.

Our first 'days' bag, which I have entered in my copy of Frank Ansell's book on mammals, is quite impressive — kudu, sable, puku, roan, hartebeeste, waterbuck, wart hog, oribi, impala, feedback, baboons, crocodiles and hippo. We also saw a couple of gnu, walking along, swinging their hips like a pair of Susie Wongs.

The wart hogs were the comics of the party — and we saw several families. They were very startled by the sight of our truck and broke into a quick trot — first the old tusker, then ma and the kids all in line ahead with their tails up like radio masts.

We got out of the truck and climbed down the bank of the river, hoping to get some good photographs of the hippos; as we approached, huge crocodiles torpedoed into the water without the slightest splash. The hippos, which were having their morning bath, 'came over all shy' as we approached and the water, which a moment before had been swirling around these cavorting monsters, was suddenly flowing tranquilly along with not a thing in sight. After a few moments the hippo came up to have a look. First one pair of pink ears came up, looking like pink heels showing through a worn out pair of grey socks. Finally, they all emerged and we were stared at by about a dozen of the beasts. After a few minutes they lost interest and returned to their games. The game park is well over a thousand feet lower than Kabompo and we found it very hot, so we returned to camp about noon and did not go out again until the evening.

The following day we were up and off very early with the objective of finding buffalo but we were to be disappointed. Apparently they had been upset by the bush fires and were also being chivvied by a lion. According to Johnny, lions are the doctors to buffalo, and they are the only creatures they fear. When lions start to go for the buffalo, they move off to

## Tribal Troubles

fresh feeding grounds, which they would otherwise not bother to do. In the course of the chivvying the feeble ones fall to the lions and so the fitness of the strain is maintained. 'This is one of the instances which show that God put all things on earth for a purpose' announced Johnny in his evangelical mode. I felt like asking whether God also made the poacher, but discretion got the better part.

Some distance away we could see a group of vultures sitting in a clump of trees. As we got nearer we could see more of them, ranged in rows like old men at the Windmill Theatre. Finally we reached a clearing and we could see that they were in fact sitting watching some swampy ground. Chikoti then demonstrated that there was nothing the matter with his eyes and pointed off to the right where he had seen five spotted hyenas, mouths open and tongues hanging out as they watched the vultures. 'Look! *Bwana*' the two Manyinga NA councillors cried as they pointed back to the vultures, '*ya ba*!' (wonderful) they said as five lions rose out of the swamp and walked up the hillside. They were absolutely filthy with black mud up to their shoulders; they all appeared to be wearing Wellington boots. As they moved off into the thicket the hyenas moved down and we all ran over the incline, quite regardless of any danger, we were so excited to see what the lions had been eating. There, was a great hippo carcass, lying on its side in the swamp. The hyena didn't waste much time and were soon dragging bits of meat up the hillside to devour away from the swamp. As we climbed back into the truck, Chikoti, our city type, hugged himself with glee. '*Bwana*,' he said, 'I didn't think animals like that could be real. I thought that they were something you could only see at the cinema!'

One of the amenities of Kabompo was a small boat with a 16-horsepower outboard motor, which was generally used for fishing and other recreational purposes. Over the period that I had been there, no emergency had demanded its use, so needless to say when one did arise there was a considerable amount of confusion. I suppose that at the time of year with the river in spate trouble ought to have been expected but in point of fact it wasn't.

## Kaunda's Gaoler

With the banks flooded and the river running fast it was not a good time to go fishing but two natives had gone out and had managed to capsize their canoe. They had taken refuge on a small island of floating vegetation that had got trapped in some growth where the river had burst its banks. Less than a couple of hundred yards below them were the cascades, the scene that was so pretty at low water was now furiously boiling white water. They screamed for help so loudly that we were able to hear them in the *boma*, way above. The local population congregated on our side of the bank and screamed back advice and encouragement but none of them ventured to go out themselves in a canoe. Obviously if anyone was going to rescue the castaways it was down to John Hart, a new cadet, and me.

We hastily got out the *boma* boat, which was in the right place, but where was the outboard? John organized a search party but it took nearly two hours to find that it had been used for another boat belonging to some fishing enthusiasts, who, since they had not been out for a while had dismounted the engine and put it into storage some way away. We thanked heaven for the brawny district messengers who could always be relied on in an emergency. By the time the motor had been mounted and petrol carried down to the boat night had fallen, we also required a pair of oars as somewhat eccentrically I was not going to take any chances of being caught out in this creek with no means of paddling.

We set off in our small craft by the light of the moon and a powerful torch. Slowly we crossed the river and worked our way towards the marooned fishermen. Those familiar with the operation of small outboards will be well familiar with the problem that we faced, turning into a fast flowing current without stalling the motor. It transpired that John was much better acquainted with outboards than I was; having manoeuvred my way close to the natives I managed to stall the motor. He politely offered to take over the helm while I hastily grabbed a paddle. A few seconds later John had got the engine restarted and brought alongside the natives who stepped gingerly into the boat for the trip back.

\* \* \*

## Tribal Troubles

In the latter part of 1961 there continued to be sporadic troubles around Kabompo, though not on the same scale as in the north. Shortly after his release Kaunda had been invited by the new colonial secretary, Mr Iain Macleod, to attend the Federation Review Conference in London and had taken advantage of the occasion to urge the need for a further conference to review the NR constitution. Macleod put forward a new set of constitutional ideas, which Kaunda and Nkumbula accepted. These were known as the 15:15:15 proposals based on the numbers of members to be elected to the legislature. In essence, the white electors would elect one-third of the members, the African electorate one-third and the final third would be arrived at through combining the electoral registers, a process that would undoubtedly have led to an overall African majority. Welensky was furious and, after Kaunda had returned to NR, succeeded in getting Macleod to change his proposals in a way that would ensure a white majority. As Lord Salisbury remarked, Macleod was 'too clever by three-quarters.' His stated goal was to achieve African majority government while preserving the federation. This goal, however desirable, was never likely to be achieved given the strength of African feeling totally opposed to the federation. This can also be seen from Kaunda's reaction to the Monckton Commission, which had been present in the federation when the first periodic constitutional review originally had been set up. Kaunda said simply that he would not give evidence to the commission because it was pointless to change the constitution of the federation when the latter was unacceptable. It was interesting that, despite this, the commission's conclusion was that the federation 'cannot be maintained in its present form' and should confine itself to overall economic planning, foreign affairs and defence while returning all other matters to the three component countries.

When the news of Macleod's volte-face reached NR, Kaunda denounced it, along with other speakers at UNIP's annual conference at Mulungushi in July, which some 3000 members attended. Kaunda specifically advocated calm and non-violence, but some of his remarks were misinterpreted and, as he mentioned in his book, 'most of the country remained peaceful, but in the Northern Province the long years of frustration spilled over into violence.'

## Kaunda's Gaoler

It was 1959 all over again but this time much worse. Cattle were killed and schools burned down in an orgy of mindless violence, carried out as far as could be ascertained by local UNIP members. Fortunately, however, it was directed at things rather than people and casualties were comparatively few, although there were a number of people killed, including some by the security forces.

UNIP leaders, supported by Kaunda, accused the federal troops and police of deliberately engineering some of the destruction and it seemed quite likely that there may have been a degree of heavy handedness comparable to that which occurred in Nyasaland and was subsequently strongly criticized by Devlin. Nevertheless, since many of the attacks were carried out in broad daylight in front of witnesses (teachers and pupils were ordered out of schools before they were set alight) it was clear enough that the vast majority of the arson attacks were carried out by UNIP members.

Considering that education was the crying need for the young population, it is hard to see how the systematic burning of schools could possibly have benefited the natives. In all probability the arsonists wanted be seen to be opposing the federal government by destroying something, and the schools represented 'a soft target' in modern parlance. Perhaps it may also have been intended as a blow against the authority of the local chief. The attitude of the ANC and UNIP to the chiefs was ambivalent. While the political parties were aware that the chiefs had opposed federation it was felt that they did not do so as positively as they might have done considering their influential position. It was also well recognized that the government encouraged the chiefs to oppose overt political activity in their areas of influence and pandered to them to ensure that they stayed broadly in line. Further, UNIP was certain that independence was going to become a reality in the near future; if and when that independence came they had no wish, and indeed no intention, of sharing power with the traditional leaders.

The difficulties were often referred to as the cha-cha-cha troubles. The apparent use of the name of a popular Latin-American dance arose from the slogans UNIP members shouted. *Kwacha* (the dawn) was their rallying cry and the echo was repeated as 'cha-cha-cha'.

I do not know that I would have described Kabompo as 'peaceful', though I certainly could not have called it 'violent' by

## Tribal Troubles

any stretch of the imagination. The district messengers were in evidence and due attention was given to preserving law and order. Possibly my earlier run-in with the chief of the Luchazi remained a deterrent.

Frances attributed a great deal of the unrest to the fact that, in Kenya, Jomo Kenyatta had been released. She felt that the natives regarded this as an expression of weakness. Certainly, there appeared to be lot of passive resistance in our area. We found that the household staff and gardener, though they turned up for work, spent their time sitting down and doing absolutely nothing, though they did expect to get paid.

Blocking the roads was a popular device in the north; but this was not encountered around Kabompo, although it was well known that the police had instituted night patrols on the road to Balovale.

On one occasion the district messengers arrested a known local troublemaker who had fallen under the influence of UNIP. He was convicted of inciting civil violence and sedition and duly imprisoned in the gaol. There was nothing particularly unusual in this but he had ideas about being a political prisoner and started his own protest in a way not unlike those the IRA prisoners held in the Maze prison in Northern Ireland employed many years later.

I first became aware of his actions during a routine inspection of the gaol one Saturday morning when I was surprised to find him wrapped in his prison blanket rather than wearing the official prison uniform. Initially, I tried to persuade him to wear the proper clothes but this did not work and I had to isolate him from the other prisoners. At the next weekly inspection, there he was again, clad solely in a blanket. We got him dressed and after some consideration I instructed the head warder to fasten a piece of wood to his arm using a handcuff so that he would find it impossible to remove his clothes. By the time of the next inspection everything seemed to have subsided, so he was returned to being with the other prisoners and it passed from my mind.

Several weeks later I received a letter from my PC enclosing a copy of a letter of complaint written in English by the prisoner. Somehow or other it had been smuggled out of the cell and posted to one of the judges of the High Court in Lusaka. The letter began with a highly coloured account of how the DC had tortured him by keeping him alone in a cell with nothing but his latrine bucket. It went on to describe how he had been made to get dressed and had then been handcuffed to one of the roof supports of the prisoners' rest hut in such a way that he could not stand up, sit down or even squat. I called in the prisoner and the head warder and confronted them, demanding to know exactly what had been going on. Rather to my surprise, the head warder acknowledged that he had exceeded his authority, but claimed that it was a legitimate punishment that he was entitled to deliver as the prisoner had behaved badly and in any case was his own nephew. At this point the prisoner's manner changed abruptly and he became very contrite. I recorded the events in the visiting justice's book with the remark that both parties had been given a warning and that there was no need for further action.

One night, one of the *boma* stores was torched. The perpetrator, who was not found, unwittingly did us a service as that particular building, which was used mainly to store worn-out tools, was boarded up and awaiting official destruction. The one person who suffered from this piece of arson was our head clerk who was on leave at the time and, having put all his worldly goods in the store, lost the lot.

The following evening a detachment of the Northern Rhodesia Regiment turned up and the atmosphere changed abruptly. It was as if a switch had been thrown. Coming down to breakfast the following morning we were startled to find cleaning in full swing: the kitchen had been scrubbed out and the stove, which had been completely neglected for weeks, had been cleaned out and polished. Dishcloths were washed and, wonder of wonders, even the mustard pots had been cleaned out and refilled. Vivian remarked that if she had not been home from school and seen the transformation herself, she would not have believed it, thinking instead that it was just one of 'Mum's good stories'.

Our daughters were at an impressionable age and nearly swooned with excitement when the major came around to the house the following evening. They took one look at him and rushed off to change into their newest clothes.

\* \* \*

## Tribal Troubles

Into this uneasy peace, our old friends the Billings of Luwingu days came on a visit. He apparently had his ear to the ground and thoroughly mystified me when he addressed me as St Sebastian. Pointing out that my acquaintance with hagiology was somewhat limited I sought clarification.

It appeared that, a few days before, a man had been arrested on the basis of statements made by someone referred to as a 'delicate source', presumably an undercover police constable (a 'Tif-Tif' as they liked to call themselves). He was subsequently charged with making threats against authority. When questioned, the man acknowledged that he had been found in possession of a bow and three arrows. When asked what he was doing with them, he said, 'This one is to shoot into the DC; this one is to shoot into the DO and this one [indicating the third] is to shoot into the Special Branch officer.' The excuse that he offered in court was that he had received orders from UNIP to act as the local hit man. He was subsequently found guilty and given a sentence of imprisonment.

The disturbances produced tragedies in our area, particularly at Balovale when some troops from the 1st NR Regiment were sent there. They arrived with their transport at the Zambezi River and attempted to cross without an experienced waterman to position the truck on the ferry. It capsized half way across with the loss of about 20 *askari*s. On a subsequent occasion another troop carrier bringing reinforcements overturned while attempting to drive through some sand a few miles from Kabompo. One of the troops was killed and several had fractures. We were very proud when our daughter, Vivian, insisted on going off with the rescue party to help.

Both the Colonial Office and the government of Northern Rhodesia were profoundly shocked by the widespread extent of the troubles and in due course an official version of the events was published, but the circulation was very restricted. The book unhesitatingly laid the blame at the door of UNIP since the vast majority of those arrested and charged with offences were members. By September London had had enough and, despite considerable blustering from Welensky, Macmillan gave instructions for talks to be reopened. Reginald Maudling replaced Macleod as colonial secretary, which also helped matters along. The violence started to subside and, by the time Maudling visited Lusaka in

November, the country was reasonably peaceful again. In February 1962 he announced what he termed an interim constitution with some minor changes to the 15:15:15 plan. Kaunda and Nkumbula accepted this as they both believed that the elections planned for that October would pave the way for an African majority government.

Shortly afterwards we had a big visit in Kabompo. Although we had been warned in advance it was still a great surprise when the paramount chief, Mwata Yamvwa, arrived around midnight with his entourage. The noise and pandemonium was considerable. They came in three large American cars, which included a current Chevrolet Impala, a present from his son-in-law leader of secessionist Katanga, Mr Tshombe. There was also a motorbus, which was painted bright yellow. With such a considerable party, the *mwata* had come with much of the necessary foodstuff for their stay. Needless to say, there was no refrigeration on the bus so all the livestock destined for the pot — goats and chickens — had travelled live. If I live to be a hundred I shall never forget the smell. Altogether there were 30 people, but fortunately we had already made plans for their accommodation.

The chief had arrived to hold an *ndaba* of his local people and when we got up the following morning we had a better opportunity to form an assessment. Actually, he was quite charming according to Frances, and if she said that it must have been true. He was wearing his famous amulet made of human foreskins. It was huge — at least three inches across in some of the thick parts. Monsieur Gomez, his Belgian government adviser who was a mine of information, came as a part of his entourage. For example, we learned that Mwata Yamvwa was a good Methodist and had only one wife, though he did have seven servants.

According to Monsieur Gomez the tragedy in Katanga was entirely of the United Nations' making. It had nothing at all to do with human rights and elections but a great deal indeed to do with the metals mined in Katanga. The parts of the Congo that really descended into chaos after the Belgian government granted independence were for some reason of no interest to the UN.

I had no means of checking whether or not it was true but Monsieur Gomez told us that Mr Dag Hammarskjöld had a personal interest because he was a director of one or more of the

## Tribal Troubles

mining companies involved. Perhaps one should not think ill of the dead.

All round, it was a successful visit. When he left, Mwata Yamvwa presented me with a particularly fine cheetah skin, which was a special mark of appreciation, while Monsieur Gomez gave Lydia a complete set of Katangese stamps, which even at that time did not look as if they would be around for long.

The visit was of considerable practical benefit. It took people's minds off the ongoing problems with UNIP and, at the time, more importantly, it induced the squabbling chiefs to drop their differences so that they could join together to render proper ceremonial greetings.

\* \* \*

To someone who has not lived in Africa, it is hard to appreciate the importance of a chief and it is easy to underestimate the force of tribalism. A legacy of precolonial days, it was given a fresh lease on life by the delegation of many local powers to the native authorities. Being a member of a tribe provided a focus for the members' lives and loyalties, particularly for the rural population, which was the majority. Possibly fans of a football club are the most comparable thing in the UK today. A specific example of the problems of tribalism arose when John Hart (who helped me to rescue the fishermen) came to the assistance of another DC. This time time, however, it ended in tragedy.

Shortly after my departure from Kabompo a native by the name of Fumbello Chilomba, accompanied by a *kapasu*, was brought before Dick Beck, the new DC, for failing to pay a fine levied by the native authority court. Beck sentenced him to prison, which should have ended the matter. However, Fumbello simply turned around and proceeded to walk out of the *boma*. The *kapasu* did nothing and the DC went after the prisoner grabbing him by the arm. Fumbello then produced a knife and stabbed the DC who fell to the ground; John Hart and Mark Sheldrake, a trainee district assistant, rushed to help and were both stabbed for their pains, Mark receiving a punctured lung. Fumbello retreated to his hut and when pursued by one of the district messengers, emerged with a shotgun and shot him, inflicting a fatal wound.

The three officers recovered in due course. Fumbello, who fled the scene was subsequently hunted down and shot while resisting arrest.

It was a dreadful ending to a very trivial affair. Personally, I felt that it had been a great mistake to lay hands on a native — remoteness, as opposed to personal involvement was part of a DC's mystique. I had known Fumbello during my time in Kabompo, for he was a well-known Lunda nationalist. I had, in fact, been urged to detain him but had decided that there was insufficient justification.

\* \* \*

The deaths of a district messenger and Fumbello were a tragic consequence of tribalism. The fundamental root of the problem was that Fumbello, a Lunda, had refused to allow his son to be educated at a Lovale school (where he would also have had difficulty with the language).

To the tribe, the chief embodied its members' consciousness, having in his persona the collective history of the past as well as being the arbiter of the present and leader to the future. Mwata Yamvwa was not just any old chief; he was the paramount chief and wielded enormous power throughout the North Western Province and the Belgian Congo.

Such a major influence can be used for good or bad, for progress and wellbeing for the tribe or for corruption for an individual's benefit. Despite the efforts of subsequent African leaders to promote centralized government after independence, the influence of tribalism continues to be a major factor. Anyone who doubts the truth of this has only to look as recently as the year 2000 to see how the political problems inflaming Zimbabwe have divided the country along tribal lines. The leaders themselves have been quick to play the tribal card whenever it has looked convenient. Post-independence violence in Nigeria, Zaire (Congo) and Rwanda has all been tribal in origin.

With the departure of Mwata Yamvwa, calm returned to the *boma* until the news got around that McTavish had escaped; this caused considerable panic among the ladies on the station since McTavish, as he was known, was a rather large python. Frank Ansell, the provincial game officer, had caught it when it was lying

## Tribal Troubles

torpidly after having eaten a duiker. Safely transferred to a cage it did not seem to mind being confined, as digesting its last meal was going to take a week or two. Besides, it was too fat to escape through the bars. What Frank forgot as he went about his work was that as the duiker got digested McTavish would get slimmer.

Needless to say, when McTavish felt hungry he simply slithered through the bars and presumably returned to the bush as we all searched high and low in an attempt to ensure that he had not taken up residence in one of our houses.

An outstanding practice of the tribes of the North Western Province was their talent for woodcarving. It was one of the first things that came to the attention of visitors because the abutments of many pontoons and bridges had been exquisitely carved with representations of chiefs and chieftainesses in their headdresses, together with *makishi* dancers in their finery. A particularly attractive carving hung on the wall of the DC's office, where it had been put by my predecessor, Roland Hill. I have subsequently heard that someone must have 'liberated' it, for it appeared for sale at a Christie's auction many years later.

At the time of my arrival I was greatly impressed with these figures and had assumed that they had been done by one of the local *fundi* in a rather generous gesture. As time wore on, however, I received some enquiries about whether it might be a good idea for more carving to be done in various places. Despite my raising no objections, nothing ever seemed to happen and slowly the suspicion began to dawn on me that maybe one or more DCs in the past had the imagination to encourage this local art form by a judicious application of the 'road vote' during construction work. I also suspected that the government auditor would not take a particularly enlightened view of the proceedings in the relatively straightened circumstances that surrounded most highway maintenance. It has subsequently been a matter of considerable regret that as a result of my lack of flexibility no further beautification of the district took place during my tour.

When I left Kabompo in 1962, a number of carvings were presented to me and they are still very much cherished. The local schoolmaster, who read a farewell address and then presented the carvings to me with the following words, headed the townsfolk:

## Kaunda's Gaoler

We give you this [an antelope] to remind you there is always meat in the plain.

We give you this [a crocodile] to warn you that there is always danger in the river.

We give you this [birds roosting in a tree] to remind you that there is always meat in the air.

We give you this [a deeply carved spiral cane surmounted with a carving of myself as a bald old man with his arms crossed at the waist] to support you when you are an old man.

Finally we give you this, which needs no explanation.

At which the crowd fell about with laughter and applause as he presented with me with an outsize bullfrog. They were, of course, aware of my imitating a bullfrog and telling the children that I could talk to them.

All of them also knew very well that I had absolutely refused to buy a copy of Kaunda's cane some years before.

Later that same year I was greatly surprised to receive a parcel from Kaunda containing a copy of his newly published book *Zambia Shall Be Free*. Inside the front cover it contained an inscription:

> To Mr C. Greenall:
> Men don't live in the past they live in the present and prepare themselves for the future.
> Best of luck
> Kenneth David Kaunda 16.10.62

# 16
# Ndola Rural (1962–64)

Returning from leave was a particularly rewarding experience because we travelled together via the Suez Canal and had an exciting opportunity to stay briefly in Cairo and to visit the pyramids. After docking in Beira in what was then Mozambique, we proceeded overland with our new car via Salisbury and on to the *boma* for Ndola Rural to where I had been posted.

It took a while to find my way around such a large district. Originally, the *boma* had been located at Mpongwe in the southern part, but had been abandoned as an administrative centre because it was very low lying and prone to flooding in the rainy season. This made transportation and communications rather difficult. The local chiefs, of course, had remained. The new location was vastly superior and also handy for the native authority offices, which were only three miles away. The *boma* and the native authority headquarters were together known as Masaiti, and had acquired the name in a rather unusual fashion. The natives noted that while he was carrying out his work, the surveyor would keep telling his assistant holding the survey staff to move it a little 'this side' then 'that side'. There were indeed 'many sides', which was rendered into the local vernacular as *masaiti*. Nearby was the border of the neighbouring district of Luanshya, home of the Roan Antelope mine.

It was an enjoyable experience meeting George Roche, the DC whom I was to replace as we had both been in the Royal Engineers and could compare notes on our wartime experiences. We discovered that we both had an interest in explosives. I learned with great enthusiasm that he had found them a particularly effective way of dealing with anthills when working on road construction. These mounds constituted a dreadful problem as the earth excavated by ants (or termites) when combined with their excretions set to something comparable to concrete and attempting to shift them with local tools was well-nigh impossible.

The *boma* had only recently been completed and our future house was still under construction. Down the road the native authority was also ensconced in a number of ramshackle buildings. It was a very different environment from the one I had recently left in Manyinga, which had been long established and where everything about the court and treasury was very spruce. The buildings that had been abandoned at Mpongwe had been constructed prior to the days of generous government grants for new buildings.

When I looked at the poor accommodation for the NA and reflected on the independence that was fast approaching, I felt that they were a meagre legacy from the empire and decided that some positive action was needed. The native authorities had been allocated grants but did not seem to have used them. They could usefully be employed to build a fitting accommodation for the various offices and housing needed. The approval of the PC was readily obtained and he whole-heartedly agreed that it was an excellent proposal. A well-known local architect, Dick Hope, was available and we eagerly set about the project, discussing our plans at considerable length with the councillors who were delighted with the idea, and who indeed were authorizing the construction.

Shortly before, Dick had gained local fame for having won a competition with his very original design for the new Cathedral of the Holy Cross in Lusaka. This was just about complete because, although it had been consecrated and the first services held in 1962, the roof was not finally in place until 1963. He used to describe his efforts on behalf of the government as attempts to create long lasting buildings to 'minimal planning standards' from permanent materials. In non-architect speak this appeared to mean functional buildings constructed on a limited budget.

The timing of my proposal could not have been bettered, for although work on the new NA buildings was commenced during the last days of the federation, it was successfully completed during the transitional period after power had been handed to the majority but before the actual arrival of independence.

My task was complicated by the fact that, with impending inde-

## Ndola Rural (1962–64)

pendence, there was going to be more work and we were going to be seriously understaffed despite all the new buildings. As a result, I had to spend a considerable amount of time finding and recruiting younger Africans with a reasonable education to become native authority councillors and to fill other salaried positions.

Other officers also seemed to be getting caught up in what looked suspiciously like the last throes of the old regime. Bryan Anderson, my former DC in Kawambwa, was now very senior and the head of the native courts adviser's department. He had been busy reviewing the powers of the native courts and had recommended some changes, including the creation of native courts of appeal. As a result, some of them were to be regazetted and the newly created Mushili native court of appeal was due to move into one of our new buildings at Masaiti.

There was a sense of urgency in the air and I planned to ensure that appropriate ceremonies marked the inauguration of the new court and native authority headquarters. It was a good opportunity for a little pomp and circumstance and we decided to stage a grand opening in the presence of as many local personages as we could invite, together with the PC and myself in full dress uniform. First, we had to take care of a long overdue ceremony — the presentation of war medals. Although the war had been over for the best part of 20 years, many of the former native members of the armed forces had never received their service medals. This was important because wearing medals would be significant for the opening.

The day came with parades and the police band providing a festive air to the occasion. We were pleasantly surprised that the local UNIP politicos who, having been kept well briefed on affairs, were out in force and seemed delighted with the prestigious new offices and no doubt claimed much of the credit for them with the local populace. They also seemed to be laughing to themselves as if more were going on than met the eye, as indeed turned out to be the case.

When all our guests had departed I was at last free to return to our house a couple of miles away and settle down for a well deserved rest with my feet up. It was not to be, however, for shortly after I had sat down revellers arrived in the street outside and started singing and chanting. When I finally went to see what was going on there was a roar and more singing of what turned out to be a song that had been composed especially for the occasion. The words could not be distinguished, but the refrain came out loud and clear: 'Greenall's here. Greenall's there, the wind of change is everywhere.' It would have been the right day for me to make an entry into local politics.

The Colonial Office in London looked at all the unusual activity and euphemistically referred to it as 'a period of gradual change'.

Attitudes were indeed changing on both sides. I ceased to receive Special Branch reports on visiting UNIP officials. In the past they would have vilified the government but now, on the contrary, they seemed anxious to be friendly and used sometimes to drop in to the office for a chat or would telephone about problems.

On one occasion I was even asked to play football for the local UNIP team and the position of goalkeeper was mentioned. The offer was diplomatically declined while at the same time I tried to promote racial harmony by a casual invitation to my home for a beer. In making the suggestion, my mind went back to the time when, as a naïve young cadet in Mporokoso, I had been visited by the then PC of the Secretariat who had taken me to one side and told me that, no matter how friendly I might become with a local African, I should never contemplate asking one into my house as it would 'scandalize local opinion' and 'make waves'.

I personally received reassurance on a number of occasions that word had gone out from their president that, whatever their personal feelings, there was to be no retaliation or violence after freedom. This principle was strictly adhered to. Such violence as there was was almost exclusively between blacks and it took place in the interim between Kaunda becoming prime minister and the announcement of independence.

Mr Maudling's intentions became clearer when he announced a transitional constitution. This was to be coupled with an interim election to be held at the end of 1962. The election duly took place and resulted in the formation of a partnership between the Federation Party, the ANC and UNIP. Kaunda became the minister of local government and Nkumbula, minister for African education. The partnership was an uneasy one as there was a certain amount of strife between the rank and file members of the ANC and UNIP. Shortly afterwards, the UK bowed to the inevitable and ceased to hope that there was a future for the federation.

## Ndola Rural (1962–64)

Permission was given for Northern Rhodesia to secede. The end was in sight, for the same right had been given to Nyasaland some time before.

With the formation of a three-party government and further revision of the constitution promised, it was apparent to everyone that independence would follow within two or three years at most. To the white colonial officers of the PA it was 'make your mind up time'. Actually, the Colonial Office had become the Commonwealth Office a little while previously, but we still thought of ourselves in that way. Some, such as John Hart who had joined me as a cadet in Kabompo only four years before, had been given every assurance in London that they would be in NR until they retired. Others had shown their hand clearly as pro-federation and a few had managed by bad luck or misfortune to make enemies among the members of UNIP. What was everyone going to do?

\* \* \*

A few had already left, either by taking retirement or seeking a transfer to some part of the world where the Union Jack still flew. The majority were to remain until the first days of independence. Our masters in the Commonwealth Office had placed a choice of two offers on the table. The first was to remain actively employed by them. Pay increases, promotions and other benefits would continue to flow as if nothing had happened. The alternative was to retire with a pension that would be frozen until 55 years of age, but to remain on the books, inactive as it were. One could then be re-employed by the government of Zambia on short-term contracts arranged by the Commonwealth Office, for two years at a time. It was a complicated arrangement but I took it, believing at the time that it would be in my best interests.

It came as a great surprise to us one Sunday afternoon while in the garden admiring Frances's sweetpeas when a Volvo sedan drove up (the only one I ever saw in NR) and out stepped Dr Kaunda, as he preferred to be called by then. He greeted us warmly and with his party officials stayed chatting for about half an hour before leaving for another engagement. It provided me with a welcome opportunity to thank him in person for his book, though of course I had already written my thanks. After his departure, we discussed what appeared to be an unexpected sign of favour and speculated that it could only mean an interesting future when he finally came to power.

With the official end of the federation in 1963 the stage was set for a further change in the constitution, which was extended to provide universal suffrage with around one million Africans on the electoral roll, and it was obvious that UNIP would win the elections that followed in January 1964. To me it was a promising sign that there were whites running on the UNIP ticket, including of course Sir Stewart Gore-Browne. In the end, UNIP won 55 of the 75 seats, leaving the ANC and the National Prosperity Party with ten seats apiece. Kaunda immediately became prime minister.

It is interesting to reflect that the federation was probably the catalyst that did more than anything else to speed the process of independence. By 1959 or earlier it was apparent to all that the predictions the ANC had made in 1953 were correct and that the federation was indeed pursuing white hegemony rather than promoting partnership. Economically, the federation was a success as far as some people were concerned. As forecast right from the start, the Southern Rhodesian members of parliament had used their greater numbers to milk the revenues from the copper mines and spend them on the infrastructure of the south to the benefit of the settlers there. Little or nothing had been done to improve the secondary education of the indigenous population. The British government, which had initially favoured federation, finally recognized that native interests were being deliberately neglected; hence it withdrew the support previously promised.

The federation never offered any public commitment to the principle that as soon as sufficient educated natives were available there would be equal participation in government and the administration. Had this been done, coupled with the ultimate prospect of 'one man one vote', I believe that the ANC and UNIP might well have been persuaded to accept federation. If that had occurred the creation of an independent state of Zambia might well have been delayed by ten to fifteen years and in the interim a locally educated and trained civil service could have come into being. The problems that soon beset the newly emergent state might well have been avoided.

What should have been a good beginning in the run-up to inde-

## Ndola Rural (1962–64)

pendence was marred in several ways. Initially, there was trouble between UNIP and the ANC when it became clear that the proportion of seats won by the latter was negligible.

The friction between the ANC and UNIP was easy to understand in that with one group having broken off from the other there was bound to be a degree of resentment. The white population, which of course included the colonial officers, was not directly involved. Nevertheless, it was a decidedly unnerving experience for residents of the urban districts to wake up each morning to find the dead bodies of Africans in the townships of the mineworkers. Since many of the matters being quarrelled over were secrets from the days of the federation, most of the time no one knew whether the disturbances were entirely over politics or, as more often seemed likely, a case of old grudges being repaid.

Kaunda's new government made considerable efforts to keep the full details of the violence secret, and with a fair degree of success because, although everyone knew what was going on, nobody was actually able to put a figure on the number of fatalities. Eventually, the two parties managed to arrange some sort of truce; again the details were kept secret.

Alice Lenshina's cult re-emerged, still with the belief that its members were invincible. Their suppression involved both the security forces and UNIP supporters and there was a high death toll. It was a disaster of the first magnitude.

After the troubles a few years earlier, the Lumpa Church had appeared to be going on its own sweet way in isolation and this was a significant factor in the forthcoming explosion. In the Northern Province not far from Kasama they had set up enclosed villages protected by palisades.

The creation of new villages was of course quite contrary to what the chiefs permitted. They also insisted that their members remain apolitical, for Christ was the only leader they needed to follow. This meant that members of the Church could not join UNIP and those who were already members were told to tear up their party cards. This was like the proverbial red rag as local UNIP officials took the simplistic view that anyone who was not a member was opposed to them. Indeed, at one time UNIP suggested that the Lumpa Church was in league with the unlikely combination of Welensky and the ANC.

## Kaunda's Gaoler

About the middle of the year a mobile police unit went to investigate one of the villages and, in a brief fracas, Derek Smith, the white inspector, was killed. The governor promptly declared a state of emergency and retribution followed swiftly as Kaunda, ordered the Northern Rhodesia Regiment to the scene. A very one-sided pitched battle ensued, which resulted in the death of numerous villagers. The sect members continued to fight even in the face of obvious defeat, presumably because they had faith in their Church's powers. This massacre was very regrettable, but worse was to follow a few days later when Lenshina's followers attacked another village; this time they had the upper hand and, after a massacre from which few survived, believed that they could celebrate victory.

The affair developed into an orgy of retaliation and retribution that went on for several months. The new government formally banned the Lumpa Church and it was obvious that it intended to act firmly. It was a great relief no longer to be in the Northern Province and actively involved, but from my office in Ndola Rural I watched and heard with horror. The troubles lasted for almost a year until a colleague of mine, Peter Bennett, showing great courage, managed to visit Alice Lenshina's home village having travelled at the dead of night. He succeeded in persuading her to surrender to the authorities, which exiled her to Mumbwa, thus ending a pointless chapter of slaughter and human suffering. The final death toll was officially put at a minimum of 700 killed, but there were many who suggested that the number was far higher. Recently (in 1998) it was reported that some members of the Church tried to sue Dr Kaunda, alleging that he was responsible for the deaths of 10,000 members.

Speaking to me subsequently, Father Etienne said that, based on his understanding of Bemba customs, it had all been predictable. In his book on the subject written several years before the foundation of the Lumpa Church, he devoted a chapter to Bemba prophetesses and Alice Lenshina was by no means the first one to have appeared.

Alice remained in detention until 1975 but was rearrested within a year or so as a result of having started to preach again. She died shortly afterwards.

## Ndola Rural (1962–64)

\* \* \*

Soon thereafter my duties were extended to include acting DC at Luanshya for a short while. I was to cover the interim period between the outgoing incumbent who had gone on leave and the arrival of his replacement, who was not due for a while. The district was clearly very well run and there was an excellent local personal secretary in place, so my presence was rarely required apart from the occasional telephone call.

This was the case until one day a routine circular arrived to say that the prime minister was to tour the Western Province. Normally this would not have caused much concern, for these visits were largely political and provided him with an opportunity to meet the various UNIP officials and organizers at the mines. On this occasion it was just as well that I paid close attention to his itinerary as under Luanshya it said 'lunch with the DC'.

The Roan Antelope mine managers were always happy to lay on a reception, even when it had to take place in the DC's house, and on this occasion they lived up to their reputation for generosity. Dr Kaunda was in particularly good spirits and was delighted when we told him how, during the previous term at her boarding school in Salisbury, Lydia had taken part as one of the speakers in a debate. The subject for discussion was that if Dr Kaunda, Hastings Banda, Sir Roy Welensky and Winston Field (the prime minister of Southern Rhodesia) were in a balloon and there was only one parachute, who was the most deserving? Lydia, speaking on behalf of Dr Kaunda, had won.

The press were also present and had somehow found out about our previous acquaintance in Kabompo. Unwittingly they provided the title for this book when they asked 'How does the Prime Minister feel about having lunch with his former gaoler?' 'I am happy to have this opportunity of meeting an old friend' was his reply, which was quoted in the *Northern News* the following day.

A rather unusual incident took place that surprised me. After Dr Kaunda had been served his meal, he leant back while one of his attendant staff proceeded to taste everything. Heaven knows what can have inspired this medieval approach! At the end of the meal a toast was proposed to the 'future President' and the same man who had done the tasting added 'for life', which prompted Kaunda to say, 'No I would not accept that.' It was an interesting little bit of by-play when one considers the subsequent history of Zambia.

It is hard to say where we would have been without the good offices of the mining companies, but they certainly operated a 'good neighbour policy' towards the surrounding areas and were always willing to help. On one occasion while I was at Masaiti an African trader managed to crash into the narrow wooden span crossing the Kafalufuta River on the road between Mpongwe and Luanshya. He destroyed part of the bridge and deposited himself and the truck in the river. A mine breakdown unit complete with a crane and other equipment had reached the scene and commenced recovery and restoration before news of the incident even reached the *boma*.

The new DC for Luanshya was from New Zealand and he duly arrived. He had not had an opportunity to get kitted up with a uniform and unfortunately he needed one shortly after his arrival. He consulted me and I offered to lend him mine for the occasion; it fitted well enough despite an obvious disparity in our sizes. Uniforms were worn so rarely that mine, which had been made to measure in wartime Britain, lasted for my entire time in Africa. With the uniform, of course, went a sword and I was able to point out that mine was a second-hand one that had saved me quite a lot of money. This clearly impressed him so I went on to repeat the old canard that if one were really short of cash, it would be possible to get by with just the handle since it never had to be drawn. Unfortunately, this did not go down well for he took it seriously and was upset at the notion that the empire and its officers were so hard up that they could not afford proper swords. In the end it was necessary for me to write a letter trying to explain that my remarks had been intended as a joke.

Although part of Ndola Rural, Masaiti was comparatively close to all the local developed centres and could never have been described as an outstation by any but the most imaginative of minds. Nevertheless, this must have been someone's thought, for Mrs Teicher, an American who had come to Northern Rhodesia with her husband to help set up the Oppenheimer College in Lusaka, was advised to visit us as an example of an outstation. Mrs Teicher was a professional sociologist and she had been speaking to some women's associations in the mining area; from there it

## Ndola Rural (1962–64)

was an easy matter to come and stay with us for a few days, supposedly to get a brief exposure to what it was like in the back of beyond. During lunch with her one day a local census enumerator turned up at the front door shaking like a leaf to complain that he could not get on with his work because a lion was following him around. It was a long while before we were able to live down the subsequent speculation that it had all been a put-up job.

On another occasion a young priest from the St Anthony's Mission, looking rather red in the face but with an ear-to-ear grin, turned up in a Land Rover. Sitting beside him was the source of his embarrassment — a young lady wearing little else but a pair of very scanty shorts and a flimsy T-shirt. It transpired that the lady was an aviator and that she had crash-landed her plane in a *dambo* (water meadow) in the wooded part of the district. The rescue plane she had hoped would spot her plight had failed to appear and she had sat shivering in the cockpit through the whole of a chilly night before being rescued by an African who, with great courtesy, had proceeded to transport her to the mission on the crossbar of his bicycle. What was rather unusual about the whole affair was that, although it had been widely circulated in the Ndola urban district that the lady was missing and believed to have crashed, no one had seen fit to tell me in Ndola Rural. The rather lame excuse the police officer in charge of the search gave me was that he had not thought that Ndola Rural was a likely place for someone to come down. The officer concerned and his wife were to become lifelong friends of ours, despite the lapse, which never became public knowledge.

\* \* \*

Senior PC Ewen Thompson, an old friend from Kawambwa days, had arranged a conference for the DCs. Rather at the last moment, he informed the group that the prime minister would be addressing us and some of the participants, believing that UNIP had been the prime mover in the violence a year or two before, planned to give him a frosty reception and grouped themselves around one end of the table. Ewen was clearly concerned about this, for he took me firmly by the arm and going to the head sat down so that Kaunda was on one side of him and I on the other.

## Kaunda's Gaoler

We were aware that, with him as prime minister, it would only be a matter of time before independence. Most of us had privately opposed federation but were equally doubtful about the capacity of the local populace to rule themselves as a nation right away.

Dr Kaunda gave an excellent and interesting speech. Clearly, he was aware of our views but we were the only sizeable body of administrators in the country and he wanted us to be on his side. An open breach could have created far too many problems. He pointed out that we had different 'political' views but that this was not a matter for personal ill will. He also stressed that he and UNIP were very flexible about their policies. As an example, he made the point that during the federal period he had campaigned against the size of the army, which he said was unnecessarily large, and that he continued to hold this view for the time being. Despite this, when independence was achieved the new government would probably increase recruitment and add two more battalions.

On a lighter note he drew attention to his choice of national dress, a 'safari suit', which was to become his trademark and which he made very popular on the world scene. He wore it that day and was rarely seen in anything else subsequently. Of course all the DCs were familiar with it as it was the invariable garb used when on tour.

At the end it was left to Ewen to make a short speech of thanks, which he did with sufficient diplomacy to partially disguise the fact that the audience had listened in silence.

Some months later, on 24 October 1964, independence was officially proclaimed and at midnight the Union Jack was ceremonially hauled down in Lusaka and replaced by the new red, yellow and black on green flag of Zambia, followed by two minutes of silence. I had just left on leave and was in the Indian Ocean standing alone on the upper deck of the Union Castle ship, the *Rhodesia Castle*, listening to the ceremony on a portable radio. For me it was an emotional moment and I was, at least temporarily, left with the feeling of where had the past twenty or so years gone to and had they all been justified? I knew that similar ceremonies were taking place at provincial and district *bomas* in all parts of the country. Later I heard that matters had deviated from the norm at Masaiti where a very old friend, Kosam Kunda was officiating and had said 'and now we will have *ten minutes* of

## Ndola Rural (1962–64)

silence in memory of all the British colonial officers who governed the country until today'. Having been in the clerical service in Kasama when I first went there, Kosam had known us all for a very long time.

It was a particularly pleasant journey home as the captain had previously served with Frances's brother and earlier still under her father, when he was the commodore.

# 17
# Kwacha: Zambian Dawn

Leave seemed unusually short compared with what I had been used to. Although the length of leaves had been reduced they were now more frequent and this was an integral feature of my new contract. On flying back to Lusaka and reporting to the Department of Local Government I learnt of my transfer to a new post as senior local government officer. I was told that we would be going to Kitwe where I would be carrying out a survey of the peri-urban areas of the Copper Belt. My arrival created a minor sensation among my old friends the district messengers — 'We have only had independence for three months and the DC's back.'

A smart new house had been allocated to us and I moved in to start the preparations for Frances's return in a couple of months.

The changeover came and from most people's point of view everything went smoothly at first and work appeared to continue as normal. A very small number of people were told that they were *persona non grata* and must leave promptly. Most of those who were opposed to independence had already left the country. There were also those who had been either particularly vocal in support of the federation or possibly members of the security services such as Special Branch, who, in the eyes of UNIP officials, had gone too far in one way or another. Other contemporaries of mine were working out their contracts prior to departure. A 20-year reunion of the 1944–45 intakes was celebrated, which was combined with a farewell party for those who were leaving.

The new house turned out to be a great success and Frances heartily approved of it. As she said, 'life was enjoyable — with roses in the garden and a television in the lounge what more do I need?' Then, after some discussion with the nuns at her school, we decided that Lydia, who was now 16, should move to a nearby boarding school in Salisbury, which in the event was a happier arrangement.

We were able to enjoy a bucolic interlude when we were asked to act as live-in caretakers for a friend's farm while they were on holiday in Europe. Fortunately, the staff and other friends knew what was involved in looking after a herd of pedigree cattle. Compared with the bush of past years, the developed farmland was quite civilized; nevertheless, wildlife did visit us and on one occasion a hippo was found in a private swimming pool from which it could not climb out. Once when we were driving home as the light was fading we were surprised to see what appeared to be an oversized black angle iron sticking up on one side of the road. Our initial reaction was to think that it was sabotage, but when we approached cautiously we realized that it was in fact a rather large black cobra with its hood fully extended. We stopped and, having wound up the windows, watched it for a while but it took no notice and after a while we drove cautiously around it.

Outside Zambia there was considerable political activity. Mr Tshombe had finally been turned out from Katanga and most of the white inhabitants had decamped to Zambia; Kitwe seemed to be awash with their cars.

In Southern Rhodesia, Ian Smith's government had made the unilateral declaration of independence (UDI), but initially it had little effect, particularly in Kitwe, which was a long way removed. Nevertheless, the president broadcast a message to the people telling them to remain calm and that there would be no problems in Zambia — though purely as a precaution additional troops had been sent to the Falls Bridge. Nevertheless, the general cost of living seemed to be permanently on the increase and, as Frances was quick to observe in one of her letters home, the shopkeepers used UDI as a pretext to put up the prices of all their stock.

The news of Mr Wilson's arrival in Salisbury occasioned a lot of comment. It was generally reported that he had arrived with a huge entourage. This, we were informed, included 90 so-called experts, plus a further 50 detectives and his personal doctor. Frances was very put out over the whole matter when she learned of its size; who did he think he was, she demanded, 'King Harold?' Certainly, no one could make out why they were all there. After all, when the Queen had visited, she had not arrived with a fifth of the number and certainly not a private doctor.

Admittedly, Frances had always favoured the federation and was opposed to premature independence, but despite this bias her observations on the general deterioration of services in Zambia were well founded. The Ridgeway Hotel, one of the best in the country, had within the space of three years begun to look dilapidated. It was not being cleaned properly. Furthermore, people who needed to reserve rooms reported widely that the booking clerks found that the easiest way of keeping their 'in trays' cleared was to tear up and discard any letters that had not been answered when they ceased work for the day. Not all her comments were negative, however; she noted with favour that the city was beginning to acquire much more of a cosmopolitan atmosphere as new blood came to the emerging nation in search of opportunities. The installation of a Canadian broadcaster at the radio station imparted much more life than had gone on before.

My work at Kitwe was complete and the news arrived that for my next posting I would be transferred to Ndola, which of course we knew well. The work I had been doing was hardly what had been anticipated at the time of my arrival in 1943, but this was post-independence Zambia and the changeover had been about as peaceful as one could have hoped. Had I made the right choice when opting to stay on to help the emerging nation with its teething troubles? Only time would tell. It was a great tragedy that independence had come about as abruptly as it had without any kind of transitional arrangements, for a serious effort could have been made to train the nucleus of administrators that Zambia needed. The problems that have beset that country for the past decades can mostly be attributed to the lack of administrative experience on the part of both the new civil servants and their political masters.

# 18
# Ndola: Yet Again

The move duly took place at the end of 1966 and we were presented with a very grand and beautiful house. It had originally belonged to a highly successful businessman and it was sited on a hill with a marvellous view, which on a clear day could extend twenty miles or more. It had a vast living room and dining room together with four bedrooms and a lovely garden. It was furnished with goods from the government store, though in honesty some of them had seen better days. In fact, the only things that at first sight were comfortable were the beds. The reason for this lay sometime in the past when a senior member of the Secretariat in Lusaka had gone visiting various outstations and seen fit to take his secretary (to whom he was not wedded) with him. Apparently, she complained bitterly about the barrack-room beds that were standard government issue at the time and were to be found in all the *boma* guesthouses. Shortly afterwards all the standard issue beds were replaced by exceedingly comfortable ones (he was a *very* senior member of the Secretariat).

No doubt in these days of enlightenment and political correctness it is wrong to cavil at the problems that can ensue from racial integration but it certainly created some difficulties for us and other European officials. Independence had brought total integration and the communal pooling of resources, including the beds in the Public Works Department store and, not to put too fine a point on it, the beds with which we had been supplied were infested with bedbugs. We were covered in shilling-sized red welts. The following day the beds were removed and replaced by fresh ones from the Public Works Department store — to no avail — all we had were a fresh bunch of hungry insects. In due course, the local municipality decontaminated us and proffered the rather unsympathetic comment that the local population was immune to bedbugs. Some years later, nostalgic memories were revived when the press corps attending an international conference in Lusaka, having confronted the same problem, registered their complaints as news headlines.

Towards the middle of 1967 we decided that it would be advisable for Frances to move back to England. She had been unwell for a few months, first with phlebitis and then a bout of jaundice and the prospect of better medical facilities was a big consideration; also she would be there while Vivian finished her studies. I was able to take a short leave to escort her home to the UK. This was a useful device because by taking just three months instead of six the balance was added to my service time. During my stay we bought a house in Farnborough and, while Frances set about getting it to suit her taste, I dashed over to Canada for a short summer visit to my sister in her lakeshore house near Toronto. On returning to England, I bid Frances a fond farewell as I set out for Zambia spouseless.

\* \* \*

Back in Ndola I discovered that my job had changed to that of provincial development officer, roughly equivalent to that of a DC. Job titles had been changed a while before and my immediate superior was Reg Thompson who was the Resident secretary (formerly a post for a PC). My arrival could have been better timed, for I was immediately expected to organize a Western Province Development Conference that was due to take place in Ndola within a week or so of my arrival. The minister of development and his adviser, who were based in Lusaka, were unobtainable because they had gone on a tour to inspect various development projects in the Northern Province.

Fortunately, I was able to familiarize myself with most of the paperwork and especially the financial arrangements for the various projects. There were a great many people involved, for, apart from the civil service side, there would be a full contingent of relevant political 'hangers-on'.

When the conference finally got under way there was little else I could contribute. It rapidly became clear that each project was to be examined in detail and wherever the progress did not satisfy the

## Ndola: Yet Again

politicians' notions, the officer in charge was left in no doubt of their displeasure. I was able to escape at one point when Reg Thompson slipped the minister for the Western Province's charge card into my hand and whispered that I was to take the development minister and his Indian adviser out as his guests for a good lunch at a hotel in Ndola.

It was an interesting meal with me, as an 'Old Cliftonian', exchanging views with what appeared to me to be two rabid communists. The minister's adviser on the other hand appeared to conclude that I had been brainwashed as a child.

The attitudes of the senior Zambian officials varied enormously from one department to the next. Many former colonial officers who had stayed on became very depressed. Some complained of never ending interference in active developments coupled with intense criticism at the slightest problem. While at the other extreme some were totally ignored and their views never sought. Several officers packed in their contracts after a few months, saying that they were not prepared to waste their time coping with the local chaos. One head of department told me that for practical purposes he had been boxed off in an office and was given no work at all. Perhaps my personal experiences were not typical but I quickly discovered that I was always treated with courtesy and everybody appeared to be delighted at my having stayed on after 'freedom'. One appeared to receive as much respect as ever with the big proviso that one did not volunteer suggestions unless they had been asked for in the first place. Unlike others, my views and advice were regularly canvassed although they had to give due weight to the socialist economics that were official policy.

This was forcibly brought home to me when I noticed that a remarkable number of new clinics were being built in the townships and villages. The reason, one of the youth secretaries involved told me, was that whenever treatment was required, even if it only meant taking medicine by mouth, there had to be a clinic with a dispenser to provide each dose, since the patients could not be relied on to follow the instructions. A clear case for a programme of education on health matters I thought, but was told that the policy had been formulated and there could be no criticism.

As far as criticism was concerned it is only fair to point out that the new bureaucrats were very conscious of their positions and tended to treat their subordinates just as badly, indeed maybe worse, than the remaining whites. I was at one conference during the hot season that was also attended by the provincial education officer, an African who was a longstanding member of the civil service. At one point during a lengthy discussion on development matters he rose to his feet and asked if he could be excused because he was feeling unwell. The minister brusquely refused and he resumed his seat, but not for long because minutes later he toppled over into my arms unconscious. The 'suicide month', as it was known, was a particularly trying time of year — I had found that citric acid tablets were a sovereign remedy but far too many people wanted to share them.

Understandably, Zambianization was the name of the game and an African assistant was posted to me to take over my position in due course. This happened rather sooner than I expected because in December 1967 I became assistant to Reg Thompson, the Resident secretary of the Western Province who had given some indication of his own intention to retire shortly for family reasons.

\* \* \*

The new post was demanding as a steady influx of young and generally inexperienced Zambians was being appointed to our office. There was also a steady attrition of personnel as no sooner had they received a minimum of on-the-job training than they were transferred, often being promoted to senior posts. There was also regular loss through marriage.

One of my first tasks on taking up the new job was to try to indoctrinate a young and well-educated Zambian woman into the intricacies of the Provincial Liquor Licensing Board, which she was supposed to manage — a complex job at the best of times. I hardly had time to decide that she was able to cope with the post on her own when she resigned to get married. The explanation was that in finding their way around the Secretariat these ladies had the opportunity to meet young and upcoming politicians from the ranks of the UNIP youth secretaries and so on — these were good catches. From the men's point of view, the Secretariat was a good place to look for comparatively well-educated partners. For

## Ndola: Yet Again

several, their education was rewarded as they relocated, accompanying their husbands to posts in Zambian embassies abroad in places such as Washington.

The laughable consequence was that, on at least a couple of occasions, it was necessary to hire temporary replacements from among the remaining Europeans. This had one immediate advantage because, for a while, I had been very conscious of the existence in old federal government files of papers with emotive titles such as 'Colonial' and 'Native'. Fortunately, our political masters kept out of the offices and the central registry or they might have had some unwelcome surprises. With the aid of our European secretaries I was able to make extensive changes. Copious new files were started and all the offending old ones were wrapped up and packaged away as being solely of archival interest.

One of the functions of the Resident secretary was his participation in all types of ceremonial occasions such as when the president came to address a meeting of his district secretaries. Afterwards, Reg gave me a brief rundown on what had transpired. It appeared that he had opened his address with the traditional criticism of the bad old colonial days and then referred to the DCs by remarking that they acted like little gods in their regions. When he got towards the end of his speech he referred to the DCs again, this time saying, 'they may have acted like little gods but they were hard working little gods, visiting the villages and I want you to be the same, get out of your offices and among our people and work hard the same as they did.' We all felt quite flattered.

# 19
# The Missing Minister: Acting Resident Secretary (1968–69)

One of the inducements I had been offered to stay on was the prospect of enhanced leave, which enabled me to make a brief visit to the UK in the spring of 1968. It was a particularly opportune moment as Vivian was getting married and I was able to perform my parental duties and give the bride away at St Michael's, Chester Square. It was also a welcome chance to be temporarily reunited with Frances and to enjoy the comforts of the lovely home she was making for our future in Orpington.

I returned to the news that Reg Thompson was retiring as Resident secretary and, rather to my astonishment, there was a phone call from Lusaka asking if I would be interested in taking on the appointment. It was an embarrassing moment for me, for although it was a plum job it was not without hazards. The Resident minister, Mr Chanda was not the easiest of men to work with; indeed, as I quickly discovered, the job had been offered to Zambians but none of them would accept it.

At least in part, the problem was that Chanda was a political appointee who had no direct responsibility to the government in Lusaka, which meant that he had power without any concomitant responsibility. Effectively, as one of the few remaining white officers, I would be the obvious target for any brickbats that might fly as a result of his actions. Consequently, I temporized, pointing out that it was probably desirable to Zambianize the post but that I would be willing to take over until a suitable person could be identified. It was also pointed out that the holder of the post should be someone who would be able to take long-term views and it was quite possible that I would not be remaining in Zambia

## The Missing Minister: Acting Resident Secretary (1968–69)

at the conclusion of my current contract, which did not have very long to run.

This was accepted and the day that Reg left I duly moved into his office as acting Resident secretary. As was later to become apparent, the members of the government were watching the goings on over the post with interest and had managed to work out the undercurrents for themselves. After allowing for a decent period to elapse in order to ensure that no one made the obvious connection and choosing a moment when I was on leave after having announced my own retirement, Chanda was removed from the post and kicked upstairs to an overseas embassy. He subsequently came to a sticky end as will be seen shortly.

To my considerable surprise and disappointment no formal announcement of my change in post was gazetted and the anticipated increase in pay did not materialize. This state of affairs continued for several months until, belatedly, the announcement appeared. At the same time I received a formal letter of appointment, my back pay and a gracious congratulatory letter.

I later discovered from friends in the accounts office that a senior personnel officer who disliked the prospect of having to ratify the promotion of a former DC had effectively blocked the appointment for a while. Amazingly, it transpired that his hand had eventually been forced by the fact that while acting as the Resident secretary I had ratified special licences for the weddings of a number of important people. Failure to confirm my appointment would have invalidated several marriages.

Most of the time there were no problems with Mr Chanda, who was a very secretive man and imbued with a strong sense of his own importance. On one occasion, however, this attitude of his looked like getting me into hot water but for a most fortunate interruption.

As has already been mentioned, the surviving members of the Lumpa Church had been pursued and harried by local UNIP officials acting in the name of the Zambian government and quite a large number of the refugees had fled from Zambia into the small section of Zaire that pointed like a finger into Zambia — the 'Congo pedicle', as it was generally known. There they had set up camp, which was a source of discomfort to the Zaire government and was also of acute concern to the Zambian authorities. This was because the camp, which was only about a dozen miles from the frontier, was much too close for comfort to the highly populated Copper Belt. Prosperous towns such as Mufulira, with substantial white and Asian populations, were virtually on the border. This proximity was sufficient justification for the government to continue renewing (every six months) the state of emergency that had been declared shortly before independence.

Secret negotiations had apparently been going on with Zaire to allow the 1st Zambian Regiment to enter Zaire in force with a view to rounding up the refugees and repatriating them to their own villages. These negotiations were so secret that not only was I totally unaware of them but so too was practically everyone else who should have been informed.

The first I heard of it was through a telephone call I received one morning from the assistant commissioner of police, Ndola. He needed to get in touch with my minister as a matter of great urgency. Could I assist him? My answer had to be that I was afraid that the minister's whereabouts were unknown. The fact that I suspected that he was off indulging in what could have been referred to as a 'bit of hanky-panky' seemed irrelevant. At this point the assistant commissioner had no choice but to confide in me. He had just been informed of the planned incursion into Zaire and had been told that buses would bring the refugees out, probably in about 24 hours. The provision of temporary housing for them would be his responsibility and he was anxious to clarify the situation.

In the absence of the minister I felt that there was no choice but to take action and I proceeded to convene the emergency security committees for Ndola and Mufulira. The first of these I chaired in the absence of the minister and made a point of attending the second. We identified a potential site for erecting temporary quarters at Bwana Mukubwa and alerted all the department heads that would need to be involved — fortunately, in the best civil service tradition we decided to take no immediate action. In the meantime I remained in contact with the assistant commissioner. He in turn was in touch with the commissioner who planned to accompany the army units.

On the appointed day the troops entered Zaire under cover of darkness and took up positions around the refugee camp without

## The Missing Minister: Acting Resident Secretary (1968-69)

alerting the occupants. The first that the latter knew of what was going on was when the commissioner, escorted by some troops, entered the camp. Everyone was summoned to get together and he made a statement to the effect that they were not welcome in Zaire anymore and must return to Zambia. There was nothing to be frightened of as the government did not wish to arrest them but merely wanted them to go back to their own home villages. To facilitate this, a fleet of buses was on its way and would arrive shortly. In the meantime, the refugees should pack up their belongings and prepare to be repatriated.

After some discussion, the refugees said that they were agreeable to going home and would get themselves ready for departure the following day. As a result of this peaceful reception the troops stood down. When the commissioner returned the following day with the coaches, however, the camp was deserted; the refugees had all slipped away into the bush during the night, presumably having decided that it was safer to find their own way home. They may have been justified. In any case, apart from a few roads, there was no clearly marked frontier.

Later, when the minister returned, I explained what had happened and the action that I had taken, fully expecting him to be critical since the emergency committees, which I had contacted, were civil servants rather than political appointees. I had also belatedly realized that they were relics of colonial days. He was not amused. 'Mr Greenall', he said, 'this is not the policy.' To be told that something was not policy was about as strong a criticism as could be made. However, he grudgingly accepted my dignified apology. I was just about to explain what problems might ensue if he absented himself without leaving an address, when the door burst open and, with no announcement, in stalked the general who had commanded the operation. He also was not amused, only this time it was with the minister. If there should ever be another operation of this kind, he stated, he would ensure that his headquarters were wherever the minister was and if the minister moved then the headquarters would simply have to move with him. I was saved from any further debate about what I had done and decided that my presence was not needed for the rest of the discussion.

It was of course quite possible that the minister had not known what was planned. Kaunda was always very careful and secretive

## Kaunda's Gaoler

over his relations with the army, retaining the post of minister of defence for himself. He realized full well that whoever controlled the army ultimately controlled the country and he took great care not to let any of his political colleagues interfere with military affairs.

From his point of view it was also very important that the army was as efficient as possible. With Rhodesia next door in the throes of UDI, his position was very difficult. He could not afford to antagonize his much more powerful neighbour but he was not willing to sacrifice his stated principle of self-government for all the black peoples in southern Africa.

It was not long afterwards that Mr Chanda managed to get himself into trouble and the boot was on the other foot when he came to me for advice.

'One party, one Nation!' was the UNIP slogan and for practical purposes it meant a one-party government. Apart from the ANC, which enjoyed solid tribal support in the south of the country, any opponents were obliged to run as Independents.

Political violence during campaigns or simply after a drinking party was nothing new and was the main reason why the mining companies segregated their workers, keeping different tribes in separate compounds.

On this particular occasion UNIP had decided to canvas the Nkana mining township where the mining companies continued to segregate their workforce. The canvassing was carried out in the usual fashion: marching, singing, shouting slogans and demanding that passers-by join them to show solidarity. The marchers had taken with them some of their senior members, including my minister, and were headed for the Lozi compound. Apart from the fact that the Lozi were opposed to UNIP, the tribe were descended from the Matabele and almost unique in Zambia in being proud of preserving their heritage as warriors (the other tribe being the Ngoni). The members of UNIP must have known what risks they were taking but decided to go ahead, possibly relying on the presence of the Resident minister to protect them and which probably would have been true if he had had the forethought to organize a police presence. It happened without warning: one minute the parade was in full swing, singing and shouting and the next they were falling over themselves in a desperate attempt to

## The Missing Minister: Acting Resident Secretary (1968–69)

flee as the enraged Lozi charged them with spears, axes and knobkerries, plus any other weapons that came to hand. Some of the more senior and elderly members of UNIP who could not move quickly enough got knocked to the ground and were quite seriously injured. The minister himself managed to get away unscathed but was subsequently bitterly attacked by members of his own party in parliament over the fracas and his undignified part in it. The questions being asked went on for quite a while and in the end it was decided to debate the incident. One of my most cherished memories is of him asking for my advice on how to handle his defence.

Not long after this event he was promoted to an overseas post, though it did not last for long. He was invited to return to Lusaka for a meeting and was arrested as he stepped off the plane. The only plausible explanation I could think of was that he had been secretly involved with one of the more extreme nationalist groups.

An attempt was made to form a new political grouping — the United National Party — by some dissidents from UNIP led by Mr Mundia, a former commerce minister in Kaunda's government who had been forced to resign his seat in parliament for not voting with the party. Using sporadic inter-party violence as an excuse, the government suppressed the United National Party and proscribed it in a vigorous manner reminiscent of the way Sir Arthur Benson had proscribed the Zambia African National Congress. Also, in a similar manner, Mr Mundia and the leaders of the group were placed in restrictive custody far from the centres of power. Mr Kaunda had learned the lessons well from his own experiences — Sir Arthur, long since retired, must have smiled to himself when he heard the news.

# 20
# Finale

The initial period of independence was a very tricky one for Kaunda to cope with. At the time of the federation the Zambian economy had been progressively intertwined with that of Southern Rhodesia and undoing these relationships was not always easy. Kaunda had to follow a very delicate path, a policy of disengagement, trying to reduce any dependence slowly but with the ultimate objective of dispensing with it. It was important for Zambia to develop its own resources, for example sugar plantations, tourism and whatever other industries were practical. It also needed an infrastructure that would give it access for exports and imports that was not reliant on Southern Rhodesia or the rather tenuous rail link through Zaire to the Atlantic. The construction of the Tanzam railroad, which took trains to my old stamping ground in Kasama, was a part of this. There is no doubt that the cost of this policy to Zambia was horrendous for a comparatively poor country. Nevertheless, this enforced modernization has paid off subsequently.

The most delicate part of Kaunda's problem was the relationship with the 'freedom fighters' who regularly crossed into Zambia. He met this by allowing them refugee status and also permitting them to have offices in Lusaka. He refused, however, to allow them training facilities and staging areas and hoped that this would inhibit any thoughts of 'hot pursuit' or pre-emptive strikes by the Rhodesian army. Nevertheless, he wanted the Zambian army to be capable of protecting the country from such action and on more than one occasion went to the British government with requests for modern equipment such as fighters and missiles.

President Kaunda was unsparing of himself in travelling around the country to see that government policies were being implemented and to look after his political supporters in UNIP.

## Finale

The one and only time I actually attended a UNIP political rally was quite an eye opener. It was to be addressed by the president and the guests of honour were two visiting Labour MPs from London whom I was asked to escort. The rally took place in Kitwe and the local party officials had booked the football ground as the only place large enough for the anticipated turnout. The venue was quite appropriate as the thousands of supporters who arrived were every bit as excited and noisy as any football crowd. The organizers were always able to ensure large numbers on these occasions as they were out at first light with bunches of activists sweeping up any and everyone and insisting that they attend.

Not being present was a serious business, for the UNIP officials clearly took the view that anyone who did not support a rally was identified as anti-UNIP. On one occasion while we were absent, our marvellous houseboy, Edward Banda, who was with us off and on for our last 12 years, was found in an empty compound when the word had gone out to go to a rally. He told me afterwards that he believed that the only thing that saved him from a serious beating was that he was able to blow the police whistle that Frances had when she was with the immigration department. At some time or other she had passed it over to him for protection. Its distinctive piercing note was easily recognizable and clearly the mob believed he was with the police and summoning help, for they made off at once.

With the noise level from the crowd at maximum pitch, the only thing that could be done was to turn the loudspeakers to their highest volume, which merely served to double the cacophony of sound. Slogans, such as 'ONE ZAMBIA! ONE NATION!' were being screamed by all and sundry. We appeared to be the only whites present and had a small enclosure to ourselves not far from a raised platform, which was the speakers' rostrum. This in turn was next to another enclosure for the party officials and the broadcasting equipment.

My companions were naturally interested in all the goings-on and maintained a steady barrage of questions that I did my best to answer. They were particularly intrigued by a bunch of well-dressed and well-behaved schoolboys who were obviously part of the UNIP movement's youth brigade.

The arrival of the president was greeted by the playing of the national anthem and the proceedings got under way as various dignitaries were introduced. The MPs were ushered onto the rostrum and introduced by the UNIP master of ceremonies in a breathless hush. 'These are our friends! These are our friends in the British government.' Finally, they were returned to me in the enclosure and after a formal introduction the president, who was an excellent speaker, made an eloquent speech, his mission upbringing clearly showing in the style of his delivery. He started by talking of party policy and then moved on to our friends' (the British MPs') humanism — a concept that Kaunda had taken to himself. Then he spoke of the Christian approach and his abhorrence of violence, hatred and racism. He talked in short sentences and paused often for the carefully controlled 'spontaneous' applause, which was deafening. Having worked up the crowd to a fever pitch, Kaunda proceeded to move on to a 'calm down' phase, reminding his audience of accidents, sometimes fatal, at previous rallies and pleading with everyone present to leave quietly and peacefully. He did not want to hear later that drunkenness and fights had marred the evening. By the time he finished one could have heard a pin drop.

All should have been well and indeed everyone started to leave in an orderly fashion. Unfortunately, the problem was that everyone wanted to get out at the same time and started to move at once. The MPs and I were swept along like swimmers trying to fight a powerful current. I grabbed one of the lady MPs by the wrist and held on for grim death as I had visions of her tripping and disappearing under the feet of the crowd. Finally, we were able to escape and make our way to the Kitwe Hilton for lunch followed by the routine motorcade (locally known as 'the thriller ride') back to the airport.

One more formal presidential visit was to take place before I finally handed over to Philimon Lyombe the Resident secretary designate shortly before my own departure. It was the occasion when the freedom of Ndola was conferred on President Nyerere of Tanzania. He was a very interesting man who had come to power a few years before Kaunda, having pursued a not dissimilar path. They were travelling together from Lusaka in the president's plane, but needless to say the diplomatic corps had turned out in force and arrived earlier.

## Finale

One of the key members of my staff was the protocol officer, a debonair young man with exquisite manners and apparently just the right amount of savoir-faire. Suddenly he appeared, breathless and agitated — 'Their Excellencies' were refusing to move into their 'line-up' and the president's plane was about to land. Taking the view that my capacity was to advise I told him not to worry, but to go back and try again and all would be well. Nothing happened and he became progressively more panic-stricken as the plane was taxiing down the runway. At this point a minion arrived from the minister with a curt instruction, 'Mr Greenall, you will attend to the problem yourself — at once'. Suddenly I felt a chill and began to sympathize with the hapless protocol officer. I had no choice but to try my own luck. Fortunately, I had the loudspeaker microphone at hand and a couple of sharp raps on it were greeted with gratifying silence. 'Would the gentlemen of the diplomatic corps please take their places as the president's plane has landed.' The US ambassador was the leader of the group, a most imposing figure well over six-foot tall; he looked round and glared at me, I smiled back with an inward prayer; there was a perceptible moment of hesitation, he smiled back faintly, turned and they all moved off.

President Nyerere gave a very amusing speech of thanks. He could not understand why the honour had been given to him, he could not see it, he could not take it away and most distressingly he could not sell it. He had his distinguished audience in fits.

When he departed, as was the custom, I was the last in line at the airport to shake hands, and was introduced by President Kaunda. Nyerere looked at me as if I were a prize specimen from a zoo: 'The Resident Secretary! Good heavens Kenneth! Have you still got one?' Then, turning to me, he gave the traditional greeting '*Mutende bwana shalenipo*' (Peace, Master, stay well) and clapped his hands just as if he were a village headman greeting the touring DC. We had a moment of laughter together before he boarded the plane.

\* \* \*

It was now almost five years since independence and, with the first throes of self-government accomplished, the Zambian government suddenly seemed to think that the time had arrived to complete the Zambianization of the administration. An offer was made for what they termed 'abolition' — presumably with thoughts of the abolition of the remaining posts still occupied by old-time white hands. The terms were quite generous and, since I had already been in receipt of similar munificence from the Colonial Office plus the inducements offered by the new rulers to stay, I deemed it was time to accept, wind up my affairs and rejoin my family. I decided to take some accumulated leave and spend Christmas with the family and start planning for a new future.

It was a short break and in January I was back in Ndola to find that changes had occurred. Peter Chanda had been replaced and a new man appointed as the Resident minister. Mr Banda was a very experienced member of the cabinet from Lusaka who at first impression appeared more than able to take care of the post. From a purely practical point of view the fact that he was a member of the cabinet meant that he was both accountable and at the same time had leverage in Lusaka. My post had ceased to exist and I was to be replaced by a permanent secretary who would take over from me. Fortunately, I knew the new man who had first worked for me as a cadet in Ndola Rural in the days before independence; so the transfer was a happy one and we were able to joke that as I had helped him into the service, he was now helping me to leave!

I was not the only one leaving and the remaining weeks went by in a veritable orgy of farewell parties. It seemed as if only a short time had passed before I was boarding the plane that was to take me from Zambia for the last time. I had lived there for the previous 25 years and it had been my life. With 15 years to go before reaching normal retirement age I was going to have to start looking for a new career. But first I was off to Paris to join Frances for a few days of celebration together.

*Kashimi kapela*

# Appendix 1
# Letter from the War Office, 23 March 1940

The War Office
Hobart Place
Grosvenor Place
S.W.1

7/Mob./3183. (Mob.2.)

Sir,

I am commanded by the Army Council to refer to negotiations which have taken place with regard to the supply of candidates for the Colonial Service during the war, and to say that the Council accept the principle that such men may be released from the Army in order to maintain the essential high standard of colonial Administration.

The Council appreciate that in time of war such candidates may feel reluctant to leave their comrades for what may appear to be a less hazardous life. I am to say therefore that candidates may be shown this letter in which the Army Council commands me to say that they consider that any officer or man that accepts an appointment in the Colonial Service may be sure that he does so with the best wishes of the Army Council behind him. They appreciate that in his new capacity he may well help the Empire more than he could as a soldier.

Instructions are being issued that leave will be granted to

candidates to appear at such interviews as are required by the Colonial Office, though the cost of travelling cannot be borne by Army Funds. Arrangements will also be made for Commanding officers to make reports on the character of any candidate for whom it is requested.

It is suggested that a copy of this letter should accompany your notice to a candidate and that he should be instructed to show both documents to his Commanding Officer.

I am,<br>
Sir,<br>
Your obedient Servant,

(sgd) P. J. Grigg.
The Under Secretary of State,
Colonial Office,
London, S.W.1.

# Appendix 2
# A Brief History of Zambia
# (Northern Rhodesia)

The history of the years immediately preceding independence has been interwoven with my own personal memories as far as it has been practical. However, a brief synopsis of the history of the country is included.

In the early part of the nineteenth century, what is now Zambia was occupied by a great number of tribes, all ethnically Bantu apart from a small number of Bushmen in the extreme southwest. It is likely that these tribes had arrived from the north and northwest as a series of waves over many centuries. This surge to the south had ceased, leaving the Lozi in the west, the Bemba and Lunda to the north and Chewa to the east as the main tribes. Then, in the middle of that century, catalysed by the wars of the Zulus under King Chaka, the Kalolo and Ngoni tribes of Zulu origin began to move back northwards. The Kalolo occupied the land that became known as Barotseland to the southeast while the Ngoni displaced the unfortunate Chewa. At that point in time none of the area had been colonized and contact with the outside world was confined to ivory bartered with the Portuguese and South Africa, together with the slave trade with Arabs via what was to become Nyasaland.

Lack of interest at that time on the part of European colonizers can be attributed to the fact that the area had not been explored and there were no known natural resources worth exploiting apart from human beings as slaves. The local population had produced small amounts of copper for centuries, but the existence of large deposits was not discovered until the early 1920s. The area had been visited by Portuguese traders, Arab slavers and, most notably by David Livingstone, whose repugnance at the brutal practices of the Arab-organized slave trade were to act as the catalyst or pretext (depending on one's point of view) for the subsequent occupation of the territory.

By the end of the nineteenth century the Bemba, along with the Lozi, Lunda, Kalolo and Ngoni, were the dominant tribes in the sense of being militant, intermittently fighting and raiding other tribes' lands. What was true then and remained true over the whole of the British colonial period was that all the tribes basically distrusted and disliked each other. The extent of the impoverished state of the area can be seen from the fact that at the beginning of the 1900s the population was estimated to be as few as one million in an area six times the size of England.

The British government of the time was suffering from a bout of what might have been called 'colonial indigestion' and was not particularly interested in acquiring new possessions that were likely to be a drain on British taxpayers' pockets. They had also provided a subsidy in the past for one of Livingstone's expeditions with a view to looking for trading opportunities and had seen no return on their investment. Cecil Rhodes on the other hand was actively pursuing his dream of a railroad travelling through a continuous strip of British possessions from Egypt to the Cape Colony. He perceived the area that was to become Northern and Southern Rhodesia as an essential link. Although Rhodes was already fabulously wealthy from his control of De Beers he thought that the area had vast undiscovered mineral wealth. The romantic in him also believed that somewhere to the north lay the mines of the fabled jewels of Ophir. The slave trade provided a ready excuse and, armed with a charter for the formation of the British South Africa Company (BSAC), he proceeded to annex the territory in 1889.

Soldiers accompanied by settlers moved north and crushed the Matabele who offered the only initial opposition. Crossing the Zambezi and moving further north the annexation was peaceful, as the tribes were easily convinced that they needed protection. The Ngoni under Mpezeni and the Lunda under Mwata Kasembe

## Appendix 2

were the only tribes that offered any resistance and this was rapidly brushed aside by military force. What was to become Northern Rhodesia took its shape from a hotchpotch of agreements between the BSAC and the tribal chieftains. The boundaries were later formalized and agreed between Great Britain and the other potentially interested powers (Belgium, Portugal and Germany). The agreements reached with the African chiefs promised, in exchange for the mineral rights, protection, an annual subsidy and education — the latter being conveniently ignored and devolved to the missionaries.

Rhodes did not find the riches he had hoped, the native tribes lived a subsistence economy, producing just sufficient food for their day-to-day needs. Further north in what was known as Nyasaland there developed a dynamic farming population and the same was also true of Southern Rhodesia. Both of these attracted substantial white populations and behind them came more education and greater prosperity. Until the discovery of vast deposits of copper and cobalt around Ndola in 1923, Northern Rhodesia remained largely backward and undeveloped through lack of funds; indeed one comparison made in the *Northern Rhodesia Record* compares the state of the territory at the end of the nineteenth century with that of Britain at the time of the Roman occupation. These factors were to be of major importance in determining the future of the country.

During the entire time that it was responsible for the territory, the BSAC never once made sufficient profit to pay a dividend to its shareholders. In order to pay for the administration it fell back on raising money through a hut tax that was very unpopular. The money raised in this way also helped to finance the construction of a rail link to the Katanga mining area in the Congo. The imposition of the hut tax also ensured that the male population had to seek gainful employment even if it entailed leaving their own tribal area (as many did). White settlers were not exempted from taxation, and income tax was introduced around 1920.

During the First World War large numbers of the native population were pressed into service, some 50,000 as porters and around 3500 as *askari*s for the military during the fighting over the German East African colonies. Many reputedly died during the conflict, further depleting a country already lacking in human resources. Even by African standards the land was relatively unoccupied.

The transition from a fiefdom of the BSAC to a crown protectorate came in 1924 as the company came to realize that there was little or no profit in the region. Sensibly, it did retain the mineral rights that were subsequently to yield a fortune.

With the takeover it became apparent that the Colonial Office was now responsible for the local population. It was important to ensure that there was sufficient food and protection, while education needed to be provided. The Colonial Office had at that time a fundamental policy that development should be funded from local sources, which were few and far between until the copper revenues boomed during the Second World War. It remained a poor country and this led to the decision to impose a native poll tax that replaced the hated hut tax.

This policy was finally changed in 1947 when a comprehensive development plan was adopted and major contributions were received from the Colonial Development and Welfare Fund that had been established by the British government. This forward-looking concept was, however, short lived, as the development plan was soon modified to take account of the views of the elected white members of the Legislative Council. The government policy on education was aimed at providing widespread elementary rather than secondary education though it continued to rely heavily on the missionaries to provide the former.

Repeated statements by members of the British government over the years indicated that it was their intention to devolve some form of home rule as soon as it was deemed that sufficient progress had been made. Shortly after the war, the then secretary of state for the colonies, Mr Griffiths said: 'The central principal of our colonial policy is to help the people forward towards responsible democratic self-government.' It was also clearly set out on a number of occasions that the interest of the indigenous peoples was paramount. Whether or not these considerations were taken seriously by senior colonial officials in London in the years leading to self-government is open to question in the light of their actions.

The nationalist movements first came into existence in the early 1940s through the creation of a number of welfare associations.

## Appendix 2

These became affiliated some years later and shortly afterwards under Harry Nkumbula became the African National Congress (ANC). One of Nkumbula's early colleagues was Kenneth David Kaunda, a well-known and highly educated teacher.

Apartheid as it was known and practised in South Africa never reached Northern Rhodesia. Although there was no formal legal status for discrimination as such, in practice it was widespread, though there were several areas (such as the mining unions) where in theory it did not exist.

Proposals to unite Southern and Northern Rhodesia first cropped up and were demanded at the Victoria Falls Conference in 1949 but were ignored by the UK. Nevertheless, the government in London was worried about risks of the northward spread of white South African nationalism and, despite considerable reservations, finally permitted Northern Rhodesia to join with Nyasaland and Southern Rhodesia to create the Central African Federation in 1953. The furtherance of the wellbeing of the native population was put forward as an excuse, despite the fact that the white settlers privately intended federation to prevent just that. Both the chiefs and the ANC universally condemned it and campaigned vigorously against it from the time the idea was first mooted in 1949.

Without having the support of the native population, few of whom had the right to vote, it was doomed from the outset. In retrospect federation probably speeded up independence since it acted as the essential catalyst that the nationalist movements lacked.

Under Sir Godfrey Huggins, the first Premier of the federation, much of the copper revenues of Northern Rhodesia were pumped into the infrastructure of Southern Rhodesia with its large population of white settlers, while the protectorate remained largely neglected. Sir Godfrey was created the first Viscount Malvern in 1955 and retired shortly afterwards following a remarkable 33 years as prime minister first of Southern Rhodesia and then of the federation. His policies were continued under Sir Roy Welensky when he became premier in 1956.

The ANC under Nkumbula appeared to lose its certain sense of direction in the late 1950s. Indeed, it was suspected among some white officials that the security forces had suborned one of its senior members. In any case Kaunda and other members of the ANC became dissatisfied with the lack of positive progress and left to form their own party, the Zambia African Congress, which very shortly afterwards was proscribed by the governor. Kaunda was first banished and then imprisoned. After his release at the beginning of 1960, Kaunda was elected the president of the United National Independence Party (UNIP), which had been formed during his imprisonment by Mainza Chona another disillusioned member of the ANC

By 1959 the British government had realized that the federation was not proceeding down lines that were in the best interests of the indigenous population and the colonial secretary, Iain Macleod, put forward plans to amend the constitution accordingly. However, he rapidly backed down as a result of threats from Welensky to declare independence. Following the announcement of the changes, UNIP started a campaign of civil disobedience and, shortly afterwards, Macleod was replaced by Reginald Maudling. A year later an interim new constitution was introduced, which enfranchized large numbers of the native population. The subsequent elections in 1963 led to the formation of a coalition between the ANC and UNIP. The dissolution of the federation and further elections at the start of 1964 gave UNIP a landslide victory and Northern Rhodesia its first black prime minister. That same October Zambia became independent with Kaunda as its president.

# Appendix 3
# A Typical District Messenger Report (Reproduced as Received)

**Report by senior Messenger Smart Table on conversation between Mr Baragwanath and Kapopo on his recent trip**

The first European who came to explore the mines was Mundungano; the second was Shabani. They reached Kapopo village, Chief Ndubeni. The village was known as Lubwakala Lesa and it was a chief's village. These Europeans came from Mumbwa; Mumbwa was called Kasabasaba before. Kapopo came to settle in Chief Lesa's area long ago. He died many years ago and is now succeeded by Sokoloko Kapapo. This man accompanied two Europeans mentioned above along with six others along the Kafue River. The names of these six men are: Ngombo, Mukatuka, Bengama, Shiyengama, Mumbelunga and Mulumbo.

None of them is still alive. They explored Kafue up to its source. They came back to Kapopo Village. They used to go to Kipushi, in the Congo, and back to Kapopo Village. It took them three weeks for the single journey on foot. From the Congo they put pegs in the Lima tribal area. The *bwanas* had one boat made from planks and two dugout canoes. On one occasion while travelling along the Kafue River water rose up suddenly and the swirling waters swept the canoe in which the *bwanas* were travelling down the stream. Life and property was saved. *Bwana* Shabani was ill, a letter was sent to *Bwana* John who was at Bilima, which is now Mpongwe asking him to supply some drugs. There were no drugs available and Kapopo treated the *bwana* by providing him with roots that were soaked in the water. *Bwana* Mudungani had six men, mentioned above, on the journey to Nkana. It took them two days from Kapopo Village. Before Nkana mine was known as Wusakili. *Bwana* Shabani was taken to Bwana Mkubwa in a hammock for treatment. *Bwana* Mundugani offered Kapopo one blanket and five pieces of clothes for the services they rendered and five others were offered three pieces of clothes at Bwana Mkubwa. These men returned to Kapopo Village.

Another European came from Mkushi. His name was Selesele alias John Chirupula. He named all of the existing mines on the Copper Belt.

One unknown European brought horses but they all died and the owner went back where he came from.

*Bwana* Mayosi and later Fisher Muchemunto, Kapalapala, Damson came from Mkushi for prospecting purposes.

Names of the mines as they were called before: Bwana Mkubwa, Chipili, Nkana, Wusakili, Mumbwa, Kasabasaba.

Bwana Shabani shot a hippo but Kapopo never remembered his name when he was interviewed recently.

This was the information that I got from Kapopo, 26 July 1958.

Smart Table

# Appendix 4
# (Letter Received from a Rhodesian Soldier in 1945 – Spelling and Grammar Unchanged)

G. M. Lovely Mutende Steamford.
The DC, Kawambwa
11 January 1945

Dear Sir,
I am respectfully writing to you this few lines of words that I may express my wishes to you sir and I am a soldier of R.A.R. and during for the time being I was a bandsman at Nkana Mine. As it goes by now I am for certain a soldier and I must firstly try to ask you as you are the mother of all the africans in that district, this I trust shall please you, sir.

Here let me say that, I have to report to you sir, that I have got my Uncle's daughter who is a school girl at Chimpempe Mission, and I want to report to you that will you please try with the almight straingth of the boma as you are our mother that you send the girl straight to Salisbury City. I am for certain expecting to come and meet her at Livingstone and while coming I want her to be leaded, by her brother Dickson Katuna. Here are the names of the men who I want you to ask an bout this girl. Dickson Katuna is the headsman and Mumporokoso is her father lives in Kabanda's chief Village, if you Sir send this girl to Salisbury I shall be thanking you always. And for certain the girl by herself is called Violet Mwansa Mumporokoso she is at the Chimpempe Mission schooling.

Sir, if you want to ask the two men written on here, that do you know Lovely Mutende? They will all try to tell you Sir and I shall now hear from you.

Sir, that girl, I ant to come here, her father is my necel uncle, and even herself knows me too. But she is not my wife yet. So I want her to be with me if you only asks the parents for certain I shall receive her and while coming to you shall give her some notice and advise her that the boy shall met you to Livingstone.

The reason I send this letter to you sir it is because I am a soldier and also a bandsman, therefore we are not allowed to come there as some of us are desating. So by the Commanding officers Law is to limit the R.A.R. band, till the war ends. So I cant help it to marry a girl of other lands is to me my pity.

I have allowed to come and meet her to Livingstone, but firstly I shall hear from you sir. Will you please try with your best to send me that girl.

If the parents disagree try to tell them that this boy, is not your nephew or not, they all know my parents too. My mother is Namatende-Lucy my father is Shimatende and myself is Lovely Mutende.

Sir, the girl I want is Violet Mwansa.

Will you also try to help them in their way upto Livingstone; I shall pay it back for certain in two months time.

I am crying to you that you may allow me to consider myself always and that we may alike other countries.

Respectfully your obident servent

Lovely Mutende Steamford.


Sir,

I am begging you that this girl may arrive here to stay with me. The law refuses we bandsmen to go on leave unless weekend leave as you know sir that I cannot reach home it is too far. So if you try to call this only two men to your office with a girl too and ask them if they have loved me for certain they shall hear you.

We are not moving from the city except to Union — and

## Appendix 4

perhaps you have heard that the R.A.R. band was in East Africa that means that when I reach Lusaka I was crying to the bandmaster and I wanted to desat.

So if you help that girl to come here, sir, sir I am swelling the almighty in heaven that I shall be thanking you for ever till my end of the life. Because I do not know what to do and am in service so anything to me am very difficult indeed. The money which they shall pay the train I shall return it back within two months time.

And I am ready at any time to receive her in Livingstone.

I have got a very wonderful displen and methidacel in all my duties. So I can keep the wife.

I don't want to marry another nations or tribe.

Please if I have made a mistake in you sir – I beg to tell me as you are our helpmeat and mother cheerful again.

There is no power more than the DC unless anything to be denied by you. That is all sir.

Respectfully etc.

Excuse me sir

That little missive may the DC give it to this two men on your presence. It is written in Chibemba. I enclose here with the letter of this two men.

# Further Reading and Background Material

Colin Baker *State of Emergency: Crisis in Central Africa, Nyasaland 1959–1960* (London: Tauris Academic Studies, 1997)
W. V. Brelsford *The Tribes of Northern Rhodesia* (Lusaka: The Government Printer, 1956)
Terence D. Carter *The Northern Rhodesia Record* (Worthing: Privately published by David Bell, 1992)
Professor Debenham *Study of an African Swamp* (London: HMSO)
Father Etienne *Customs of the Bemba* (unpublished private papers)
John Hudson *A Time to Mourn* (Lusaka: Bookwood Publishers, 1999)
Kenneth Kaunda *Zambia Shall be Free* (London: Heinemann, 1962)
Christina Lamb *The Africa House* (London: Viking, 1999)
*Northern Rhodesia Police Association Newsletter*
Robin Short *African Sunset* (London: Johnson, 1973)
Peter Snelson *To Independence and Beyond* (London: Radcliffe Press, 1993)
*The Northern Rhodesia Journal* 1955–64 (Lusaka: The Government Printer)
Tim Wright *The History of the Northern Rhodesia Police* (Bristol: BECM Press, 2001)

# Index

1st Zambian Regiment, 190

Abercorn, 7, 16, 26
Abyssinia, 30
Accountant General's Department, 12, 77
Accra, 132
African Affairs Board, 100
African District Council, 54–5
African Lakes Corporation, 59
African Mineworkers' Union, 109, 110
African National Congress (ANC), 31, 55, 99, 101–3, 108, 116, 130, 132–3, 142, 146, 158, 170, 172–3, 192, 205–6
African Provincial Council, 55
African Representative Council, 103–4
African Staff Association, 110
African Welfare Association, 55
Agriculture, Department of, 71, 115, 119
All African Peoples' Conference, 132

Anderson, Florence and Bryan, 46, 54, 169
Anglo–Belgian Border Commission, 55
Angola, 116, 149
Ansell, Frank, 154, 164
Army Council, 1, 199
Atlantic Ocean, 194
Attlee, Clement, 100

Balovale, 113, 116, 120, 134, 140–1, 144, 159, 161
Banda, Edward, 195
Banda, Hastings, 133, 135, 175, 198
Bangweulu, Lake, 51, 59, 78, 80, 82–3, 89, 93
Barotseland, 111, 201
Beachy Head, 5
*Beans*, 78
Beck, Dick, 163
Beira, 167
Belfast, 7
Belgium, 203
Bellington, 46
Bemba, 14, 17, 19, 22–5, 30,

39, 42, 46, 48–9, 64, 69, 73–4, 76, 80, 87, 90, 115, 122, 127, 138, 147, 150, 174, 201–2
Bennett, Peter, 174
Benson, Sir Arthur, 16, 51, 110, 135, 193
Biafra, 129
Billing, George, 88
Billings family, 161
Boer War, 9
Bredo, Dr, 64
Brelsford, Vernon, 85
British Empire, 2, 9
British South Africa Company (BSAC), 9, 22, 139, 202–4
Broken Hill, 28, 46, 56, 95–7, 102, 104–5, 107–8, 117
Brown, E. L., 4, 5
Bryant, Mr, 5
Bulawayo, 10, 28
Burma, 31, 32
Bush, Mr, 102
Bwana Mukubwa, 190

Caergwrle, 8
Cairo, 11, 58, 167
Cambridge, 1, 7, 9, 49, 52, 67, 73, 83, 85
Canada, 102, 184
Canterbury, Archbishop of, 112
Cape Colony, 202
Cape Town, 9–10, 28, 68–9, 72, 74, 113
Cape Town Air Race, 26
Carmel, Mother, 79
Cathedral of the Holy Cross, 168

Catholic Church, 48, 147
Cavreille, Battle of, 3
Central African Council, 99
Central African Federation, 97, 103, 205
Chaka, King, 201
Chalimbana, 13
Chamber of Mines, 110
Chambeshi River, 15–16, 80, 82–3, 93
Chanda, Peter, 127, 188–9, 192, 198
Chester, 8
Chester Square, 188
Chewa tribe, 201
Chiengi, 62, 85
Chikoti, 153, 155
Chilomba, Fumbello, 163–4
Chilubi Island, 79
Chimpempe mission, 61, 209–10
Chimpili Plateau, 45
Chinjavata, James, 115
Chinsali, 23, 56, 147
Chiswick, 1, 8
Chitambala, Frank Makarios, 136, 140–1
Chitambo, Chief, 80
Chitimukulu, Chief, 22, 30
Chittenden, Cecile, 75, 83
Chittenden, Micky, 75, 76, 83
Chiwala, Senior Chief, 151
Chokwe, 119
Chona, Mainza, 142, 206
Churchill, Winston, 9, 51, 64
Clifton College, 6–7, 19, 21, 51, 185
Close Association Conference, 99, 100

## Index

Club House, 12
Colonial Development and Welfare Fund, 204
Colonial Office, 1, 3, 7, 12–13, 25–6, 54, 73–4, 98–100, 128–30, 146, 161, 170–1, 198, 200, 204
Commonwealth Office, 171
Commonwealth Society, 8
Congo, 50, 58–9, 62–3, 65, 78, 82, 123, 129, 162, 164, 189, 203, 207
Conservative government (UK), 100, 146
Constitution Party, 133
Convention Peoples' Party, 128
Copper Belt, 78, 93, 108–9, 130, 153, 180, 190, 208
*Cornwall*, HMS, 2
Coton, Superintendent, 104
Creech Jones, Mr A., 98
Cunningham, Dr, 79
Cunningham, Peter, 5
Cyprus, 7, 140

Dalhousie, Lord, 41
Dalmeny Park, 7
De Beers, 202
Debenham, Professor, 67, 73, 80, 83, 85
Department of Local Government, 180
Devlin (of West Wick), Patrick Arthur Devlin, Baron, 146, 158
Devonshire Course, 73

Dominican order, 95, 116
Dublin, 27

East Africa, 70, 203, 211
East India Company, 9
Eastbourne, 3
Edinburgh, 8
Egypt, 40, 202
Elizabeth II, Princess (Queen), 70, 101, 102, 182
Elizabeth, Queen (Mother), 70, 106
Elizabethville, 63
*Empress of Scotland*, 28
Etienne, Father, 38, 76, 90, 174
EverReady, 69
Evetts, Julian, 57
Executive Council, 11, 95

Falls Bridge, 181
Farnborough, 184
Federal Party, 101, 104
Federation Party, 170
Field, Winston, 175
Field Survey Company, 2, 7
First XI, 134
First World War, 2–3, 6, 17, 30–1, 56, 58, 203
Fisher, Charles, 91
Flanders, Michael, 127
Forestry, Department of, 70, 115
Fort Rosebery, 51, 78, 81, 91–3, 138
Fort Widley, 7
Foster, Robin, 10

Franklin, Harry, 69, 105, 133
Free French, 30
Frost, Denis, 93

Game, Department of, 37, 115
Gandhi, Mahatma, 133
George V, King, 11, 64
George VI, King, 70
Germany, 30, 203
Ghana, 128, 143; see also Gold Coast
Gibraltar, 9
Gibson and Weldon, 73
Glieman, Mr, 21
Gold Coast, 128; see also Ghana
Gomez, Monsieur, 162–3
Goodfellow, Derek, 75
Gore-Browne, Sir Stewart, 55–6, 69, 95, 104, 172
Gow, Abe, 118
Greenall, Cynthia, 91
Greenall, Frances, 1, 7–8, 15, 25–9, 33–4, 45, 47, 50–3, 55, 57, 59–60, 67, 69, 72, 74–5, 79, 83, 85, 89–91, 105, 110, 113, 115–17, 123, 127, 138, 141–2, 148–9, 151, 159, 162, 171, 179–82, 184, 188, 195, 198
Greenall, Gerald Vyvyan, 3, 6
Greenall, Lydia, 84, 91, 116–17, 149, 163, 175, 180
Greenall, Thomas, 37
Greenall, Vivian, 52, 59–60, 69, 79, 84–5, 91, 116–17, 160–1, 184, 188

Guildford, 79
Guthrie, Professor, 74
Gymkhana Club, 12, 17, 54

Hall, Mr, 5
Hammarskjöld, Dag, 162
Hampstead, 7
Hart, John, 115, 156, 163, 171
Hastings, Sir Patrick, 27
Hatchwell, Mr, 12
Hatfield, 15
Hawaii, 61
Health, Department of, 91, 111
Heath, Tony, 51, 91
Hill, Roland, 114–16, 165
Hope, Dick, 168
Household Cavalry, 26
Howe, Gilbert, 20–1, 55
Hudson Bay Company, 20
Huggins, Sir Godfrey, 97–100, 103, 105, 205
Hull, 9

Ibo, 129
India, 13, 30, 103, 124, 133
Indian Congress, 103
Indian Ocean, 2, 178
Information, Department of, 105
Inns of Court, 73
International Telephone Exchange, 26
Invershin, 8
Ipusikilo, 76
IRA, 159
Isaac, Bunny and Mary, 58, 70
Isangano, 79

Jelf, Philip, 84

# Index

John Henry, 149–50
Johnstone Falls, 48–9, 66

Kabompo, 25, 41–2, 50, 76, 113–22, 134, 136–7, 140–4, 148, 150–2, 154–5, 157–9, 161–3, 165, 171, 175
Kafalufuta River, 176
Kafue Game Park, 151, 154
Kafue River, 70, 152, 207
Kafulwe, 61
Kalambo, 47
Kalolo tribe, 201–2
Kalungwishi River, 16
Kangomato, 82
Kansenga, 50
Kapalala, 78, 81, 93
Kapepwe, Simon, 133
Kapitabane, 83
Kasaba, 79
Kasabasaba, 207–8; see also Mumbwa
Kasama, 14, 15–18, 20–2, 25–6, 28–30, 32, 35, 37, 45, 51–4, 56, 61, 68, 74, 83–5, 87, 91, 93, 101, 111, 147, 173, 179, 194
Kasembe, Senior Chief Mwata, 50, 54, 202
Kasempa, 152
Kasenga, 63
Kasoma, 87, 88
Kasomo, 147–8
Katanga, 162, 181, 203
Kaunda, Betty, 140
Kaunda, Kenneth, 13, 56, 99, 101, 103, 108, 114, 130, 132–3, 135–44, 146, 157–8, 162, 166, 170–5, 177–8, 191, 193, 194, 196–7, 205–6
Kawambwa, 16, 45–50, 52–4, 58, 65–6, 73, 169, 177, 209
Kenya, 5, 14, 57–8, 129–30, 159
Kenyatta, Jomo, 129, 159
Kikuyu tribe, 129
Kilwa, 59, 62
Kings College, 2
Kitwe, 91, 112–13, 117, 180–2, 195
Kitwe Hilton, 196
Knight, Christina, 7
Knight, Mrs, 69
Knight, Roy, 1–2, 5–7
Kunda, Kosam, 178

Labour, Department of, 107, 111–12
Labour Party (NR), 95, 104
Labour Party (UK), 74, 100, 195
Lammond, Willie, 49, 66
Lancaster House, 100
Lander, Tony, 114
Legislative Council (LegCo), 11, 55–6, 95, 99, 103, 204
Lennox-Boyd, Alan T., 112, 146
Lenshina, Alice, 146–8, 173–4
Lewanika, King, 101, 120–1
Livingstone, 11, 108, 209–11
Livingstone, David, 11, 17, 48, 60, 80, 83, 202
Lloyds, 3
Loloma, 142

217

Loluma, 150
Lomu, 48
London School of Economics (LSE), 73–4
Londonderry, 27
Lovale, 76, 115, 122, 142, 164
Lozi tribe, 119–21, 192–3, 201–2
Luangwa River, 60
Luanshya, 167, 175–6
Luapula River, 49–50, 59, 61–3, 78, 80, 82–3
Luapula Valley, 48
Luchazi tribe, 119, 150–1, 159
Lumpa Church, 146–8, 173–4, 189
Lunda tribe, 48, 50–1, 119, 121–2, 127, 163–4, 201–2
Lunga Bank, 82–3, 88
Lupososhi River, 79
Lusaka, 10, 11–12, 17, 21–2, 53, 58, 61, 68–70, 72, 74–5, 96, 108, 111, 137, 142–4, 159, 161, 168, 176, 178, 180, 183–4, 188, 193–4, 196, 198, 211
Luwingu, 22, 51, 67, 73–81, 89–93, 95, 101, 136, 151, 161
Lyombe, Philimon, 196
Lyttelton, Oliver, 100

McAlpines, 109
Mc Gibbon, Dr, 142
McInnes, Cadet, 114, 137
Macleod, Iain, 146, 157, 161, 206
Macmillan, Harold, 144, 146, 161
Macrae, DC, 65, 92, 93
Macrae family, 45, 62, 65
McTavish (python), 164–5
Madagascar, 30
*Maizie*, 78
Majuba Hill, Battle of, 51
Mambalima, 48–9
Manpower, Department of, 26, 95
Manyinga, 120–2, 151–2, 155, 168
Masaiti, 42, 167, 169, 176, 178
Matabele tribe, 192, 202
Matongo Island, 90
Matopo Hills, 70
Mau Mau, 129
Maudling, Reginald, 161, 170, 206
Maze prison, 159
Mbikusita, Mr, 101
Mbunda, 119
Mediterranean, 9
Middle East, 68
Mofu, 79
Mombeshi River, 126
Monckton Commission, 157
Mongu, 111
Moscow, 141
Moshi, 152
Mount Nelson Hotel, 72
Mozambique, 167
Mpezeni, Chief, 202
Mpika, 30, 85, 93–4
Mpongwe, 167–8, 176, 207
Mporokoso, 43, 45, 50, 57–9, 61, 63–5, 68, 78–9, 170

## Index

Muchemunto, Fisher, 208
Mufulira, 190
Mukula, Pambi, 61
Mulenga, 80
Mulungushi, 157
Mumbwa, 174, 207–8; see also Kasabasaba
Mundia, Mr, 193
Munkanta, 54
Munyaka, John, 121–2
Mushili, 169
Musonda, 136
Muspratt-Williams, Group Captain, 68–9
Mwalole, 22–3, 25, 30
Mwamba, Chief, 22, 34
Mweru, Lake, 58, 62–5, 85

National Archives of Zambia, 62
National Prosperity Party, 172
Native Affairs, Department of, 30, 89, 102, 108
Naylor family, 91
Ndola, 46, 74, 77–8, 81, 91, 94, 107–9, 112–13, 177, 182, 184–5, 190, 196, 198, 203
Ndola Rural, 62, 167, 174, 176–7, 198
*Neleus*, SS, 9
New Zealand, 176
Ngoni tribe, 192, 201–2
Nigeria, 5, 129, 164
Nkana, 192, 208–9
Nkrumah, Kwame, 128, 132
Nkumbula, Harry, 56, 101, 108, 132–3, 157, 162, 170, 205

North Western Province, 134, 164–5
Northern Ireland, 159
Northern Province, 14, 17–18, 22, 35, 55–6, 77–8, 111, 114, 123, 129–30, 138, 146, 157, 173–4, 184
Northern Rhodesia African Congress (NRAC), 101
Northern Rhodesia Regiment (NRR), 30–1, 51, 160, 174
Nsalushi Island, 85–8, 90
Nsamba, Chief, 88–9, 92, 151
Nyasaland, 97, 99, 130, 132, 135–6, 146, 158, 171, 201, 203, 205
Nyasaland African Congress (NAC), 133, 135
Nyerere, Julius, 196–7

Operation Longjump, 134
Oppenheimer College, 176
Orpington, 188
Orwell River, 113
Otto Beit Bridge, 70

Paarl, 113
Palestine, 7, 104
Peachey, Derek, 26
Plymouth Brethren, 48–9
Pook, James, 85–7
Port Elizabeth, 78
Port Said, 126
Portugal, 203
Premier Hotel, 72
Pretoria, 9
Provincial Liquor Licensing Board, 186

Public Works Department, 113, 183

Queen Alexandra's Nursing Service, 58
*Queen Mary*, 9

Rennie, Sir Gilbert, 91–2
Rhodes, Cecil John, 9, 11, 70, 202–3
Ridgeway Hotel, 182
Roan Antelope, 167, 175
Roan Antelope Mine Hospital, 91
Robinson, Chimpempe, 61
Roche, George, 167
Rome, 48
Royal Air Force (RAF), 58, 68
Royal and Ancient, 107
Royal Artillery, 3
Royal Empire Society, 8
Royal Engineers (RE), 7–8, 51, 167
Royal Navy, 3
Rwanda, 164

St Andrew's Preparatory School, 3–6, 19
St Anthony's Mission, 177
St John's Wood, 3, 7
St Peter, 48
Salisbury, 113, 116, 144, 148, 167, 175, 181, 209
Salisbury, Lord, 100, 157
Samfya, 51, 81
Santa Maria medical mission, 79
Sardanis, Andrew, 139–40

School of Oriental and African Studies (SOAS), 73–4
Second World War, 22, 204
Second XI, 134–5
Selous, F. C., 19
Seventh Day Adventists, 61
Sheldrake, Mark, 163
Shimumbi, Chief, 88
Shiwa Ngandu, 56
Short, Robin, 40, 119, 150–1
Sikufele, Chief, 119–21
Simms, Edna, 19, 46
Simms, Reverend, 19, 138
Simpson, Simon, 17
Size, 29, 34, 52–3, 57
Slater, Sister Elaine, 25–6
Smarti (puppy), 47
Smith, Derek, 174
Smith, Ian, 181
Smuts, Jan Christiaan, 9
Snelson, Peter, 41
Solwezi, 113–14, 134
Somaliland, 30
South Africa, 9–10, 22, 72, 97–9, 108, 144, 201, 205
South African Air Force (SAAF), 12, 17, 68
Special Branch, 129, 133, 135, 138, 146, 161, 170, 180
Suez Canal, 167
Suffolk, 113
Swan, Donald, 127
Swiss Cottage, 3

Table Mountain, 9
Table, Senior Messenger Smart, 207, 208
Tanganyika, 64; *see also* Tanzania

*Index*

Tanganyika, Lake, 58
Tanzam railroad, 194
Tanzania, 17, 196; *see also* Tanganyika
Teicher, Mrs, 176
Territorial Council, 55
Thompson, Ewen, 177–8
Thompson, Reg, 184–9
Toronto, 184
Transport, Department of, 103
Tredwell, Gordon, 30, 93–4
Truscott, Doris, 3, 6
Truscott, Roy, 3, 5–6
Tshombe, Moise, 162, 181
Tungati, Chief, 87

Uganda, 7
Unga, 87–9
unilateral declaration of independence (UDI), 181, 192
Unilever, 70
Union Castle Line, 69, 113, 178
United National Independence Party (UNIP), 55–6, 141–2, 157–9, 161, 163, 169–73, 175, 177–8, 180, 186, 189, 192–3, 194–6, 206
United National Party, 193
United Nations (UN), 162
Uys, Johnny, 152–5

Victoria Falls, 70, 98–9

Victoria Falls Conference, 98, 205
von Lettow, Commander, 30

Waddington, John, 93
Walilupo, Lake, 80
Walker, Johnny, 10
Washington, 187
Welensky, Roy, 56, 95, 97–9, 103–4, 157, 161, 173, 175, 205–6
Welwyn, 15
West Africa, 64, 70
Western Province, 175, 185–6
Western Province Development Conference, 184
White Fathers, 38, 76, 79
White, Charlie, 114–16
Williams, Bill, 17, 19
Wilson, Harold, 181
Witchcraft Ordinance, 41
Wolverhampton Hippodrome, 125

Yamvwa, Paramount Chief Mwata, 50, 121, 162–4

Zaire, 50, 164, 189–91, 194
Zambezi River, 70, 161, 202
Zambia African Congress, 138, 206
Zambian African National Congress (ZANC), 133–5, 137–8, 142
Zambian Air Force, 46
Zimbabwe, 46, 164
Zulus, 201